The Making of a Community
The Vail Way

The Making of a Community
The Vail Way

John Horan-Kates

The Vail Leadership Institute exists to develop values-based leaders and organizations that produce higher levels of results by leading with purpose.

Inspirational Works is the publishing arm of the Vail Leadership Institute.

For additional information, visit our website at
www.inspirationalworksllc.com

Print information available on the last page.

Rev. date: 10/29/2015

CONTENTS

DEDICATION

To my wife, Pamela Sue Horan-Kates, who has stood by me
for almost forty years, providing a solid foundation
to my wild dreams and ideas.

FOREWORD

Vail is unlike any other place: it was not born from a mining history like Aspen, nor a cowboy ranching legacy like Steamboat Springs. It didn't erupt from bubbling natural mineral springs like St. Moritz. It was a new town, a blank canvas. An experiment in self-creation, as much an idea as a place.

As early residents, we were refugees. Fleeing the urban known for the mountain unknown; coming from our various roots to a place that profoundly shaped us as we shaped it. Today, at 50 some years old, Vail has evolved from sheep pasture to ski area to international resort to bonafide year-round community for those drawn to the dream of a place to explore, start or raise a family, retire, find adventure, reflect, or begin anew.

In his book, ***The Making of a Community – The Vail Way***, early Vail Associates executive and Vail Leadership Institute founder John Horan-Kates, having both observed and collaborated with many of Vail's pioneers, reflects on what makes Vail *Vail*, attempting to decode the enigma. This work is not an exercise in self-congratulation, but for the purpose of sharing the leadership lessons inherent in Vail's success. Though much has been written about Vail, this book chronicles a different story – how the lives and endeavors of its residents co-conspired to build a real and enduring community at the foot of an epic ski mountain.

Telling the story of a place is risky, as community history is never simply a matter of fact, but also of interpretation, perspective, and selective inclusion or omission. I remember being challenged by town leaders for my use of what I thought was a friendly comparison between Vail and its then more famous neighbor Aspen. That Vail was the ambitious, aggressive, and athletic "Sparta" to Aspen's mature, refined, and artistic "Athens" seemed apt, and not altogether unflattering. Not everyone agreed.

But nothing motivates like criticism. And Vail, as it evolved, sustained its fair share. "Shake and bake Bavaria" was the most annoying – that Vail, with no history of its own, had simply copied the motifs of European alpine villages in a bid for instant patina and charm. What couldn't be argued, and what remains Vail's most authentic pedigree, is the post-war entrepreneurship of 10th Mountain Division veterans who brought recreational skiing and a mountain ethos to Vail, as well as the European ski racers and hoteliers who were among Vail's first risk-taking residents.

Nature and time have been kind to Vail, burnishing its reputation as home to some of the world's best skiing and snowboarding, as well as dining, lodging, and shopping. It has a roster of Fortune 500 business executives and Olympic medalists, destination orthopaedic medicine, the Bolshoi Ballet, a corporate-community philanthropy, a locally funded environmental science campus, multiple Bravo cultural events, and more. How it got here, that special Vail DNA – what the Vail way includes, is thoughtfully examined within.

Like many in the Gore Valley, my life and family have been profoundly impacted by Vail – how I think about community, leadership, service, sustainability, and purpose. I've come to value and believe even more deeply that there truly is a Vail way. Living at altitude inspires and requires a higher level of consciousness and commitment. To whom much is given, much is expected.

Perhaps the Vail way can help us find our own way in a confusing and unpredictable world. As Pete Seibert said, "after summiting the mountain, keep climbing."

Terry Minger
Boulder, Colorado

September 28, 2015

PREFACE

This is a story of entrepreneurs who created something incredible out of nothing. It's about how the commitment to a vision built a flourishing community in just fifty years. It's a history of quests, trials, and failures, of how innovative and dedicated people acted on their vision. It's the story of realizing a dream.

Entrepreneurship is the process of creating and building something believed to be of value to others. It's a French word coined by economists who expounded the doctrines of Adam Smith, often cited as the father of modern economics.[1] Entrepreneurs are most often linked to a commercial enterprise, but on deeper investigation that definition is too limiting. So, the stories contained here cover variations on the entrepreneurial theme: the classic business entrepreneur, the social-sector leader, the government variety, the faith-based entrepreneur – even athletes. Projects, programs, and organizations are started in all sectors by visionary leaders who see what others don't.

Entrepreneurs go beyond just ideas – they create successes. The Vail way is an expression of how pioneering impresarios created a world-renowned community out of open sheep pastures and the surrounding national forest. It's the story of how people did it, not only in the beginning but also today as the community continues to evolve. It's partly a story of building organizations or institutions that make up our community, but more important, it's about the people.

The entrepreneurial process begins with an idea and is deeply rooted in action, much like the admonition in the Bible in the book of James that says "faith by itself, if not accompanied by action, is dead."[2] Vision without action is just a dream. Entrepreneurs are moving targets – they are constantly pressing ahead developing the necessary resources. They spot opportunities, take risks, deal with uncertainty, and exercise initiative.

Entrepreneurs, people like Pete Seibert and Bob Parker, drew heavily on leadership principles like collaboration, commitment, courage, and innovation to create breakthroughs in Vail's early years. And lest we forget, there's plain hard work, the kind Thomas Edison spoke of when he said, "Opportunity is missed by most people because it is dressed in overalls and looks like work."[3]

Vail has been propelled by passionate people. Unlike most entrepreneurs, these people were more interested in the mountain lifestyle than the pursuit of money. They understood what Edison described. But they also benefitted from various cultural factors that were a recipe for success: the enthusiasm of the returning World War II veterans who spawned the boomer generation; the economic expansion that these two groups wrought; new ski equipment and trail grooming; the condominium laws that opened vacation-home ownership to many; the growth of jet travel and the interstate highway system; and the convergence of anti-war sentiment, marijuana use, and the sexual revolution that fostered a free spirit and willingness to experiment.

Most of Vail's founders were military veterans, many from the famed 10th Mountain Division who fought in the Italian Alps in World War II. They trained at Camp Hale, not twenty miles south of what would become Vail, to prepare for winter mountain warfare. They are part of what's called "the greatest generation" not only for their sacrifices in combat but also for the economic juggernaut they built when they came home. They were hardened by combat but passionate about the mountains and skiing.

Colorado's Gore Valley had been a sleepy, verdant sheep pasture until 1957 when those soldiers saw the potential. With the help of Earl Eaton, a crusty rancher who grew up in nearby Squaw Creek, Pete Seibert found the perfect place for his life-long dream of building a ski resort. This high mountain valley, with soaring peaks all around and Colorado's dry snow and clean, crisp air, promised the renewing benefits of an adventurous lifestyle.

The Gore Valley certainly had promise, but what would become known as Vail Mountain was the real jewel. And the Back Bowls would be truly unique in American skiing. Shirley Welch, in her book **Vail: The First Fifty Years,** describes what created this distinction: "Back in the 1860s, drought besieged the area. Then lightning struck the bowls on the south-facing side of the mountain, and fires raged, burning entire hillsides. Over the next 75 years, heavy snowfalls returned and the remains of the burned forest decayed, leaving mountain slopes devoid of trees. These open bowls remained invisible from the valley floor."[4]

Pete Seibert knew what he was looking for, but it took Earl Eaton, who had hunted in these bowls for years, to mention that hidden nugget of information. They both knew Vail Mountain would be special.

The Gore Valley in 1957

I landed in Vail in 1974 and have lived and worked for more than forty years alongside many of these pioneers. Along the way, I felt the tug to understand more clearly how it all happened. While I called upon other community leaders to comment on the various sections in the book, this narrative is largely my observation of how the Vail Valley evolved. Hundreds of people could have been highlighted in this story; I chose mostly those I came to know.

Much like the Disney way, the Marriott way, or the Toyota way, this book begins to describe a "Vail way." It explores the motivations that drove the founders and those who have followed. After learning about these other "ways," I asked myself, "Is there a secret sauce here that can be shared? What has worked – and what hasn't? Who were the people – the leaders – who helped make it happen?"

I think the Vail way is rooted in entrepreneurship – it's a way of going about building community. The Vail way is demonstrated regularly through the virtues – the values, principles, and attitudes – exhibited by entrepreneurs. Beyond the vision, there's resilience, trust, focus, and teamwork. Every step of the way, in every sector of the community, there are apt examples of how this way of thinking created something extraordinary. Over time, an entrepreneurial mindset pervaded those who followed the founders. An attitude approaching invincibility was present in many; in fact, Rod Slifer, a two-time mayor of Vail said he kept hearing, "We can do this. We're not sure how, but we can do it."[5]

My initial hope is to describe a perspective that will encourage teams of people to be truly entrepreneurial. My longer-term intent is to define the kind of culture needed to build vibrant communities. When I first read Stephen R. Covey's classic work *The 7 Habits of Highly Effective People*, I was struck by his audacious challenge:

> *"What if we could get model communities in this country, and model institutions, schools, businesses and governmental units, to become islands of excellence in a sea of mediocrity? What if they could become models and then transport what they learn to others so that this whole spirit of stewardship, of servant leadership, of working at the empowerment process through structures and systems could take root and flourish?"*[6]

These sentiments motivated me to uncover and describe this supposed Vail way. I believe this approach is embodied in many companies, governments, and nonprofits up and down the fifty-mile corridor that follows the Gore Creek, which empties into the Eagle River, and then finally flows into the mighty Colorado. Numerous communities, towns, and neighborhoods make up the greater Vail Valley. Some of these towns and their more vocal residents see themselves as autonomous, but most broad-minded people recognize that they are really part of something larger, bound together by the Vail economy and a shared love of the mountains. Vail still has the appeal, the cache.

This culture is anchored in a handful of characteristics that have been present from the beginning. And I believe these attributes are applicable to other individuals, teams, organizations, and communities regardless of their particular focus.

Here are several key principles that I observed along the way:

- **Commitment**: the state of being emotionally or intellectually bound to a course of action or person. It's about persevering in something arduous, in this case, acting upon one's ideas. Pete Seibert, as a teenager, had the idea of building a ski resort, and he never wavered in his passion for this dream. He and the other founders, people like Pepi and Sheika Gramshammer, Sally Hanlon, and Dick Hauserman, had the strength of character to follow their instincts. They believed in their vision and chose to take huge risks. They demonstrated that the discipline to act on one's passion – to get things done – is a foundational concept in Vail. It started with the first shovel of dirt in 1962 and has continued as more entrepreneurs have stepped forward and put their ideas, their money, and their futures on the line. Pete and his World War II buddies embodied how another visionary, Dr. Robert Jarvik, the inventor of the artificial heart, described leaders:

"Leaders are visionaries with a poorly developed sense of fear and no concept of the odds against them.[7]

Having a vision is an inspiring thing. It's a picture of what it will look and feel like when you are achieving your dream. It can motivate a few people or many. A vision can evolve simply from something you read or see or from a comment that a friend makes. Whatever the seed, for visions to come alive, they must be articulated. Some people write down their dreams – others just keep talking about them. Either way, they begin to take on a life of their own. In his book ***Visionary Leadership***, Burt Nanus defines vision as "a realistic, credible, attractive future for your organization. The right vision jump-starts people to move forward." [8]

Leaders see what others don't. They look for what is coming next. And while visioning is a skill that helps us paint vivid pictures, for it to be significant, it requires an executable strategy that evolves in relationship with others. For a vision to be fully realized, leaders must build trust with those around them. They've got to invest the time to engage others deeply. It's one way that leaders develop followers – just as the Man from Galilee did.

• ***Collaboration***: the willingness to engage others in one's ideas. From the very beginning, everyone saw that Vail would be a whole community effort. Because they were fairly isolated from Denver, the founders had to rely on one another – for a telephone or a band-aid – or just the basic necessities. They realized that helping others achieve their goals was a way to achieve their own as well. As the story in Chapter 7 conveys, the evolution of the Vail Valley Foundation embodied this spirit. So does the story of Kim Langmaid in Chapter 8.

Collaborating involves working with others to achieve a common purpose. It's often referred to simply as teamwork. But collaborating is how big things get done. David Gergen, a counselor to four U.S. presidents reminded us, quoting an old African proverb, "If you want to go fast, go alone. If you want to go far, go together."[9] Inherent in this strategy is recruiting people who share your passion and are willing to work in unity for the whole – people who know how to cooperate. And once you've got the team, you have to spend time with them building relationships, much like the 10th Mountain Division soldiers did during World War II.

When teams work in an other-centered manner, creativity often results, community is built, and opportunities are seized. A key aspect of collaboration is the willingness to surrender tight control. While strong teams are often made up of individual players, these individuals must meld together to benefit from their combined strengths. They must share resources and responsibilities. In Jim Collins' best-selling book *Good to Great*, he expounds on the notion of "getting the right people on the bus, and then getting them in the right seats."[10]

The Vail Valley is a good example of an "intentional community," formed by people who sought an alternative lifestyle. They are people who share certain values, like a commitment to family, the environment, and adventure – especially skiing. They had, and still have, a deep, collective determination to create something special. They know how to collaborate.

- *Innovation*: striving to create the very best. In Vail's case, it was to be world class – to deliver "first quality." From the early founders, who innovated almost daily, to today's well-educated residents, people believed in the notion of first-quality services, facilities, and organizations. Led by Vail Associates in the early days, and built upon by hoteliers, restaurateurs, and others, the community has always set high standards of guest service and environmental sensitivity. Their commitment to innovate has paid wonderful dividends – both in a financial sense, but also in the experience of the mountain lifestyle.

Innovation is the process of finding and applying better solutions to existing needs. It's that valuable leadership practice that unites capabilities with novel ideas and applies them to an existing situation in a way that results in something different and impactful. Vail Associates (VA) innovated from the beginning and today's Epic Pass is evidence that that process continues.

In the organizational realm, a positive, collaborative culture allows innovators to translate ideas into tangible improvements. Whatever one wants to call them – work groups, skunk works, teams – the ability to work together is central to innovation. Setting aside one's ego is an important cultural attribute that makes for the best atmosphere for innovation. And having an open culture versus a controlling, central authority generally makes for better results.

According to Clayton Christensen of the Harvard Business School, "disruptive innovation" is the key to future success in business. But we know that great ideas in any organizational setting are worthless unless they are well executed. Sometimes innovations come in giant leaps, but more often they evolve through many small steps. Either way, an innovation that is a catalyst for growth must be delivered well.

Walter Isaacson, in his book *The Innovators*, says, "Innovation occurs when ripe seeds fall on fertile soil…innovators glean insights from a variety of experiences, conversations and observations and that they usually flow from multiple sources, from a collaboratively woven tapestry of creativity."[11] It's usually a group effort. Pete Seibert was the instigator, he articulated the vision, but it took a "whole village" to create the Vail Valley. Sometimes, but rarely, innovations are sparked by a lone creator, but more often they result from what Isaacson calls "an evolutionary process that occurs when ideas, concepts, technologies ripen together. There is no conflict between nurturing individual geniuses and promoting collaborative teamwork."[12] The Vail Valley's success with three World Alpine Ski Championships over twenty-five years is evidence of that.

- *Service to Others*: the act of helping people and promoting a sense of community. This core concept is embedded in the Vail way. It's the instinctive desire to nurture both people as well as the environment. As the community grew, business owners and residents saw that visitors were like guests in their home; there was no doubt that Vail was in the people business. Many realized early on that there was something special about the clear mountain air, the wildlife, and of course, the dry, light Colorado snow. Guarding these natural assets has always been foremost. And many recognized that this place provided opportunities for renewal and rejuvenation that could be transformative. This principle, serving others, is about being good stewards of every dimension of God's creation.

Serving is a holistic approach to work, an attitude that promotes a sense of community. When we are serving others, we are helping them grow. Servant leadership is the term often used today to describe this way of thinking and working. Robert

Greenleaf, the best-known advocate of servant leadership said, "It begins with the natural feeling that one wants to serve, then conscience choice brings one to aspire to lead."[13] It's interesting to note that servant-leadership is not really a new concept – it's been around a long time, and many of our most exemplary leaders have followed this approach. Greenleaf refers often to the example of Jesus who "did not come to be served, but to serve"[14] and to Mother Teresa, Abraham Lincoln, Martin Luther King, Jr., Mahatma Gandhi, and Eleanor Roosevelt.

The stories about the Vail Valley Medical Center, the governments of the Vail Valley, and the various compassionate organizations described in Chapter 3 are indicative of this serving principle – and of the Vail way.

- *Courage*: the quality that enables one to face challenges with confidence and resolve. Vail's pioneers had this quality in spades, as have so many other economic and social entrepreneurs over the past fifty years.

Courage is a manifestation of a positive attitude. When you are courageous and step out to meet a test, you signal to those around you that you can be counted on to do what is required. Bob Parker, a marketing guy, exhibited this trait when he stepped forward to create a natural gas system in the summer of 1962 to avoid the proliferation of those ugly white propane tanks.

Courage in leading goes well beyond the physical prowess or endurance we tend to think of first. A more subtle dimension of courage is the ability to admit your mistakes versus hanging on to being right. Giving up control of a project and delegating authority and responsibility takes courage. Jack Marshall did it with the final Beaver Creek planning by assigning it to Bob Parker.

Another dimension of courage is the way we respond to fear, certainly the fear of danger but more importantly in organizational life the fear of failure or the fear of what others will think. Then there's the fear of being isolated or seeming awkward. It takes courage to bet on your ideas and take a calculated risk in spite of your fears. The Vail founders understood this.

Courage is about the willingness to step out, to be bold, maybe even audacious – to step into the arena. Pepi Gramshammer's resolve to build his *gasthof* with virtually no money took guts. William Hutchinson Murray, crediting a Johann Wolfgang Goethe couplet, said,

"Whatever you can do, or dream you can, begin it.
Boldness has genius, power and magic in it. Begin it now"[15]

Courage is definitely part of the Vail way.

Initially, the founders were all part of Vail Associates (VA), the master developer of Vail. And Vail Resorts, the successor organization to VA, has continued to be not only the major employer but also the major investor in the community's most significant asset – the mountains. While Vail started as a "company town," within a few short years the natives were getting restless to form a town government and move to establish the other institutions, such as a chamber of commerce, a hospital, and an interfaith chapel that were all needed for a growing community. Much of this story is told in Chapter 3.

People now come from all over the country and from around the world. Some establish a second home here, and their contributions to the community have been significant. They come typically for the skiing, but they stay because the people drawn to the Colorado mountains are a powerful, interesting, entrepreneurial bunch. They stay for the clean air and clear water and the beauty of the Almighty's creation. And, as much as we might boast about the Vail Valley, we have our share of problems, and there are various issues that need continuing focus. The prescriptions for these challenges, if approached with the same vigor that built the place, will move us toward becoming an even more vibrant community. The final section of the book touches briefly on these issues.

One final aspect of the Vail way is less about entrepreneurship and more about lifestyle. I refer to it as an attitude of being healthy, active, and engaged. People who have chosen the Vail Valley seem to be committed to an alternative, sustainable standard of living. These qualities exemplify a way of life that takes full advantage of the mountains – both winter and summer. From the beginning, Vail was about having fun, experiencing the joy of being with like-minded people, and chasing that cute girl – or guy. Whether it is going up the mountain on snowshoes or a mountain bike or coming down by every imaginable device, being outside in the clear, fresh air is central to our way. And residents have tended to be caring people who blend head with heart. The intuitive, relational, and spiritual dimension of people is evident. As the community has grown, the softer side of human nature, the recognition that it takes both character and competence to be successful, is surely part of that secret sauce that makes the people of the Vail Valley different.

It is my hope that these stories will be an inspiration to others from near and far as they build their teams, businesses, organizations, and communities. Most people familiar with the Vail story know the key role played by Pete Seibert and many others in getting Vail off the ground. The accomplishments that they all realized have been told in book and film many times over. This book is an effort to describe how and by what means and manner – in what way – it was accomplished.

My interest in telling these stories is linked to my own sense of purpose, which I have described over this forty-year period as "building spirit-filled community." It grew out of a desire to leave big-city life behind, to put down roots, and be part of something special. The residents here have shaped the community's character, and Pam and I have been fortunate to be part of it. By understanding how Vail came to be, by providing some context for envisioning the future, I hope teams of people will be inspired to grow in their own way. My own experience and observations convince me that there definitely is a Vail way.

John Horan-Kates
Vail, Colorado

November 25, 2015

Introduction

My Entrepreneurial Story

"The most important truth to be found in this landscape is that earth's power and human understanding once built a long history together. Maybe if we bring a willingness to embrace what the land has to teach us of limits and possibilities, it can be rediscovered in our own lives, here in a place where earth meets sky in the long dream of life."

T.H. Watkins

The Lake Creek Valley where we built our home

Many people have asked me, "Why are you writing this, and whom is it for?" And I've asked myself, "What gives me sanction and authority to undertake a project like this?"

While my interest in writing is linked to my purpose – to build spirit-filled community – I also wanted to record what I've observed along the way and the lessons I've learned in Vail. At first, I thought the Vail way might have applicability for other small communities, but that felt a bit arrogant; in fact, just the expression "the Vail way" caused some people to comment that it sounded a little pompous. But still, I wanted to better understand how "good community" is built.

Then Harry Frampton, my colleague of thirty years said, "You should do it for us." As we discussed this approach and I thought about it, I realized that "us" was really locals – the business people, resort community employees, and homeowners – who ought to know how the Vail Valley came to be, how it happened. I felt that documenting the history around the many entrepreneurs who invested themselves in making this place so special was a worthy project. As I settled on the entrepreneurial focus, I recognized that I've been one most of my life.

Before Colorado – Earning My Way

I grew up in Detroit, a great place to be away from. My parents didn't believe in allowances, so I started working when I was eight with a paper route. Sundays were the hardest because I had to get up really early to deliver the Detroit News to about sixty houses. Later as a stock boy at Hudson's, Detroit's major department store, I made enough to have my own spending money – but not much more. My dad was a small businessman running a wholesale and retail dog food distribution business; we never had a lot but always enough. He provided pretty well. Maybe I got the entrepreneurial bug from him. But remembering my upbringing helps me see the dramatic distinctions between a Midwest urban existence and what I came to appreciate as an alternative mountain lifestyle.

All through high school I wanted to be the first in my family to go to college. Going away to school without a scholarship was out of the question financially, so I ended up commuting to Wayne State University in downtown Detroit. I worked more than I studied, and I graduated in December 1967 with a bachelor's degree and no debt. I had paid my own way.

Within four months, I was in Navy Officer Candidate School (OCS) in Newport, Rhode Island. Even with all the Vietnam War protests, I felt enlisting was the right thing to do. I believed that when the country called, you went, and I ended up on the Me Kong River serving our riverine troops. It was an awesome learning experience, mainly because I didn't know jack-shit (a technical Navy expression). My administrative tendencies kicked in with the fifty guys I was leading, and I found that being well organized was a decent way of staying on top of things. About halfway through my tour, it dawned on me that maybe I ought to make a plan for my future. Where was I headed after the Navy?

I thought, "Why couldn't I become vice president of marketing for Vail?" What a cool thought. My degree was in marketing, I loved skiing, and Colorado was clearly the best. I wrote it down along with a few other goals, like salary, housing, and investment options. It was pretty sketchy, but I had a direction, assuming I got home in one piece.

The USS Jennings County in the Me Kong River

Perhaps the most meaningful take-away from this experience was that serving was an honor. I still feel good about having taken some measure of responsibility back then. I believe in the sentiment, "freedom is not free."

After Vietnam, I was stationed at the Alameda Naval Air Station across the bay from San Francisco for two years. The Kirkwood Meadows ski area was on the drawing boards in 1971 and I thought maybe I could land a job there. The weird idea popped into my head that maybe I could make a deal on a job. So, at a lunch in San Francisco with the CEO, I blurted out, "I'm willing to work for free for three months setting up your accounting system if you'll give me a shot at a job at the end of three months." To my amazement, he said, "You've got a deal."

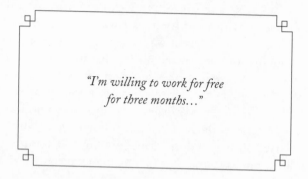

*"I'm willing to work for free
for three months…"*

Before long, I was business manager, marketing director, and controller all rolled into one. My offer seemed like a reasonable risk, perhaps because I could sense the possibilities. Even though I didn't realize it at the time, opening Kirkwood involved overcoming pretty much the same hurdles that Vail's founders had encountered ten years earlier. Being in on the ground floor was pretty exciting – we were literally creating something from scratch. When I started, Kirkwood was still largely untouched – no roads, no lifts, no trails. It was a clean slate.

While I wasn't the lead guy in Kirkwood, I started to understand what a significant entrepreneurial venture involved. I spent the first year helping develop the financial projections needed to secure a development loan. I had a vague remembrance of debits and credits, but I had no idea of how cash flow linked to the income statement or the balance sheet – but I learned. Accounting wasn't really what I wanted to do, but our CPA chided me by saying, "If you want to learn the business, learn the numbers." And he was right.

Landing in Vail – A Vision Realized

After Kirkwood's first ski season, I was offered the position of marketing director at Keystone ski area. It was a stepping stone that served as an introduction to Colorado, but ultimately it was not the right fit. I arrived in Vail in August of 1974 as the number two in marketing.

When Harry Bass bought controlling interest in Vail Associates (VA) in 1976, my dream came true. Given Bass' personality and management style, most of the top executives moved on to run other ski areas. It didn't happen exactly this way, but it seemed like Jack Marshall, then VA's president, called down the hall one day and said, "Come in here – we've made you VP of marketing." That kind of rocked my world.

My wife Pam and me on the cover of the Vail Trail, Christmas 1977

In rapid succession, I was thrust into various leadership roles: encouraging a creative and enthusiastic marketing department, chairing the board of the Vail Resort Association, and serving on the board of Colorado Ski Country. Even more important, Pam Horan and I tied the knot – both taking the name Horan-Kates – and shortly thereafter we designed and built our log home in Lake Creek. I was "entrepreneuring" a more complete life.

One of the most significant influences at this time was my introduction to Werner Erhard and his confrontational, but nevertheless valuable, Erhard Seminars Training, or simply "est." In the 1970s, est was all the rage. It was written up in national magazines and talked about widely at cocktails parties around Vail – mostly about how it was "California mumbo jumbo," except to those who had actually experienced its transformative effect. My major takeaway was the commitment to periodically get away and "take a look" at my life. I wanted to reflect on what was important and see if I was really making a difference. This willingness became an annual event, sometimes with Pam, sometimes on a business-sponsored retreat, but always in a reflective way. Regardless of form, these retreats and this eagerness to learn opened doors to many thought-leaders and many perspectives over the next thirty years.

An example of how est influenced me was in response to how Harry Bass micro-managed and pushed away many of VA's best leaders. Many left to run other ski resorts around the country, and, for a fleeting moment, that possibility occurred to me. But having reflected on my values, I knew I was really in the "Vail business" rather than the "ski business." I wanted to make a difference locally versus globally. So I decided to sink my roots even deeper.

A big break came with the opportunity to work with President Ford in developing the Vail Valley Foundation. Much of this story is told in Chapter 7, but from an entrepreneurial point of view, it was the chance to cast a big vision with a team of prominent, experienced people. I may have been in over my head, but because of Ford's involvement, we latched onto Vince Lombardi's renowned challenge: "If we strive for perfection, maybe we can achieve excellence."[1]

President Ford at Beaver Creek

The Vail Valley Foundation was a wonderful ride, but when it ended in 1987, I started a company that became East West Marketing where

I led a team of seven for about ten years. But I didn't like the agency business (clients were too fickle), so I shifted much of my energy to creating programs where I had an ownership stake. One of the most successful was Wedel Weeks with Pepi Gramshammer; part of that story is told in Chapter 3. It was a blast, and we made a decent profit. And much like my relationship with President Ford, I rode Pepi's coattails.

One of the things that entrepreneurs do is start things. In 1996, I was asked to lead the Beaver Creek Arts Foundation in building what became the Vilar Center for the Performing Arts. It was a little bit like "herding cats" given the prominent eighteen-person board, all of whom were working like crazy to raise the many millions needed. But it was very interesting work.

A similar situation unfolded when I was asked to chair the building of Vail Christian High School in 1998. In this role, I began to understand the importance of the spiritual dimension in leading a group of strong-willed individuals. I learned that God can be a powerful antidote to an unhealthy ego. We all have egos, but entrepreneurs are especially challenged to keep theirs in check. This experience helped me see that I needed some work in this regard.

The final building block in my proactive life in Vail was the development of the Vail Leadership Institute. More than all the other experiences combined, the Institute served to solidify and clarify my entrepreneurial perspective. I learned a ton during this twenty year run, but none more important than patiently building relationships of trust. The full story is told in Chapter 10.

This somewhat self-indulgent litany is simply intended to outline the perch from which I have developed my perspective. Entrepreneurs build stuff, and as I look back, I recognize I've spent some time doing just that.

CHAPTER 1

THE FOUNDERS' DREAM

*"The future belongs to those who believe in the
beauty of their dreams."*

Eleanor Roosevelt

Vail Village in 1963

The founders of Vail were a risk-taking, can-do bunch. Many of them had lived those qualities in the trenches and mountains of Europe during World War II. The camaraderie of training and combat created tight bonds, and while many of them had vague ideas of what a skiing future might hold, first they wanted to get home alive. Their discipline, commitment, and resilience exhibited their entrepreneurial spirit, and these qualities are indicative of the Vail way. This chapter is the story of three of Vail's founders; I called them "the three amigos."

FOUNDING CHRONOLOGY

March 1957: Pete Seibert and Earl Eaton discover Vail Mountain

May 1959: TransMontagne Gun Club formed

December 1962: Vail Mountain opens

August 1966: Town of Vail formed

June 1967: Vail Resort Association launched

June 1968: Vail InterFaith Chapel opens

December 1967: Vail Clinic opens

Pete Seibert, Bob Parker, and Bill Brown

PETER W. SEIBERT

It all started with Pete Seibert's dream. As a teenager in Sharon, Massachusetts, he and his buddy Morrie Sheppard, whom Pete would later hire as Vail's first ski school director, talked constantly about building a ski area. And Pete never lost the passion for this vision. It was fueled in mountain warfare training in Colorado, where he experienced the Rocky Mountains' light, dry snow.

The 10th – The Dream Percolates

At Camp Hale, only twenty miles from where Vail would be built, America's ski troops, the 10th Mountain Division, trained intensively on alpine maneuvers and survival. They learned about living in the mountains from Finnish and Norwegian "old timers" for whom skiing was a way of life. These Nordic and other experienced mountain people – former ski patrolmen and ski racers – helped these young soldiers cultivate a love of the outdoors and a passion for skiing.

On their rare free weekend, they headed to Aspen or Loveland to enjoy the thrill of big-time skiing. In Aspen, still a sleepy former silver mining town, they tested their new-found skill with a trip down Roch's Run, which would later be made famous during the 1950 World Alpine Ski Championships. And, of course, there was chasing any girl in sight.

Training at Camp Hale

Pete's dream most certainly grew during this time, as soldiers always talk about what they're going to do after the war. Those who know the freedom and exhilaration of skiing understand how Pete and his fellow soldiers became enraptured – passionate really – about the sport. Skiing was a rejuvenating experience given the constraints of military life.

The dream percolated after the war even as Pete recovered from massive wounds to his leg and face from the assault up Mount Terminale in the Italian Apennine Mountains. He always seemed to wear a slight smile, which in reality was due to his multiple surgeries. But his whole demeanor conveyed an upbeat and enthusiastic way in spite of those injuries.

Aspen – Still Percolating

In 1946, Pete headed back to Aspen, this time to work on the ski patrol and to regain his skiing legs. His work on the mountain, both summer and winter, helped him see what was required to build and maintain ski runs. By 1947, his determination and athleticism brought back his racing form, and he won the coveted Roch Cup. While Aspen was fun and exciting for four years, Pete could see that his dream of building his own ski area wouldn't be realized in Aspen. As he said in his book *Vail: The Triumph of a Dream*, "I knew there was only one way – work at it."

So he left Aspen to further prepare himself. He enrolled in L'Ecole Hoteliere in Lucerne, Switzerland, in 1950 to learn the fine art of hospitality and service. Even then, he was thinking of what it might take to operate a first-class resort. He knew the Europeans had a leg up on us in hospitality from his years in Italy and Germany. And he knew typical American ski area cuisine was served with ketchup and mustard on paper plates. This time in Lucerne galvanized his commitment to the dream – to build something that would rival Europe's best.

Following hotel school, Pete returned to Aspen. There he found work as a ski instructor and, before long, a wife – Betty Pardee. Aspen was also the perfect place to meet potential investors, people he knew he would need. Like plants need water, ideas need money. In late 1955, Pete had landed the job as general manager of Loveland Pass, a rustic and rough ski area where he learned the operation from top to bottom. It was good training, the kind where you got your hands dirty fixing rope tows and clearing parking lots. Before long, the job as assistant manager at Aspen Highlands had opened up, and Pete was back in Aspen. And Earl Eaton was there too. Here the two of them began to lay the groundwork for Vail.

Earl Eaton – The Finder

Earl was a crusty rancher from Squaw Creek, a tributary of the Eagle River, who shared Pete's desire to find the perfect mountain. His connection to the 10ᵗʰ Mountain Division came from having helped build the sprawling Camp Hale facilities. Earl was soft-spoken, but when he had something to say, it was plain common sense. Pete described the search in *The Triumph*: "We had explored a dozen or more sites, including the Collegiate Peaks west of Salida, Monarch Pass, and the San Juan range in southwest Colorado, as well as a hill or two in the Eagle Valley. We came away convinced that none were up to the standards of the mountain we wanted. But we were never discouraged."[2]

Earl Eaton and Pete Seibert – Circa 1958

Then in early 1957, Earl suggested they explore the terrain that would become Vail Mountain. It had remained undiscovered from other ski area dreamers because you couldn't see the back bowls from the highway. Once he and Earl had skied the now famous bowls, his dream kicked into high gear. They wanted a big mountain, with gentle slopes for the average skier and plenty of steep grades for experts. Pete knew immediately this was the place.

But like any new business venture, there were a multitude of hurdles and challenges – money, land, permits, and people, to name just a few. There had to be a plan, but it required initiative and flexibility. When these two pioneers laid out their idea for Vail, almost everyone thought they were crazy – most claimed it would never work. There was nothing in the valley but sheep pastures and a few run-down ranch houses. It was a hundred miles from the nearest city on a treacherous two-lane road. I-70 was barely on the drawing boards.

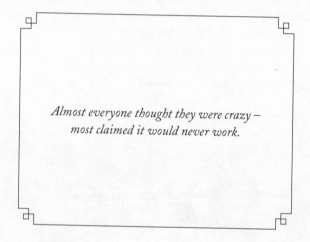

Almost everyone thought they were crazy –
most claimed it would never work.

A Small Deception – The Dream Begins to Take Shape

For the next few years, Pete put the key pieces in place. In 1958, rotary-dial, party-line phones were in use, Ike was still president, and microwave ovens were many years off. Pete was operating the old-fashioned way, and that included building a team and selling the vision. It would take a village of Type A risk takers.

And, as always, there was the need for money. Even though Pete didn't have much to speak of at that point, he had skied with several people who did – or who knew where to find it. There were numerous investors (see the Glossary) throughout the early years, but George Caulkins, a Denver oilman, stands out. Pete sold George on his vision in 1960 by letting him experience it – by skiing the incredible terrain. Every entrepreneur needs a "money man," and George conveyed his own passion for the idea to his friends and colleagues. Pete was astute by giving these partners, for a measly $10,000 investment, a home site to build on and four lifetime ski passes for their families. They were hooked. And those initial investments grew like crazy over the years, eventually becoming worth millions. Ben Duke, one of those early investors, said many years later, "It was probably the smartest investment I'd ever made."

George Caulkins – the "money man"

Many of these founders were soldiers, enthusiastic amateurs, but shrewd, and it showed as they went about acquiring the land the resort would need. First, they formed a shell corporation known as the TransMontagne Rod & Gun Club to mask their real intent. Once the key parcels at the base of Vail Mountain were locked up, they began the equally difficult work of securing the permits to operate the ski area on federal land. The U.S. Forest Service didn't think there would be demand for another ski area in Colorado. Paul Hauk, the regional forester, repeatedly denied the use permits saying, "With Loveland and Aspen just opened, there's no market. Plus we have to give these other resorts a chance to get off the ground." Pete pushed back, arguing that the federal government had no business restraining trade in that way.

After several agonizing attempts, plus a nudge from the Colorado congressional delegation in Washington, Hauk finally relented. But he required the company to first raise $1.5 million to guarantee the project's completion. This was a huge sum back then, when you could buy a Volkswagen bug for $1,800 and a typical urban house might cost $25,000. But Pete committed to raising the $1.5 million and that launched the next phase of fundraising. These obstacles may have seemed daunting at the time, but they'd seen more difficulty in war. Discipline and commitment experienced in Europe carried the day.

There were innumerable situations where these pioneers had to take risks requiring initiative and courage. For example, the nearest electric utility declined bringing power to the valley, so they formed their own cooperative, which is now Holy Cross Electric. Just about everyone involved had stories of where their passion kicked in and pushed them forward. There was no instruction manual – in many cases they were just winging it. It was, as the *New York Times* wrote in a November 1962 article about the new ski resort, "an incredible frenzy of organized chaos."[3] But like Disney magic, they were creating something out of nothing.

Pete Seibert – always smiling

Everyone acknowledged that Pete was the visionary. He was full of ideas and passion, but handling the details was not his strong suit. He was being pulled in multiple directions, so he called upon others to keep the dream in motion. It quickly became clear that all kinds of people would be needed to build a new community from scratch. Architects, builders, plumbers, bankers, doctors – people of all stripes. The challenge was to build a team, and after Earl Eaton, Bob Parker was the next addition.

COMMENTARY ON PETE SEIBERT

From my point of view, Pete didn't really have a recognizable management style. He thought about problems swiftly, figured out that we had only so many resources, and quickly decided. To get everything done by a certain date, his approach was absolutely necessary. He was a ski racer, after all.

But he was also a dreamer. While others were building in the village, he was dreaming about Blue Sky, what we called SuperVail. While some were trying to improve the skiing, he was dreaming about where the downhill course should be. Moving on was his byword.

Seldom has a dream become so successful. All from a guy who wasn't supposed to recover from his truly terrible war wounds

Bob Parker
Retired Senior Vice President – Vail Associates

ROBERT W. PARKER

Another 10ᵗʰ Veteran – A Journalist Who Spread the Dream

Bob Parker grew up in the out-of-the-way hamlet of Geneseo, New York. The country was just settling down after World War I, and Warren Harding was still president. In this small village in the Genesee River Valley, the farming values of hard work, putting in a full day, and being punctual made an impression. The farm taught Bob about how animals instinctively knew things that we humans couldn't understand, and it planted the seed for a love of wildlife, the natural world, and, ultimately, his love of exploring mountains. A deep military heritage anchored Bob with a patriotic sense that would eventually become real for him in World War II.

But before the war came the Great Depression. It's hard to imagine the impact that this era had on people, but it hardened Bob. He had concluded early on that there were many things more important than money, like nature and the outdoors, and they were beginning to pull on him.

Not long after Pearl Harbor, Bob read about the new 87th Mountain Infantry Regiment being formed by Minnie Dole, the founder of the National Ski Patrol. It turned his life upside down. Bob was immediately drawn to this group of soldiers that was to ultimately become part of the now famous 10th Mountain Division. This was not a gut wrenching decision – Bob knew he was called to serve.

If anything, World War II was a team endeavor, and soldiers learned to work together and came to appreciate the ultimate team attribute – trust. But war is hell – there's the horror of death alongside the desire to survive. The sights and sounds and smells stay with you forever. For those never called to serve in this way, it can be very difficult to understand the requirement to take another's life. Bob's poem, "Not Proudly," written in 1949, tells of his own pain and the futility of war.

> Not proudly, facing the enemy,
> But quietly waiting in a farm doorway
> For the fury of war to pass, and let
> Him go home, he was shot from the opposite
> Window, and fell, twisting into the sunlight,
> And lay, propped on his own pack, while
> His blood ran among the cobbles
> Of the yard.
>
> Only three chickens,
> And a preposterous hissing goose

INTERNATIONAL SKI RACING

Both Pete and Bob were racers themselves, and they understood what major ski racing events could do for Vail's image.

For Bob, this inclination flowed naturally from his earlier career as a journalist. He knew instinctively it was better to have others recognize your efforts rather than toot your own horn. For Pete, having recovered from war wounds to win Aspen's Roch Cup meant ski racing was in his blood.

Decades before many of us at the Vail Valley Foundation reintroduced World Cup racing to the community, these two pioneers had planted seeds by supporting the International Cup Races on Vail Mountain.

Their foresight ultimately flowered into the World Alpine Ski Championships twenty-five years later. And these events in 1989 and 1999, and again in 2015, secured the Vail Valley's international reputation.

We saw the possibilities, but only because they had shown us the way.

To see him die. A small wind lifting
Loose straw, a barn door slamming dully,
Closing in that moment for the last time,
Echoing in the corridors of his mind
For the last time that any sound
Would come to disturb the
silence that was there
in the beginning.[4]

After the war, many of the veterans of the 10th began to form the backbone of the ski industry. Their passion for the mountains took root at ski areas, ski equipment manufacturers, and ski shops. While Pete headed to Aspen, Bob's inclination to write took him to the magazine world. There he met Merrill Hastings, the publisher of *Skiing Magazine* and later *Colorado Magazine*, both based in Denver. Bob served several years as editor of *Skiing*, and in 1959 Pete pitched him on the idea of Vail by saying, "It's got open bowl skiing, fantastic snow, and it's only one hundred miles from here." Bob could tell Pete was serious.

Merrill Hastings, for his part, was a long way from a dreamer. He was a tenacious salesman and a tough boss, and it was these qualities that would eventually propel Bob to Vail. During the 1962 World Alpine Ski Championships in Chamonix in the French Alps, he pushed Bob too far. Merrill's aggressive nature led him to establish a policy that strictly prohibited employees from fraternizing with the magazine's competition – "the enemy" in his mind.

Following the races one day, Bob was having drinks with the other journalists covering the events, and Merrill learned of it. He sent word down for Bob to report to his room immediately. Bob sent back word that he'd be there "as soon as he finished his drink." Between the bar and Merrill's room, Bob concluded that his policy was an unreasonable and unnecessary intrusion. Merrill stood firm, and Bob said, "Fine, I quit." This was to become vintage Bob Parker – standing tall for what was important.

Bob's first move was to call Pete Seibert. When Pete had pitched Bob in Denver, he had included an offer to work for Vail, but the timing wasn't right. Now it was. Pete's immediate response to Bob's query was, "You're hired. Report to the Bell Gondola Ltd. in Zurich and wait for instructions." Bob was a gentleman about leaving *Skiing Magazine*. He maintained a good working relationship with Merrill, who became a big advocate for Vail, building a home on the Vail Golf Course and promoting his adopted hometown with vigor in his magazines.

Within a few weeks, Bob was fully engaged in his responsibilities as Vail's first marketing director when it became clear that Vail's gondola delivery from Europe was in trouble. A several-month delay would throw the critical planned opening of Vail Mountain into jeopardy, so Bob was called upon to expedite the process. Pete said, "Bob didn't argue; he just went ahead and fixed the problem on his own." Negotiating with Bell Gondola was obviously a long way from marketing, but with dogged persistence he re-routed shipments, hired professional expediters, persuaded customs officials, and got the components to Vail just in time. This was just the first of numerous instances where Bob took the initiative to get things done. Job descriptions didn't mean much back then.

A Complete Leader – Much More Than a Marketing Guy

Pete looked to Bob again when he observed the number of ugly white propane tanks beginning to litter the new village. Bob agreed: Something had to be done or before long they'd look like a run-down trailer park. So he developed a whole underground pipeline design, found the subcontractors, and built the system. This was a "marketing guy" who could think and act well beyond ads and press releases in supporting Pete's vision.

While Bob was a leader in his own right, he was a good team player as well. It became clear that all kinds of people were needed to build a new community from scratch. While Bob humbly credits Pete as the "real visionary," he and the other unsung heroes fought for aspects they felt would make Vail unique. In Bob's case, he lobbied hard for building Chair 5 in the back bowls when several Vail Associates (VA) directors urged that that money be used to finish the Lodge at Vail. But Bob was thinking about the quality of the skiing experience, and he knew the back bowls would differentiate Vail from the competition.

Bob Parker in the gates

Bob was not only hardworking but also valued doing the right thing. He fought for the Vail golf course in the early years when VA directors thought it wasn't that important. He knew early on Vail would need to develop summer tourism to be viable as a community. He blended pragmatism with a willingness to compromise, and this quality gave him credibility. Pam Conklin Pettee, his publicity director in the mid-1970s commented, "Integrity was the most observable quality I saw in Bob. He was a good leader and mentor because he inspired trust and respect. He had a rock-solid foundation, and he stood firmly on it. There was no shifting sand under Bob's feet."[5] The first nine holes of the Vail Golf Course got built, and that launched Vail's second recreational offering.

Everyone worked like crazy in those early years, sometimes to the detriment of family and one's own financial future. "We had no idea what we were doing, but we kept pushing ahead,"[6] Bob said. When he describes these early years, he talks less about the projects and more about those fearless people. He tells of the teamwork and how everyone worked fourteen hours a day, seven days a week, and gave way more than 100 percent. They were working on a dream. Before long, these pioneers sensed that Vail would survive the early challenges, and they began to create the backbone of the community. When it became clear that VA couldn't afford to provide all the municipal services necessary, they formed the Town of Vail – and Pete and Bob were right in the middle of it.

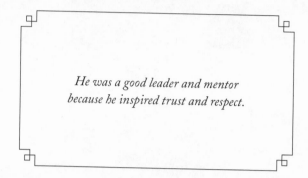

He was a good leader and mentor
because he inspired trust and respect.

Creating a municipality was no simple matter. It included an initial charter, various ordinances, taxing authority, and a ton of other details. Pete and Bob had to make the difficult management decision to give up control. Clearly, forming a town had major financial implications, but it also set the tone for a collaborative community versus a company town.

Community Organizations – He Knew How to Collaborate

Next came the Vail Resort Association (VRA). In the mid-1960s, many businesses were just getting off the ground. It was a rag-tag collection of entrepreneurs struggling to stay alive while enjoying the long winters and deep powder for which Vail was to become famous. The VRA was part chamber of commerce, part promotional arm. Since Bob was the only guy in town with a marketing budget, he collaborated with small business owners like Gaynor Miller, Otto Kean, Joe Stauffer, John McBride, and others to put Vail on the map. It was just another chapter in the series of "bringing people together."

Visionary leaders can often see what others can't. Bob said, "I could see the potential from my first day on the mountain."[7] And he shared that vision with people around the country and the world through words and pictures. He engaged others and built trusting relationships over a very long period of time – more than thirty years. He was a serious thinker, an accomplished writer, editor, and poet – and a man of action. He is known throughout Colorado and loved by those he touched.

As a guy who understood the press, he was in charge of preparing for President Ford's first visit to Vail as "leader of the free world." It was a hectic time with the White House Press Corps demanding every conceivable thing – rooms, restaurant reservations, Ford's daily itinerary, photo shoots, and lift passes. It was wild. But Bob and Pam Conklin were calm, professional, and thorough – and amazing to watch in action.

Bob was a mentor to many in VA. He had a remarkable way of holding your attention with penetrating eyes. He had a deep baritone voice and a practiced way of spreading out his words – plus a liberal use of "ahs" – that kept people listening while he wove his point masterfully into the conversation. He was hard to argue with because he was so thoughtful.

Bob was an early advocate for the environment, a perspective born in his early years on the farm. He became VA's conscience, dedicating himself to open space, helping organize the new town's government, and fighting for the Eagles Nest Wilderness area. He knew he didn't have all the answers, so he embraced other opinions. He sought expertise from experts. He served under four presidents at VA, and in every case, he took the newcomer under his wing, introduced him to the community, and guided him through the political minefields.

The Ski the Rockies Marketing Directors.
Parker is in the first row, second from the left

Bob was more than promotionally oriented: He grasped the larger national and international business picture. As one of the founders of Colorado Ski Country, he sensed the need to establish the ski industry as a force in the Colorado economy. But he knew he couldn't argue his way to recognition without the facts. So, he lobbied and got support for the first-ever Economic Impact Survey for the ski industry. Everything changed when the results showed skiing was Colorado's second largest industry behind agriculture. The Denver news media started paying attention, and the survey changed the tone of conversations with state legislators. This analytical, research-oriented side of Bob would come out again and again as Vail grew and became more influential. He was more of a well-rounded executive than just a marketing guy.

When some of the other major resorts in neighboring states wanted to ride that bandwagon, Bob helped create Ski the Rockies, another cooperative marketing organization that took this thinking beyond Vail and planted the seeds of Vail's international following. Forming this organization was out-of-the-box thinking at the time, and it became a key element of Vail's marketing strategy. Herman Kretchmer, director of the Breckenridge Resort Association and an important behind-the-scenes leader in Colorado, called Bob "the dean of ski area marketing – the person who created a profession."[8]

In the early 1970s, Bob worked with Dudley Abbott and Reverend Don Simonton to create the Colorado Ski Museum to honor ski industry pioneers in time for the 1976 Colorado Centennial Celebration. The museum started in a tiny building that had served as the phone company's initial switching station but grew to become a community attraction. Before long, the museum added the "Ski Hall of Fame" to its mission and has since inducted hundreds of these skiing pioneers. The ski museum has become a community gathering place honoring those who started it all.

The current Colorado Ski Museum

Bob was the first chair of the board of the Vail Associates Foundation, a board that read like "who's who." (More on the foundation in Chapter 7.) Directors included President Ford, as well as Tom Watson, the son of IBM's founder; Jay Pritzker, of Hyatt fame; FitzHugh Scott, chief architect of Vail Village; Dick Swig, of San Francisco's famous Fairmont Hotel; and others. Bob chaired these meetings with bigwigs like he'd been doing it all his life.

While the development of Beaver Creek was Bob's major focus during the early 1980s, he somehow found time to help launch the 10th Mountain trail and hut system. Working with Fritz Benedict of Aspen, Jean Naumann, Buck Elliott, and others, Bob served on the first board of directors of this budding association. With a dozen huts scattered throughout the White River National Forest, Bob helped keep our environment in the forefront of adventuring souls.

Bob's contributions to building Vail came from a credible, humble presence that drew upon that famous axiom that "it takes a village." He described his approach when he said, "Bringing people together of similar interests has always been my *modus operandi*."[9] He talked about others, never about himself. He persevered through the hardships of war, through the many ups and downs of VA ownership struggles, and through the challenges created by state and federal bureaucracies to get Beaver Creek open. His thinking and his actions have left an indelible mark on people, facilities, and institutions.

In 1985, Bob finally "hung it up" from corporate life and moved to Santa Fe. As he entered this new season, an early passion from his years on the farm resurfaced. He enrolled at the University of New Mexico and pursued a master's degree in archeology. Through the mid-1990s, he led a variety of digs in the Four Corners region, some previously undiscovered. It was a passion that had lain dormant all those years.

At his retirement, Harry Frampton, then president of VA, said of Bob, "He has been a stabilizing force over many years. From the beginning of Vail to the launch of Beaver Creek, Bob's mark was undeniable."[10] Some leaders can cast a big vision, but it takes patience, perseverance, and commitment to see it through. Bob Parker is one of those Vail visionaries.

WILLIAM R. BROWN

Sarge Brown – A Maverick Leader

And then there was Sarge Brown, the toughest of the "three amigos." It said "Bill" on his rarely used business card, but you called him "Sarge." He was born in Cascade, Idaho, and grew up in McCall where his father was a U.S. Forest Service district ranger. A football and skiing scholarship took him to the University of Idaho where he majored in physical education. He was an athlete for sure, and his love for the outdoors was like a father's love for his son. In many ways, Vail Mountain became his baby.

He served in the 10th Mountain Division in Italy and earned two Silver Stars for valor, but unlike Pete and Bob, Brown stayed in the Army and achieved the highest possible enlisted rank of Command Sergeant Major. When an enlisted man achieves this rank, there is something special about him – he can get stuff done. Bill had shrapnel all over his body – in his legs from Italy and in his arms from Korea. In all, he had been awarded five Purple Hearts. He was gruff and demanding but supportive once he saw you could deliver on your commitments. Like so many of the founders, Sarge was a maverick, unique in his approach, and you could see he was strong by just looking into his eyes. His complexion was ruddy from combat, some of it in sub-zero conditions, and then there were those hard-drinking years. And he loved to wear turquoise jewelry, but no one quite knew why.

Sarge Brown in a training exercise

For his last posting in the Army, Bill spent eight years at Dartmouth College as head of Mountain and Winter Warfare Training for their Reserve Officers Training Corps (ROTC) program. It's no wonder that he landed at Dartmouth. This small New England college had been the largest single contributor to the 10th Mountain Division, so they knew what they were getting. He said, "It was the best job I ever had in the Army."[11] Many alumni of that program remember the military rigor Bill brought to training. Tom Washing, who was in the ROTC program at Dartmouth when Sarge was there, said, "I can remember as a freshman trembling in my boots every time he walked by – he scared the hell out of all of us. Then I realized he just loved to terrorize the young guys. Two minutes later he would be walking around with a big grin on his face."[12]

Mountain Ops Director – He Brought Military Discipline

By 1966, Pete Seibert realized he needed to hand off the building of the mountain to someone else, and Brown was Pete's first choice for the position based on their shared 10th Mountain experience. He started by supervising the trail crew, taking on slopes and trail maintenance, and, soon thereafter, the ski patrol. Right from the beginning, Bill ran the mountain the way he ran his platoons. He was in charge – no question. When you saw a fleet of his snow cats coming down the mountain in formation, it was like seeing a group of Sherman tanks coming at you. It was military precision with near-perfect spacing and snow flying up behind them. And he maintained his military bearing in his appearance. Art Kelton remembers walking by the barber shop one day, and Bill was getting out of the chair saying, "Damm it, I told you to cut it short."[13] Brown's traditional "flat top" cut had left barely anything, but he wanted it "short."

THE RUSSIANS

In 1983, John Garnsey and I travelled with Bill Brown to Sydney, Australia, as part of our campaign for the World Championships.

To secure the three Russian votes, we decided to invite them to dinner. Never mind that none of us spoke Russian nor did any of them speak anything but very broken English. It's amazing what lots of hand-shakes and nodding heads can do in thinking the other guy will understand you. But what really helps is liquor.

We thought it would be cool if we ordered vodka drinks straight away. When the waiter brought everyone vodka and tonic, we got "nyet" from the Russians. They meant bottles of vodka... for everyone.

Garnsey and I were toast before the main course and in bed by 10:00. Bill stayed with them until 2:00. We got their votes!

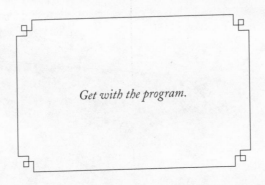

Get with the program.

None of the senior executives, vice presidents on up, would mess with Bill's guys or his equipment without checking with him first. He could pull it off because he ran a tight operation, and he delivered. Once you got to know him, though, he was a teddy bear. Paul Testwuide, ski patrol director under Bill and ultimately his successor, called him "tough, but soft-hearted." Commenting on Bill's infamous "0600" meetings, Testwuide said, "If you were there at six o'clock, you were late. Being there ten minutes early and being ready to go, that was being on time in his world."[14] That military bearing was ingrained in Bill – being precise, presenting yourself well, and giving and following direction was how he ran Vail Mountain. He set high standards for everyone, but he held himself to those standards first. His most illustrious line was, "Get with the program."

Bill would beat on the marketing people to get them out on the mountain. He said, "If you are going to sell this place, you have to understand it – you have to know it backwards and forwards. You have to speak from your own experience. So get out from behind that desk."[15] They were on the chairlift with him the next day. And he was right: Product knowledge was one of the best arrows in one's quiver. It's interesting that a guy as tough as Sarge Brown actually wanted everyone out "testing the product."

At Christmas in 1974, when the newly minted President Ford brought his family to Vail (plus nearly the entire White House Press Corps), the lead Secret Service agent, Larry Buendorf, stopped by Bill's office to tell him how the security operation needed to function. Before Buendorf could get out more than a few words, Sarge said, "Sit down, son, and let me tell you how it's going to work." Buendorf said later of that meeting, "I knew right away this guy was the real deal."[16] As time went on, he found Bill to be tough, in charge, and totally organized.

Were they sharing state secrets or ski racing tips?

In the early 1980s, a group traveled around Europe with Pete, Bob, and Bill promoting Vail and Beaver Creek. Pete and Bob were familiar with many of the people in the various places they visited. And Bill was tight with all of the ski racing officials, in part because he had been a fairly successful racer in Europe after the war and because his reputation for preparing the best race courses was legend. They all wanted to know how he did it. He held court with confidence talking about his crew, his snowmaking systems, and his fleet of snowcats. "We can do whatever you want. Just let me know." He could say this because he controlled most of the resources needed to deliver. He also knew when to hold his ground. During one campaign meeting for the World Championships, the Iranians promised their support if we'd give them one of our used chairlifts. Bill handled that one easily by saying, "We don't do business that way."

John Garnsey, who worked for Bill Brown on the race crew before joining the Vail Valley Foundation, remembers him this way: "He had a drive for excellence – it was his passion. He ingrained in us a culture of 'doing it right the first time.'" Garnsey tells the story of Brown's "file 13" program. He demanded that your desk be organized and that papers be filed properly, and if they weren't, he'd throw everything right in the trash – file 13. Garnsey said, "I came into my office one day and it was completely clear of everything. I knew Bill had been there. It only took one time – I got organized."[17]

Bill went to be with his maker in 2008. His memorial service, like Pete's, filled the Ford Amphitheater – probably 3,000 people. It was moving to see him honored for his service to the country and to our community. The stories told at the service brought tears, but laughter as well. He was dearly loved. His legacy was Vail Mountain, arguably the best-run ski mountain in the world. His trail design approach using "the big iron" (Bill's phrase for the gigantic D-8 bulldozer he used) supported by "rock-pickers" in the summer, his use of snowmaking, and his grooming techniques with his fleet of snowcats were known throughout the ski industry. Harry Frampton, president of Vail Associates in the 1980s said, "Bill helped establish a culture of excellence on Vail Mountain."[17] And more lasting than these techniques was Bill's way of treating people. He taught everyone how to be both considerate and responsible – how to get the job done...right.

The "three amigos" influenced so many people, each in his own way. They embodied the proverb "iron sharpens iron." All three have been inducted into both the National and Colorado Ski Halls of Fame. What is obvious fifty years later is the shared passion they held for skiing generally and for Vail specifically. They loved the place, and it showed. The commitment to their work was rock-solid – it came more clearly through their actions than their words.

Pete Seibert taught that it was essential to have a vision that you were passionate about. Bob Parker imparted that you could do more collectively than you can on your own. And from Sarge Brown, it was being committed to a job well done. The diversity of their perspectives and the trust they had for each other were special ingredients in how much they accomplished. Their friends and colleagues respected each of them immensely and were blessed to have known them.

COMMENTARY ON BILL BROWN:

He started out with the Slopes and Trails Department, but before long he assumed responsibility for almost everything on the mountain. Almost everyone responded to his "military precision," but they also knew there was a heart in that tough body.

Brown's techniques were legion. He used his "big iron" (a huge bulldozer) pushing things to the limit. Everything was hurry up on "his" mountain. Bill Brown was bluff, hearty, and direct, but you could always count on him in a pinch – always.

Robert W. Parker
Retired Senior Vice President – Vail Associates, Inc.

I hope this story has surfaced a few thoughts about the Vail way. To further the thinking, here are several action steps from this chapter worth considering.

Also, the Questions for Dialogue, and the space to write, are intended to stimulate your thinking and generate conversations with friends and colleagues. Talking about your perspectives with others is a good way to learn.

ACTION STEPS:

- Sell your vision. Pete, Bob, and Bill showed us how.
- Be resilient in making adjustments along the way.
- Stay committed, and keep moving forward.
- Understand what moves you, then follow your instincts.

QUESTIONS FOR DIALOGUE:

- What is your long-term vision? For your work? For your community? For your life?

  _____

  _____

- What are you really passionate about? And to what extent are you willing to take risks to see it through?

  _____

  _____

- What does it mean to be fully committed to something?

  _____

  _____

- And what gets in your way of being fully committed?

  _____

  _____

CHAPTER 2

AUSTRIA COMES TO COLORADO

*"Some people dream of success, others stay awake
and make it happen."*

Unknown

Gasthof Gramshammer with flags flying

Sometimes you need independent "lone rangers" to build a true community. Pepi Gramshammer filled that bill, and he still does today. He likes to do things his way. Born in Kufstein, Austria, he grew up during World War II surrounded first by German soldiers, then by the Americans. He was hungry most of the time and already a scrapper at the age of nine. He made friends with both sides looking for a little extra food for his family. Following the war, he began an apprenticeship as a cheese maker high in the Alps and then coached ski racers on Stelivo Pass in Northern Italy.

Before long, however, ski racing grabbed ahold of Pepi and thrust him down the classic race courses throughout Europe – the Hahnekamm, the Laberhorn, the Zugspitz, and others. He became a member of the Austrian National Ski Team in 1955, and ski racing became his passion.

THE GRAMSHAMMER CHRONOLOGY

January 1955: Pepi joins the Austrian National Ski Team

March 1960: Races in the Pro Tour in Sun Valley

January 1962: Skis the back bowls and names a run "Forever"

May 1964: Builds Gasthof Gramshammer

December 1973: Becomes the ski instructor to Vice President Ford

January 1981: Helps start the Jerry Ford Celebrity Cup with the Crystal Ball

June 1982: Builds the Potato Patch Club

February 1985: Leads the Vail Ambassadors to Biomio, Italy

December 1987: Launches Pepi's Wedel Weeks

October 1999: Inducted into the Colorado Ski Hall of Fame.

BUILDING A HOME

Pepi arrived in America through the Pro Racing Circuit, and he was winning many of these races, just as he had in Europe. One of the stops was Sun Valley, where he reconnected with Sigi Engle, the ski school director, who hailed from Kitzbuhel, the seat of the famous Hahnekamm Downhill.

Then, following another pro race at Loveland in the spring of 1962, Pete Seibert invited Pepi to check out Vail. He was hooked the moment he finished that first long run through the powder of Vail's back bowls. His long walk out that day gave the run its name – Forever. He could see the possibilities with Denver nearby and linked by the interstate highway that was winding its way up the mountains like a snake. And then there was the Colorado snow.

Pepi on the front page

Gasthof Gramshammer – Building at the Crossroads

Pepi and his wife, Sheika, established one of the community's first lodges, Gasthof Gramshammer. They actually wanted to open a ski shop first, but Dick Hauserman and his wife, Christy Hill, had a several-year exclusive on their boutique, Vail Blanche, so the Gramshammer's built a twenty-room lodge instead. It was patterned after the quaint Tyrolean lodges they knew so well. The ski shop and Sheika's nightclub came a few years later.

Gasthof Gramshammer in the making in 1964

It was small and intimate – heavy stucco walls, rich wood finishes, and an inviting fireplace. The exterior was a wild yellow that would normally shock one's senses, except that in Vail Village's alpine style, it fit right in. In fact, together with the Lodge at Vail, it began to set the tone for much of what Pete had envisioned.

Pete Seibert wanted the Gramshammers to build adjacent to the gondola, but Pepi had the foresight to select a site not immediately at the base of the lifts, but rather at the crossroads of the two main streets. He could envision the village that was still on paper and wanted to be in the middle of the action. Gasthof Gramshammer now sits in the heart of the community with a sunny outdoor patio that is constantly full.

The Gramshammers ran a tight ship, doing much of the work themselves. And Pepi was shrewd for a cheese maker turned ski racer. He had very little money, but like many entrepreneurs, he had his share of street smarts. And he had gotten here early – in 1964. That was the same year John Glenn orbited the earth and the Beatle's landed in America.

He possessed the wisdom to hire an attorney, John Ferguson, to structure a deal where investors (most notably Howard Head, the innovator of metal skis and oversized tennis rackets) would help him build the hotel in exchange for complimentary stays at his choosing. And knowing that he really wanted control of his enterprise, Pepi asked Ferguson to structure the investments as loans. That provision allowed Pepi to buy out his partners over time and be independent. Within eight years, he was out of debt and since then has funded all his expansion and renovation from profits. And as Frank Lynch, one of Pepi's long-time friends aptly said, "Pepi has *all* of his investments tied up in cash."[1]

When you walk through Pepi's bar (it's actually Sheika's part of the business, but everyone says, "Let's meet at Pepi's"), the walls are covered with photos of celebrities and friends that the Gramshammers have hosted over the years. The thing is, they really are their friends. Both Pepi and Sheika are gregarious and truly interested in their guests. Probably most notable were Betty and Jerry Ford.

DON'T MESS WITH SHEIKA

I met the Gramshammers in 1974 just after arriving in Vail. Sheika gave me an early indication of the Gramshammer way when she had a minor policy disagreement with the town fathers.

She wanted to remove an Aspen tree, those spindly little "quakies" that grow like weeds in Colorado that was blocking the view of her restaurant guests. Someone in the town's planning department said, "No, you can't cut down trees without specific approval. We just don't allow that in the village."

The next day the tree was gone, and Sheika said, "It must have been those midnight loggers again. I'm so sorry."

You don't want to mess with Sheika.

FRIENDSHIPS

The President's Friend and Instructor

Pepi became President Ford's ski instructor and guide when Ford was still a congressman from Michigan. They were fast friends. Ford was a fairly good skier, but Pepi made him even better. He described Ford's ability this way; "He was a solid skier with strong legs, probably from his football days."[2]

Ford loved the exhilaration and freedom of flying down Born Free, one of his favorite runs. When he became our thirty-eighth president, things got a little more complicated given the security demands. They still skied the whole mountain, but now there was a small entourage in tow. Over the years, the Gramshammers were with the Ford's on almost every visit. The president enjoyed Pepi's engaging way and infectious personality. And they were simpatico on their politics. Pepi was living the American dream and credited our democratic, free-market economy to statesmen like Ford.

The former president and Pepi

And Pepi was community-minded too. His involvement with the Vail Valley Foundation took off like a rocket with the opening of Beaver Creek, Vail's neighboring ski resort in 1981. (More on the Foundation in Chapter 7.) President Ford had agreed to launch the skiing counterpart to his wildly popular golf tournament, and Pepi helped dub it the Jerry Ford Celebrity Cup. Pepi was a huge part of making it happen: Not only did he convince many of his ski racing buddies to come, but he helped with fundraising as well.

When the Foundation approached Pepi with a new fundraising idea, he responded in his usual fashion. If the Foundation could get the Town of Vail to contribute $20,000, would he be willing to match that through some kind of fundraising event. Without hesitation he said with his disarming Austrian accent, "Ve do dat."

No one was sure what to expect, but the Gramshammer way kicked into high gear. Within days, the Crystal Ball was launched. Pepi had some funny ways of saying things; for example, "You should come, because it's de-taxable." This would be no routine rubber-chicken dinner. Pepi and Sheika pulled out all the stops, and in the end they handed the foundation a check for $100,000. That was one of those moments when the foundation knew for sure that it had a tiger by the tail – both Pepi and this new event.

To advance the valley's ski racing interests, a group of individuals (myself included) traveled in January 1982 to Kitzbuhel, Austria, not far from Pepi's birthplace. He knew everybody. The delegation met with all the skiing kingpins, and Pepi did most of the talking – in German, his native tongue. There was no containing him. Pepi was always asked to make the toast at the various dinners; it wasn't mentioned in advance but just sprung on him. He was always so enthused about Vail and so proud of his adopted home. He had this cute little grin, with a kind of child-like wonder about him. He was so genuine there's no way you couldn't love him, and pretty much everyone did. He was passionate about Vail and knew in his bones that world-class ski racing would build Vail's reputation – and probably his business, too.

In Kitzbuhel, he wrangled an invitation for the Vail delegation to inspect the Hannekamm race course. As a result, we found ourselves in the starting gate of the most treacherous downhill course in the world with a bunch of International Ski Federation (FIS) officials – many of whom had influence on future race venue selection. The Austrian Army had foot-packed the course, and it was rough. Our group was used to the beautifully groomed runs in Vail – this was different. Rocks, twigs, grass, and ice showed through everywhere. The incredibly steep Mousefolle section of the course was pretty much like falling off a cliff. The shared sentiment was, "These racers must be nuts!"

Pepi and Bill Marolt, head coach of the U.S. Ski Team, were off making a few controlled turns. The group was side-slipping, hanging on for dear life. It was scary, but we could see immediately why this was the premier race course in the world. It was a huge deal in Europe – sixty thousand crazed ski racing fans jammed into every nook in Kitzbuhel. Frank Gifford and Bob Beattie covered it for *ABC Sports*. Now we were energized, and we could see the possibilities for Vail. Could we bring this kind of excitement to the valley?

Schmoozing the FIS – Bringing the Best to America

The euphoria around the Ford Cup would ultimately lead to a worldwide campaign to bring the World Alpine Ski Championships to Vail and Beaver Creek. The event is similar to the Olympics but on a smaller scale with men and women from virtually every alpine country. There would be national and international television and presumably a large economic impact. The championships were awarded based on a national voting system much like the Olympics.

To win the bid, you had to woo votes and sometimes negotiate or arm-twist with FIS reps from countries around the world. There was intense competition from several European communities, and Vail was hardly known, particularly compared to Aspen where the championships had been held in 1950. It was exciting – and Pepi was super-excited. Having lost his chance to compete in the Squaw Valley Olympics in 1960, he felt that bringing the championships to his adopted home would be another way of participating at this international level.

In February 1985, Pepi proposed the creation of the Vail Ambassadors, a lobbying group of fourteen couples who traveled to Europe. Our primary purpose was to schmooze the FIS. And we did that in spades, and it was fun.

We flew to Paris as guests of TWA, one of our sponsors. After two days to acclimate, we arrived in Bormio, Italy, site of the 1985 World Championships, ready to make our case. The trip ended with three days in St. Moritz, our sister-city, including an evening at Willy Bogner's house. But the major outcome was realized at the Bormio Opening Ceremonies.

Vail Ambassadors in Bormio; Elizabeth Juen, Sheika Gramshammer, JoAnn Crosby, Beth Slifer, and Pam Horan-Kates

While the Bormio opening ceremony wasn't quite on the Olympics scale, it nevertheless included music, flags, a parade of athletes, fireworks, and the requisite speeches. It was small but still grand. We knew we were at an important event and felt the emotion. On the way out of the stadium, Bobby Albrittan, a colleague of Jack Crosby's and a part-time Vail resident, pulled me aside. He said, "I get it now; I see what we're trying to bring to Vail. I'd like to contribute $50,000 to the cause."[3] That simple offer, followed by several drinks, resulted in the creation of the Friends of Vail. Before we touched down back home, we had six commitments at the same level. Before long, we had twelve couples in the club. From there, the Friends of Vail grew to become the Vail Valley Foundation's funding backbone.

Our campaign culminated in our formal pitch before the FIS Congress in Sydney, Australia. Once again, Pepi was right there shaking hands and singing Vail's praises. In time, this whirlwind effort resulted in winning the award for the 1989 World Championships, which would advance Vail's international reputation. The mayor of Vail at the time, Paul Johnston, said when accepting the award, "This is an honor. You can count on us to organize it well." [4]

There were many good reasons why we won this prestigious event. Vail and Beaver Creek had great terrain and the best course preparation because of Bill Brown's expertise in moving man-made snow around. And we had a strong organization with wide community involvement. But more importantly were Pepi's friendships with the right people. They knew him and trusted him. And more than any of these other reasons, the general consensus was that the FIS gave the World Championships to Pepi. There's more on this event in Chapter 7.

> *They knew him and trusted him.*
> *And more than any of these other*
> *reasons, the general consensus*
> *was that the FIS gave the World*
> *Championships to Pepi.*

Pepi's Wedel Weeks – Getting Ready for the Season

In 1987, Pepi and I decided to launch a business together. He called it Wedel Weeks, wedel being German for "wagging," which describes the motion that expert skiers made back in the day for quick, controlled turns – as in the wagging of the dog's tail.

The idea started in St. Anton, Austria, in the 1950s as a way for skiers to tune up their technique and equipment early in the season. And it helped fill otherwise empty hotel rooms. It was a good marketing strategy and sounded like fun.

Pepi secured rooms from three other hotels, convinced VA to help with discounted lift tickets, and put the arm on several ski equipment companies to participate. It was an attractive package, especially when Pepi convinced the best ski instructors – mostly his European buddies – to join the team. They were excited because they would otherwise be idle, so this was extra income.

It was a blast all around. Great people, lots of fun, and it was profitable. The Bogner fashion show on Wednesdays was a highlight for many, with the instructors serving as

WEDEL WEEKS

By the twelfth year, people were clamoring for slight changes. As a marketing guy, I was trained to listen to the customer, but Pepi wasn't buying it. In fact he wasn't budging. He'd say, "Dis is da program."

So, after much agonizing, I decided to sell my half of the business to Pepi. The only problem was Pepi wouldn't let me go. It took three years but he finally relented. It was a good run, and I have fond memories. Pepi continues to operate Wedel Weeks, albeit less actively, because his age and his health have slowed him down. But he's as feisty as ever.

As a leader, Pepi had a unique style. He didn't have a written plan, and he never carried a day planner or cell phone. That wasn't his way. He used to say, "If it's important, I'll remember." That usually worked – but not always. One time we had a meeting set for 10:00 AM. I was there on time – but no Pepi. I waited a few minutes, then decided to look around. I found him on the roof fixing loose shingles. It needed to be fixed so he just handled it. He used that infamous approach of "managing by wandering around." He spent time talking to his guests as he walked through the restaurant. He went skiing with them. He was guest-oriented – but he also knew the company's cash position.

He is a true entrepreneur!

models. Pepi cajoled people by saying, "You have to buy 'deese tings' because I have a very expensive wife," which Sheika was. The last night was a farewell dinner where the instructors organized skits and poked fun at Pepi by imitating his funny mannerisms.

At 83, Pepi still leading a Wedel Weeks group

It became like family. Lots of interesting people from all over, great ski instructors, and some really great early season skiing. Many of those who participated have continued to visit Vail, and some actually moved here.

Beyond Gasthof Gramshammer, Pepi was an investor in other Vail Valley projects, like the Potato Patch Club and the Arrowhead development. To foster his passion for ski racing, he started with Anderl Moleter, another champion ski racer from Austria, the Red Lodge Racing Camp for aspiring racers. This camp then spawned a whole complex call Rock Creek Resort that included a lodge and conference center. Pepi figured it was a great place to stash Gasthof Gramshammer profits.

Skeika and Pepi living their dream

In 1990, he was inducted into the Colorado Ski Hall of Fame and received several awards from the Austrian government. He's a celebrated guy, but down to earth. Fast forward to February of 2015 when Vail and Beaver Creek hosted the World Alpine Ski Championships once again. And Pepi was right there pulling for the Americans, but in his heart hoping the Austrians would make a good showing.

He and Sheika have an amazing story. They still live above their business in Vail Village. Pepi talks a little funny, but he's a real entrepreneur.

I hope this story has surfaced a few thoughts about the Vail way. To further the thinking, here are several action steps from this chapter worth considering.

Also, the Questions for Dialogue, and the space to write, are intended to stimulate your thinking and generate conversations with friends and colleagues. Talking about your perspectives with others is a good way to learn.

ACTION STEPS:

- Have courage in your convictions. Consider what Pepi built.
- Invest what little you may have in something you believe in.
- Manage by wandering around; interact with people face-to-face.
- Make friends and invite them into your work and your life.

QUESTIONS FOR DIALOGUE:

- To what extent are you willing to take risks?

  _____

  _____

- Who's an entrepreneur you admire? What is it about his o her approach that you like?

  _____

  _____

CHAPTER 3

A COMMUNITY IS CONCEIVED

"Community is much more than a place on a map.
It is a state of mind, a shared vision, a common fate.
Community is not where we live but how we act toward each other."

Richard Lamm

Community members in dialogue

Many people dislike aphorisms – they are just too simplistic, too cliché. But remembering that "necessity is the mother of invention" applies nicely in the case of conceiving the Town of Vail. To Pete Seibert, it was an economic and cultural necessity to urge the formation of a municipality.

By Vail's third ski season of 1964-1965, Pete – and almost everyone else – could see that Vail was catching fire. The back bowls were truly unique in American skiing, and the national press was spreading the word. But with this growth came challenges like snow plowing, parking, water, fire protection, schools, and housing for workers, just to name the most obvious. It might have seemed overwhelming except that everyone was so excited and passionate about building the place that the necessities were second fiddle.

However, executives at Vail Associates (VA), together with early business owners like Marge and Larry Burdick, John McBride, and architect FitzHugh Scott, began exploring the various ways to off-load some of the costs of this new resort. Colorado law authorized special districts, so a water district was formed as well as the Vail Fire Protection District. But the major move was the formation of the Town of Vail. The leaders of this first municipality set the tone and laid the groundwork for how the rest of the Vail Valley would evolve. They were collaborative and innovative – they envisioned a "new community with good government."

COMMUNITY CHRONOLOGY

August 1966: Town of Vail formed

August 1969: Vail InterFaith Chapel opens

December 1970: LionsHead opens

June 1971: Vail Symposium launched

November 1977: Ford Park established

April 1978: Town of Avon formed

December 1980: Beaver Creek opens

November 1991: Arrowhead opens; Bachelor Gulch follows in three years

June 1996: Eagle Airport expands

April 1999: Eagle Ranch launched

August 2006: Miller Ranch completed

November 2005: Arrabelle transforms LionsHead.

THE MOTHER SHIP

The Dobson and Minger Show –
Crafting Good Government

Terry Minger wasn't the first town manager; Blake Lynch served initially in that capacity for several years. But it was Minger who, over the next decade, brought focus to the challenges of moving from a resort to a community.

Terry Minger at a Vail Symposium gathering in the early 1970s

Terry Minger was brought up on the dusty plains of Kansas and had honeymooned and learned to ski in Vail in 1965. He was a gifted student who sharpened his environmental leadership perspective, first with an undergraduate degree at Baker University, then an MBA from the University of Colorado, followed by a MPA (Masters of Public Administration) from the University of Kansas, and finally as a Loeb Fellow at Harvard. He returned to Vail in 1969 at a youthful age of 27 following a stint as assistant city Manager in Boulder, sometimes known as the "Republic of Boulder" for its independent-minded residents. There he helped plan and implement an ambitious community open space program, including the passage of the nation's first sales tax funded acquisition program. He brought a progressive leadership philosophy honed by Boulder's culture of student unrest, hippie mentality, rising technology, and college intelligentsia.

What Minger stepped into was a hailstorm of entrepreneurs wrestling with passionate skiers who weren't quite sure what they were creating. Was it just a ski resort catering primarily to well-heeled Texans? Was it the temporary home to young baby boomers escaping the pressures of urban life and the raging Vietnam War? If Vail wanted to become a community, what would it take, and what kind of culture would be required? These questions fostered a father-son-like relationship between Minger and Dobson. Dobson confided in Minger that, at times, the reverse was also true.

John Dobson came to Vail in 1965 with his effervescent wife, Cissy, from Vermont after selling their successful lumber business. The Dobson's owned the landmark Covered Bridge store. They were a dynamic couple – intelligent, innovative, and totally engaged in building their new retail business. John was most creative walking around a room pontificating as he puffed away on the ever-present cigarette. And he was keen on the politics of building a new town.

Minger and Dobson clicked immediately and fed off one another as they bounced around ideas about this new town. They could both see the success of Vail – the LionsHead expansion had just been completed – and they could sense the nascent struggle as to whether Vail was a resort or a community. To wrestle with this fundamental issue, one of their strategies was to create the Vail Symposium. It was to be as Don Berger, a local journalist described it, "a conscientious citizen effort to formulate goals and ideals for the purpose of guiding future change in the municipality."

The Vail Symposium – Celebrating Mountain Communities

Of course, there were other more worldly issues that Dobson and Minger wanted on the agenda – issues like the environment, energy, and economics – but the question of how Vail might evolve was their unstated goal. They wanted a forum to constantly re-examine and re-evaluate important questions and policies. They invited dignitaries like Jerry Ford, Robert Redford, and John Lindsey, then mayor of New York City, who by reputation attracted locals and members of the burgeoning second-home owners' community. Their underlying intent was to foster intellectual conversation that would help build a culture beyond skiing. By elevating the dialogue, Minger hoped to foster a community. He wanted both a "think tank" and a "do tank." Of course there was push-back from people like John Amato, a local entrepreneur and attorney who said, "Hell no, Vail is a business." [2]

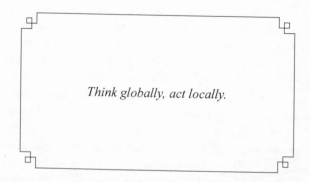

Think globally, act locally.

The Vail Symposium was seen as an opportunity to "celebrate mountain communities as the last best hope to escape from the urban center and reconnect with the natural world." [3] During this tumultuous time in the early 1970s, when the protest culture was in full swing, the symposium provided a venue, as speaker Rene Dubos said, for participants to "think globally, act locally." [4]

Robert Redford at the 1974 Vail Symposium

Among many ideas flowing from the first symposium was one concerning "home rule," a governance structure that sanctioned local control. A Home Rule Commission was formed and in September 1972 a charter was approved by the voters giving town fathers more control over bonding, sales tax, and later, a real estate transfer tax. Describing the leadership of Vail's early town fathers, current town manager, Stan Zemler, said, "Being bold and taking risks is no sure path to popularity, but an inspection of the community's defining moments reveals a pattern. Actions that can now be seen as visionary, ahead of their time, required commitment and resolve." [5]

Ford Park – The Result of Tumultuous Planning

By the late 1960s and early 1970s, Vail was seeing significant growth in skiers but alarming growth in condos. The people who had chosen a slower lifestyle, one more connected to nature, saw the pace of development as threatening. In response, community leaders undertook a comprehensive master-planning process called The Vail Plan. Residents from every sector of the community debated, argued, and cajoled one another on topics like pedestrian access, parking, open space, recreation, architectural guidelines, and parks. In the end, numerous policy decisions were implemented that preserved Vail's pedestrian-friendly image, including the Vail Village parking structure. Among many trend-setting improvements, the development of Ford Park stands out.

The debate around Ford Park was simply one manifestation of the "resort versus community" issue. The developers who were responding to the rapidly growing housing demand came up against those who felt "enough is enough" and that we needed to preserve some of the natural attractions that had brought them here. And because this land, just East of Vail Village known then as the Antholz Ranch, was directly in the view corridor of the spectacular Gore Range – it was a prized location. The debate raged for over a year with lots of shouting matches along the way. But in the end, and certainly looking back with several decades in the rear-view mirror, the voters made a good decision.

Ford Park has become a jewel in Vail, particularly in summer, and manifests a favorite local expression: "Winter is why we came, but summer is why we stayed." Not long after the town acquired the property, planning for an outdoor amphitheater began. Fred Meyer and John Dobson took the lead and engaged an architect to design a modern performing arts facility. They raised enough money to build the seats that people sit on today, but a downturn in the economy stalled the project. The seats became overgrown with grass and tumbleweeds, and many people forgot about the project. Several years later, Meyer and Dobson approached President Ford about naming the facility in his honor, and, with his concurrence and active involvement, the Vail Valley Foundation took over the project and raised the remaining funds. The result was the Gerald R. Ford Amphitheater that opened in 1987.

The amphitheater may be the most visible part of Ford Park because of the Bravo Colorado music festival, but the Vail Nature Center, the Betty Ford Alpine Gardens, the world's highest botanical garden, and the several athletic facilities and fields operated by the Vail Recreation District make this a huge community asset. The collaborative approach of several entities fostered by the Town of Vail is indicative of the kind of culture the town fathers were trying to create. And it was pointing toward a Vail way.

The entrance to the Betty Ford Alpine Gardens

The Vail Chapel – An InterFaith Community

The interfaith concept started as the Vail Religious Foundation in 1963 when the founders recognized that the makeshift locations for a church (like the Casino Nightclub) just wouldn't do – even though attendance was supplemented by some holdovers from the night before. And similar to the need for schools and grocery stores, this nascent community needed a church. But what tradition, what denomination?

The town fathers, including Ted Kindel, John Dobson, and Rod Slifer, all mayors of Vail, put their heads together and concluded that a collaborative, sharing approach made the most sense. The Catholics could probably have pulled it off on their own, but Father Tom Stone of Minturn's St. Mary's Parish was a progressive thinker – and a pragmatist. He asked, "Why should a budding community stretch its thin charitable resources on multiple churches?" So together with Don Simonton, the first Lutheran pastor who had been recruited to start a "recreational ministry," the organizing group decided to do a little research on interfaith initiatives. Unfortunately, there weren't many to be found – except on military bases and a few college campuses.

The Catholics worked with the Lutherans, and later with the Jewish congregation, in a way that would have made God smile. Simonton said of the fundraisers, "They will surely get lifetime passes in eternity." [6] As the chief fundraiser, Rod told people, "If you donate to our building fund, your chances of getting into heaven will be very much improved." It was the easiest fundraising he'd ever done, with a little help from above.

Among many, Simonton was the glue. Tom Vucich, who was married to Blondie by Simonton in 1977, said of him, "Many can say they love Vail and the mountains, but Don added the dimension of an ever-present and loving creator whose work can be seen in all that we do and experience in our community." [7] In addition to pastoring, Simonton was a ski instructor, historian, and author with his wife June. Although most pastors don't think this way, he was a social entrepreneur.

The Rev. Simonton making his rounds

As in so many other civic situations, VA stepped up and donated the land. They broke ground on the Vail Chapel in 1968. Before long it was christened the Vail Interfaith Chapel serving as home to multiple faiths that each maintained their individual services and yet found ways to cooperate. Over time it became a community-gathering place – the spiritual heart of Vail – where life's most meaningful moments were celebrated.

In 1986, a similar effort was undertaken in Beaver Creek to build their interfaith chapel, with many of the same faith groups coming together. President Ford chaired that campaign raising more than $7 million. And then in 2007, Brooks Keith, the Episcopal priest, who possessed the founders' cooperative spirit and saw the fruit of the collaborative mentality, made a conscious decision to advance this interfaith movement with a third chapel in Edwards. This effort not only embraced the interfaith concept but added a "community center" as well, making it a much larger and more expensive facility. For a broader description of the Beaver Creek Chapel, check out the video at *www.beavercreekchapel.com/content/about.*

The collaborative nature of the interfaith movement is yet another demonstration of the Vail way. And it doesn't stop with shared facilities. The pastors and rabbis have organized joint programs where shared questions or concerns could be openly discussed. A good example occurred following the tragedy of September 11 when Father Brooks organized a "community gathering" featuring clergy from the Christian, Jewish, and Muslim faiths. It had a healing effect emphasizing a shared spiritual perspective.

And there are other offshoots from these interfaith roots. One very powerful but largely invisible outgrowth was the formation of the Vail Pastors Network. This network was a result of a trip for many Vail Valley pastors, all from different denominations, to attend the Leadership Summit conference in Chicago sponsored by Michael Barry, a resident of Cordillera. Attending the conference together allowed these "men of the cloth" to see that the distinctions between their various "flavors" were minor. They could see the possibilities of working together on community projects, like Minturn's Senior Care Center or promoting a free Thanksgiving dinner at 4 Eagle Ranch for the needy or sponsoring the interfaith concert at the Ford Amphitheater called Uplift. Another dimension of the interfaith movement was the development of Vail Christian High School as mentioned in the adjacent sidebar.

The Beaver Creek Chapel

LionsHead – A Misstep Reborn

With the obvious success of Vail Mountain, Pete Seibert wanted to keep expanding. VA had the land and that part of Vail Mountain was within the U.S. Forest Service permit, so going west seemed natural. Everyone was feeling jubilant – especially VA's real estate people. With the ink on new zoning and architectural design regulations barely dry, the nascent Town of Vail certainly wasn't going to stop this fast-charging economic train.

But all was not well at VA. The rapid growth had severely challenged Pete and his management team. Cash was tight, as in a ski racer's suit. As

A NEW SCHOOL

Just after opening the Vilar Center in 1997, I was asked to help start a school. With my interest in learning and a re-emergence of my faith, and mostly to ensure that our kids, Conor and Brooke had that foundation, I agreed to help form the board for Vail Christian High School.

It happened this way. One Sunday, Pastor Dan Rolhwing announced enthusiastically that he had just received a multi-million dollar donation from a part-time parishioner from Chicago. The donor had given him complete discretion on the use of the money, and Dan wanted a Christian high school.

The somewhat daunting thing was that as he made this announcement and asked for help, he was looking right at me. It was like I had received a tap on the shoulder. The Lutheran's refer to it as "being called." As we left the church, Dan asked me, "Will you help?" I responded, "Absolutely."

The school opened in 1999 to young people of many faiths and denominations...even kids of no faith from China and Korea.

LionsHead construction unfolded, what some remember as "controlled chaos,"[8] the VA Board of Directors made the classic decision to replace their visionary founder. LionsHead opened in 1969, but the company was bleeding. The change in leadership was devastating – but necessary.

While it was not obvious at the outset, only a few years later this cold feeling settled over the embryonic LionsHead "village." Was it the six-story condo buildings? Or was it the wide spaces between the buildings resulting from an interest in more "green space"? Or was it both? Pete had been influenced by his time in France and many of those alpine resort villages were "high-rise" concrete edifices designed to withstand avalanches common in the French Alps. One of the architects, Rigo Thurmer, thought the high-rise approach made economic as well as design sense. Whatever the rationale, it was different from Vail Village. Nobody knows for sure, but perhaps Pete was reacting to the growing criticism that Vail Village was "plastic Bavaria."

Nevertheless, LionsHead continued on this path – more condos, more concrete, more skiers. The design wasn't a hot topic at Donovan's, but most people knew it wasn't quite right. The retailers complained, and the restaurants struggled. Many of the early Vail pioneers scoffed at LionsHead as being "way out of town." It wasn't until 1978 that the town responded to the problem. Meetings were held and expensive consultants were hired. But there wasn't much you could do – the die was cast – or so many felt. A feeble attempt was made to put lipstick on this "pig" by adding landscaping and dramatic sculptures, but it wasn't enough.

Before long, the focus was down valley on Beaver Creek

ROB LEVINE SHOWS THE WAY

While the complex planning and approval process for Arrabelle was winding its way through town hall, Rob LeVine, the GM of the Antlers Lodge, was taking things into his own hands.

Rob asked his nonprofit homeowners' association board to go at risk for $20 million to expand and renovate the Antlers. Although it wasn't an easy ride, they designed and built a new front to this 1970s condo-hotel that completely changed the character of that part of LionsHead. The heavy stucco, European look that had always set Vail Village apart was now visible in LionsHead.

Even though a similar design for Arrabelle was already under way, people could see that Rob and his colleagues had set in motion a new tone. Within a few years, Montenaros, Lion Square Lodge, and many other properties in LionsHead got on board.

Rob LeVine was ahead of everyone else – and still is!

and LionsHead languished. It wasn't until the late 1990s that the town and VA (now Vail Resorts) could muster the energy and the finances to rethink the mistake. Even the exhaustive community planning process called Vail Tomorrow in 1997, as positive as it was, couldn't change LionsHead's image. But it wasn't just the town and the merchants that were interested in fixing LionsHead; the ski company saw the need as well.

In March of 2000, the town commissioned the Vail Leadership Institute to undertake a comprehensive, year-long study to determine how the LionsHead Parking Structure might be redeveloped. It was labeled a "Community Crossroads – Where Culture, Recreation, and Learning Meet." The effort involved hundreds of meetings and tons of analysis of what might be possible.

In the end, the team proposed a $97 million project to include a conference center, a performing arts theater, a second covered ice rink, and a youth center. Additionally, some commercial space was proposed, including a coffee shop and bookstore. Part of the thinking was to build something that connected Vail Village and LionsHead. The pitch to the town was for roughly a 50/50 funding split, with half in TIF (Tax Increment Funds) and half raised in private contributions. The team was confident – the town council was not.

The idea died quietly only to be resurrected a few years later when a conference center-only referendum for $50 million passed voter scrutiny. And a few years later another vote overturned that referendum in a recall election. Part of the debate was that core issue; did we want to be a resort that attracted more business, or a community for the people?

Arrabelle – Vail's New Dawn

It wasn't until 2003 that Arrabelle changed the game for LionsHead. Much of the credit goes to Adam Aron, then CEO of Vail Resorts (VR), who devised the bold plan.

This step-child to Vail Village had been a headache from the get-go. Pete Seibert's concept for a second village was inspired by his experiences at the high alpine resorts in France, particularly Avoriaz, Courehevel and Tignes. Many called it "noveau franco." Maybe Pete was influenced by the "cultural elite" who were sensitive to the criticism that Vail Village felt like plastic Bavaria. Perhaps a more modern design, like those high-rise resorts in France, would provide some diversity. But by most assessments, LionsHead was a bust. It was cold, colorless, and uninviting. Aron's task was to fix it.

The new Antler's Lodge

Talk about a complex undertaking; this challenge included multiple condominium associations with vocal owners, numerous businesses, town building regulations, and high-profile architects and designers. While all this activity was taking place in 2001, terrorists were flying planes into buildings, and the prospect of war in Iraq was hanging in the air.

Arrabelle would require a decade of agonizing planning and more in construction. The disruption to existing retail businesses was considerable, not to mention the noise. The excavated hole-in-the-ground where the old LionsHead Gondola building stood was huge. The project was massive in so many ways: financially, architecturally, not to mention the sheer scale of it. But it changed LionsHead so dramatically that the area shed its prior cold status for the inviting style that had given Vail Village its distinctive feeling. The architects reverted to the Bavarian; heavy stucco walls painted wild colors, shuttered windows, and tight pedestrian walkways. Even though the development was extensive, somehow the scale was brought down. And while Arrabelle was VR's development, other property owners caught the vision and brought their worn and tired exteriors into the twenty-first century.

The story of the Antler's Lodge is told in the adjacent sidebar, but there were many others who got on board, painting their exteriors, adding much needed landscaping, and generally changing the face of LionsHead. VR even went so far as to change the name of LionsHead to Vail Square. It only took thirty years, but this huge collaboration between private interests and the public sector has paid off. Many would say LionsHead was a painful experience, but in the end, patience, commitment, and teamwork paid off.

Arrabelle at Lions Square

Unfortunately, it wasn't all good news. Arrabelle had huge cost overruns, technical issues with architecture, and lawsuits for ice and snow damage. It cost some people their jobs. Jack Zehren's firm was hired to complete an extensive redesign of the roofs to mitigate ice and snow damage, all of which cost a significant amount for the remedial work.

COMMENTARY – THE MOTHER SHIP

The men and women who moved to Vail in those early years were original and adventuresome. Vail was the adventure. For those who stayed, the journey continues.

Beneath the surface of great skiing, comradery, hard work and even harder play was the knowledge that we were a fledgling community whose success was predicated on that of Vail Associates (VA) and the Mountain. Vail Associates agreement was to provide the best of skiing experiences and those in business would create matching "bests" in lodging, retail and hospitality. The recognition that we needed services to match our mountain, brought a community together to evaluate how. The sense of democracy, and of cooperation birthed a "Vail way" of process. The financial status of VA opened the door for the foundation of the Town of Vail. We turned to a community forum format for seeking answers as to how to proceed.

Early on Vail developed a process of going outside for dialogue, study and research to address the issues in our development: town planning, water and land management, urban planning and design. The Vail Symposium gave us the forum under the auspices of Terry Minger and the town, with topics like "Resort vs Community", "Agenda for Tomorrow", and "Alternatives for the Rocky Mountain West". Community consensus has given Vail a method to "think globally – act locally".

Elaine Kelton
Former Owner – RamsHorn Lodge
Former Chair – Vail Symposium

DOWN VALLEY

The Town of Vail was growing like a weed, and the cost to live the dream was rising too. By 1970, the market forces of supply and demand were making it more and more difficult to call Vail home, especially for the work-a-day people who made the resort hum – ski patrolmen, and ski instructors, and hotel and restaurant staff. They began to look down valley, first to Matterhorn, and for many, further down valley, which meant Minturn, Eagle Vail, Avon, Edwards, and all the way down I-70 to Eagle and Gypsum. These market forces and the resulting migration caused resentment toward the mother ship; Vail was starting to look like a place only for the wealthy. But employees weren't the only ones migrating. Vail Associates (VA) was looking carefully at Beaver Creek.

Beaver Creek Resort Company – A Private Municipality

Vail's sister mountain was actually in Pete Seibert's sights in 1959. It took until 1968 to convince Willis Nottingham, the rancher who controlled the several thousand acres leading up to the ski mountain, to sell, extracting $5.6 million. When the possibility for the 1976 Winter Olympics came along, Beaver Creek was selected as the site of the alpine events. Then the Colorado voters erased that possibility, and VA went back to the drawing boards. While a more complete story of the

---

BEAVER CREEK GETS THE VILAR CENTER

In 1997, Harry Frampton asked me to join John Boll to lead the Beaver Creek Arts Foundation to build the performing arts center. It was a huge project with broad-based community support.

When Alberto Vilar heard about the project he offered to make a multi-million dollar naming gift. He invited me and Pam to his New York offices to finalize the deal. Over lunch in his luxurious conference room he told us why he was contributing to so many charitable causes – mostly to the performing arts. In that his business was managing tech stock funds, he knew what Bill Gates and the other tech moguls were worth – but they weren't giving back. He said he wanted to set an example to the super-wealthy. I found that very interesting then, but even more so when Gates and Warren Buffet formed the "billion dollar club" ten years later.

When Vilar was convicted of fraud in 2006, I just scratched my head – it didn't add up for me. Given what we'd heard, I guess I was just bamboozled.

Beaver Creek development is told in Chapter 6, one part of the story is how the ski company planners viewed the "resort versus community" question.

Just a few short years after the Olympics were sent packing to Innsbruck, Austria, Harry Bass took control of VA following a failed hostile takeover attempt. Those who thought Bass may have rescued the company from "outsiders" soon discovered his controlling business philosophy. Harry Bass was from west Texas and grew up in the hardscrabble life of oil drilling. He was tough, detail-oriented, and controlling. And he wasn't that fond of government either.

When it came to forming a municipality in Beaver Creek, Bass called upon Kevin Conwick, a senior partner at Holme, Roberts & Owen, a leading law firm in Denver. Conwick managed to shepherd enabling legislation through the Colorado system creating "service corporations." This suited Bass just fine in that it allowed the formation of the Beaver Creek Resort Company (BCRC) with the power to "assess" businesses, homeowners, and visitors. This assessment capability was essentially taxing authority called "civic assessments" and "common assessments." And because VA had set up the Resort Company, they controlled the board, thus creating a private municipality. It was unique and innovative. What Bass had learned from talking to Vail Resort Association (Vail's chamber of commerce) members was that not all businesses were on-board in promoting Vail skiing. Many said, "that's VA's responsibility – let them pay the freight." Most of the management team at VA agreed with Bass on this point, wanting full involvement from every business – not just the community-minded.

From the outset, the debate raged as to whether this "private municipality" was a good thing or overbearing. Pepi Gramshammer was asked to replicate his *gasthof* in Beaver Creek but declined saying, "I don't be part of dat." Almost everything was managed by VA – community planning, real estate sales, architectural design, marketing, transportation and parking, and of course, all recreation starting with skiing and golf. Control was the watchword.

The upside was that Beaver Creek had put in place, at the beginning, sources of revenue – assessments – that mitigated the cost of many of these typical governmental services. Certainly there were deficits in the early years that VA picked-up, but by 1990, the BCRC was in the black and building-up substantial reserves. This war chest was coveted by virtually every ski resort in Colorado.

The discussion still exists today as to whether the company-town model is preferable to the more community-minded approach in Vail. As in many aspects of life, there are those who lean one way or the other

– either more left or right – with more who see the benefits of both, who advocate for working together to promote the whole. It took ten to fifteen years for the Beaver Creek development to really catch on, but as more people built homes and joined the Beaver Creek Club, a community began to emerge – gated as it was. When the Vilar Center was proposed in 1997, the Beaver Creek lovers stepped up and fairly quickly raised the $12 million needed to build the 530 seat performing arts center. It has become a jewel to them.

Looking back at the evolution of Vail and Beaver Creek, one can see the differences. Some prefer Vail to Beaver Creek – some see it the other way. There is a rivalry of sorts but also cooperation. At each of the three World Alpine Ski Championships – in 1989, 1999, and 2015 – the two communities worked incredibly well together with some events held in each. Thousands of volunteers turned out each time to augment the relatively small paid staff.

The impact around the world was significant. Each neighborhood along the Eagle River, including Minturn, Avon, Arrowhead, Edwards, and all the way down valley to Eagle and Gypsum, is distinct and appeals to a slightly different demographic. Some definitely know they're connected to Vail – others say "we're unique – we're not part of Vail." But a thirty thousand-foot view reveals that the vast majority of people are here

THE HK'S PUT DOWN ROOTS

Many of the pioneers loved Vail and wanted to stay – but most had little money – so they built their own homes. In 1977, I suggested to my wife Pam that we look at Lake Creek. She said, "You're nuts, there's no way we could afford it." But much like Rod Slifer, I said, "We can do this."

That decision began what has become a thirty-five year process of putting down roots and building a home. We did it ourselves, mostly anyway. We engaged a family friend who was a carpenter to live with us. Even though we didn't have a clue, he knew what he was doing. But we learned. We helped set the logs, pounded nails, lined up subcontractors, and served as general laborers, mostly cleaning up.

We were "in" in six months, but by no means finished. We used every cent we had, plus 1st Bank's construction loan.

But for us, building our home didn't happen all in one shot.

We've been making improvements every year, sometimes additions, sometimes renovations. It's been an on-going process, but one that has given us great joy.

Much like building Vail, it's been a labor of love.

because of the mountain lifestyle, and Vail is the epicenter. Certainly from an economic perspective, most jobs are connected to the resort recreational opportunities. When traveling out of state, almost everyone answers the "where are you from" question with "I live in Vail, Colorado." Vail is the icon. So, taken together as parts of the larger Vail Valley, this community is pretty amazing. One tiny aspect of this story is Miller Ranch.

Miller Ranch – A Multi-Stakeholder Collaboration

As the community evolved, the single biggest issue that consistently surfaced was housing. On one end of the spectrum were apartments for workers on the mountain and in the village. There would always be college kids wanting to spend a winter "playing" before settling into a career. Over the years, the supply of apartments grew in response to demand, with the latest shortage creating yet another "housing commission" to address the problem.

At the other end were homes for the entrepreneurs who were building the place. Many executives or business owners built their own homes in the off season out of necessity. Eagle-Vail and Singletree became the go-to neighborhoods for many locals. But the biggest need was for those in the middle – employees who were middle managers, running hotel front desks or managing retail stores. These were people who saw the possibilities and loved the lifestyle but were making only modest salaries. Many of these people were young couples who wanted to put down roots to build a family. Government leaders knew there was no way to move from resort to community without these young families. Thus Miller Ranch was conceived.

In 1998, the Eagle County Commissioners, the Town of Vail, the Town of Avon, and the Eagle County School District grabbed the reins of a unique opportunity. The discussions started when Tom Moorhead was the town attorney for Vail and concluded when he took the position as county attorney. In Edwards, there were several small ranches that were lying mostly dormant. Through a series of joint meetings, both staff and people the staffs called "the elected's" hammered out a comprehensive master plan for what would become known as Miller Ranch. Moorhead said, "The result is what can happen when public entities work collectively for a broader public purpose. There were individual interests that were put aside to achieve a goal that could not be achieved by any of the entities individually. [9]

There were two two-hundred acre parcels just east of Edwards between the Eagle River and I-70. What the planners saw was the prospect of creating something responsive to our most pressing needs. The housing would include apartments for rent, deed-restricted townhouses, and small, single family homes for sale. The key overarching word in the housing discussion was "affordable." And tying it all together would be schools and recreation.

With considerable foresight, the planners assigned parcels for schools ranging from elementary to middle school to high school with a charter school and a special needs facility tossed in. And capping off the possibility for the full array of learning from children to young adults, the planners included land for Colorado Mountain College.

A street level view of Miller Ranch

On the recreation side, Miller Ranch would include all the typical athletic facilities included in schools – baseball diamonds, a football field, and playgrounds. Separate from the schools, the recreation district would build soccer fields, a skate park, a full field house, biking and hiking trails, and even a dog park. Everybody was happy.

It is very cool to drive through, or bike through, Miller Ranch on any day of the week and see the vibrant activity. Kids of all ages and families of every stripe. It's a little noisy, but it's energetic. And it's a beautiful example of entrepreneurial collaboration at the governmental level. From a community culture perspective, Moorhead said, "A number of community leaders who had been together in Leadership Vail Valley made this happen." [10]

COMMENTARY – DOWN VALLEY

Like Eleanor Roosevelt who would "rather light a candle, than curse the darkness", Vail found solutions as needs occurred. Housing for a growing employee population, expansion of the Vail skiing experience through Pete Seibert's dream of a sister resort Beaver Creek, took us "down valley" founding the communities and towns between Vail and Eagle. Participation became key. Though Vail was the engine which fueled the growth in Eagle County, we had to learn to cooperate in an arena where we weren't the sole decision maker.

The Miller Ranch land purchase comes to mind. This 400 acres was originally jointly purchase by the Towns of Vail, Eagle Vail, Avon and Eagle County to provide housing for Avon. Eagle County now owns Miller Ranch which is the campus of educational facilities for early childcare, the Eagle County School system, Colorado Mountain College, as well as Eagle County's largest public-private affordable housing development.

Elaine Kelton
Former Owner – RamsHorn Lodge
Former Chair – Vail Symposium

CREATING MORE VIBRANCY

By the mid-1980s, in spite of a struggling economy, it was obvious that rapid growth in the Vail Valley was a reality. Alongside this growth came an array of "place-based" philanthropic organizations whose collective purpose might be described as "helping others." The social sector of the community was flourishing. Beaver Creek was starting to catch on, and Bachelor Gulch and Arrowhead were on the drawing boards. Still, the continuing major challenge was housing for worker bees. Many were looking as far west as Eagle and Gypsum for affordable places. Both of these communities had long histories dating back to the late 1800s, but they were sleepy with little in terms of new accommodations. Entrepreneurs stepped in with two major developments that pulled the down-valley communities more into the resort orbit. And social entrepreneurs were busy as well.

Compassionate Organizations – Sharing our Strengths

By 1987, the Vail Valley Foundation was thriving with Ford Amphitheater programming, President Ford's World Forum, and the 1989 World Alpine Ski Championships coming. And there were other nonprofits in the cultural arena that were offering interesting programming like the Bravo Colorado Music Festival, the Vail Symposium, and a maturing Colorado Mountain College.

CHICKEN PIE FOR THE SOUL

One morning, sometime around 2008, when we thought the world was coming to an end, Pam had her "bolt of lightning" moment. During her morning prayer-time, she got the word to start a business. Then the next thought was her mother's chicken pie recipe.

One thing led to another and before long she was making pies for people in need. At first it was people recovering from cancer, then it was someone who had lost a parent, then it was someone celebrating – like a closing for one of her real estate clients. As others around town heard of the idea, they began ordering pies.

Her chicken pies have become quite popular, especially when recipients learn that they have also been prayed for during the making. She charges $35 for a pie (I say it's way underpriced), and all of her profits go into providing pies for those who can't pay.

It's a pretty cool ministry.

What began to define the Vail Valley as a place of compassion, however, was the flourishing social sector – those nonprofits designed to help others. The outpouring came from a broad-based constituency including many of the Vail pioneers and successful local business people, but the generosity of second-home owners was exceptional and has made a huge difference. The Vail Valley Foundation led the way with its Friends of Vail program opening the eyes of social entrepreneurs to what might be possible. The Bravo music festival built on this expression with robust support from music lovers. And the Vail Valley Medical Center, as mentioned in Chapter 9, grew with help from many of the same people.

Some have said the Vail Valley has too many nonprofits, but consider the good work of the Vail Valley Charitable Fund and Vail Valley Cares, both of which operate like a United Way – and we even have a chapter of that national organization here. Then there's Round-Up River Ranch, a summer camp for children with chronic illnesses built in affiliation with Paul Newman's Hole in the Wall camps. This ranch on several hundred acres was built in a short span with a seven-figure challenge grant from Denny Sanford. Next, think about SOS (Snowboard Outreach Society) that started as the brainchild of former County Commissioner Arn Menconi to serve inner-city kids with a values-based leadership program on snowboards. Vail Resorts' Echo Promise program got behind SOS, and it is now at twenty-five ski resorts around the country. Thousands of underprivileged kids get a chance to experience the mountains each year. How cool is that!

And there are many other wonderful nonprofits like the Swift Eagle Foundation that provides funds in emergency situations, the Youth Foundation that serves K-12 students, the Bright Futures Foundation serving abused women, and the three interfaith chapels mentioned earlier. Then there's Starting Hearts, an organization founded by Lynn Blake, who after surviving a sudden cardiac arrest and being rescued by Vail Fire, launched an effort to put AEDs (Automatic Electronic Defibrillators) all over the valley. A more recently established nonprofit that has garnered tremendous support is the Vail Veterans Program.

Cheryl Jensen had been a selfless volunteer helping a variety of good causes when in 2004 she conceived the Vail Veterans Program. It all started after meeting Army Captain David Rozelle who had lost his leg when a landmine exploded under his Humvee in Iraq. The idea was to help restore and transform military service men and women who had been severely injured while serving in Iraq and Afghanistan while defending our freedom. It started with skiing and snowboarding but evolved over the years to include everything available in the mountains from horseback riding, golf, mountain biking, river rafting, fly fishing, and even rock climbing. With an impassioned community, Jensen provides opportunities to rebuild confidence and create life-long relationships for wounded warriors and their families. Most veterans come directly to Vail from military medical centers like Walter Reed National Military Medical Center in Bethesda, Maryland, Brooke Army Medical Center in San Antonio, Texas, and the Naval Medical Center in San Diego, California.

Daniel Riley, retired Marine corporal on a mono ski

Jensen's vision is to become the standard for outdoor recreational therapy. One way the program does this is by involving the whole family. The injured vet and his or her spouse and children are included, thus creating a bonding experience not available in very many places. And Jensen has raised the funding and access to Vail's vast array of facilities such that the entire experience is without cost to the veteran, his or her family, or military medical staff that attends each program. It's a gift from the whole Vail community. Jensen commented, "The Vail community has embraced the service and sacrifice of those who have served. The wounded warriors that attend feel deeply connected to this community as it is a place of healing for them and will forever hold a special place in their hearts." [11]

The Vail Veterans website asks these questions: "Can mountains heal people? Can they open our hearts? Create a lasting memory?" The mountains have always been a place of renewal and rejuvenation, and now there are thousands of our nation's vets who can attest to that power. This array of world-class therapeutic activities taps into the freedom the mountains bring out in people like Corporal Kevin Dubois who participated in a summer program in June of 2015. He commented, "We are very humbled by the generosity of the Vail community. I did not think it would be possible for me to learn to ski after losing both my legs in Afghanistan in July 2011. The experience has given me more hope during my rehabilitation and reassurance that I can still do the things I love." [12]

The Messersmiths (Brian, Katie, Joseph, and Ethan) at 4 Eagle Ranch

Much of this book – perhaps too much – has been devoted to the building of the physical plant. And while infrastructure is critical, the Vail Veterans Program reminds us that the people dimension of the Vail way is just as important to a vibrant community. Kudos to Cheryl and every other social entrepreneur!

The Eagle Airport – Connecting to the World

As accessible as Vail was, being right on I-70, community leaders wanted to improve the transportation link because getting people over Vail Pass wasn't always that easy. With George Gillett in the driver's seat at VA and international demand growing, particularly following the 1989 World Championships, he put together a team of people who could work on the problem. In this case, the consummate entrepreneur knew he needed governmental help.

A key member of that team was Dick Gustafson, an Eagle County commissioner who shared Gillett's passion for working this challenge. Prior to the 1980's, Eagle County Airport was a tiny local facility run by a private Fixed Base Operator (FBO). Beyond the occasional twin-engine charter, the airport served mostly local private pilots flying small single engine Cessnas. Pretty small potatoes.

At this time, two other ski communities were developing direct-flight programs. First, Crested Butte started flying jets from Atlanta into Gunnison Regional Airport with Johnson Flying Service, friends of the Callaway's (of the Callaway Gardens family), then owners of Crested Butte. And then Steamboat, another secondary player in the Colorado ski industry, developed high-profile programs with American Airlines. Everybody was envious. Vail needed to get on board, so Gillett enlisted Gustafson to take the lead in getting a multi-million dollar grant from the FAA to expand the little airport that could. At the time, many people were scratching their heads trying to understand how it would be possible for big, commercial aircraft to get into this little airport. But almost anything is possible if you put the right heads together. The other critical person was Kent Myers.

Myers was a gregarious, good-natured Texan transplanted to Colorado, first to Winter Park and then Steamboat as marketing director. At Steamboat, one of Kent's biggest challenges was getting skiers there. This cowboy-oriented resort was at least three hours from Denver over two-lane highways that could be a little treacherous. Myers convinced American Airlines to bring skiers into the Yampa County Regional Airport directly from several major markets, initially Chicago and Dallas, by guaranteeing a breakeven result. There was no small amount of jealousy around Colorado for what Myers had pulled off.

Jets lined-up at the Vail-Eagle Regional Airport

Gillett and CEO Mike Shannon, their competitive juices flowing, moved smartly past envy and hired Myers to do something similar for Vail and Beaver Creek. The direct-flight program was a complicated game, but Myers knew how to play. First there was the technical side; could 757s be accommodated? Then there was the little matter of funding those lengthened runways, so Shannon and Gustafson lobbied Senators John Glynn and Frank Lautenberg for financial support from the FAA.

Then there was the task of convincing American Airlines that there was a market. And lastly, according to Myers, the most difficult step was getting American to actually schedule aircraft to fly these new routes. The marketing guys at American loved the idea, but if the schedulers couldn't work Vail into their system, you were screwed.

Myers added, "Shannon wanted to limit the financial risk of guaranteeing the air service contracts, but VA wasn't strong enough to leverage a big entity like American Airlines. So we came up with idea of trading American the unused advertising on Gillett's TV stations, which had a huge audience across the country." American bought into the idea – it was a win-win. American Airlines received over $1 million in TV advertising, and the Vail Valley had nonstop jet service from several cities that winter. Without government backing, both at the local level and in Washington, it never would have happened.

Within a few years, the airport served direct flights from numerous points around the country requiring an expansion of terminal space. Flights weren't cheap, but many people were willing to pay for convenience. In addition, the Vail Valley Jet Center sprang up accommodating private jets and charter air service, and a blossoming rental car business was launched. Adjacent to the airport proper, industrial warehouses were built housing many construction and transportation businesses, freeing up more valuable land up-valley. The whole airport initiative has been a blessing to the community.

Eagle Ranch – A Neighborhood for Locals

By 1995, the Vail Valley was well established as a tourist destination with plenty of hotel rooms for skiers plus second homes for the more affluent popping up like wild flowers. Many of the people being left behind were those in the middle – local managers and administrators making modest salaries. These were the people needed to run the resort community but who were being squeezed. Seeing this need was yet another entrepreneur, Jen Wright.

Jen Wright landed in Vail in 1967 working for Vail Associates first in their accounting department and then in real estate development. He is the quiet, visionary type. In everything he's done in the Vail Valley (Potato Patch, Arrowhead, and MountainStar), he has given others the credit. Most people don't know it, but he was the guy behind the scenes in Eagle Ranch as well.

Jen Wright

Wright and his associates at East West Partners could see and feel the need for more affordable housing. They studied similar developments, like Seaside in Florida and Kentlands in Maryland, both iconic examples of "new urbanism" conceived by land planner Andres Duany. Wright said, "The scale for Eagle Ranch was based on the classic template of small towns in America; tree lined streets with sidewalks on forty-five to fifty foot lots. We interjected new amenities into the layout with open space, walking and bike paths, and golf." [13] The planners wanted a more traditional community that felt like home, at least as boomers remember it. Modest homes with front porches, alleys, and backyards where the dog could run. A place where young families could build a life.

The Town of Eagle had been sleepy since its founding in the late 1800s with small ranches eking out an existence. It was, however, the county seat and home to the airport, so it had some reasons for being. As Vail grew, more and more people looked west and landed in the smattering of small homes built after World War II. North of town was open land with a handful of small ranches. Wright saw the potential and began amassing the pieces of a new community.

Today, Eagle Ranch is one of the great small communities in Colorado. Young families, singles, second-home owners, and retirees have discovered the lower altitude and milder climate of "down valley." The small retail center, movie theater, medical facilities, fitness center, and new schools are all part of what has attracted so many. With a library, county fairgrounds, lots of recreation, and a senior center now in construction, this little community provides the diversity of lifestyle that so many are seeking today. Eagle Ranch has the convenience of urban in a relaxed and comfortable environment. As the trees grow and landscaping expands, it will feel like it's been there a really long time.

Eagle Ranch neighborhood

But there's a problem, and it results from our free-market economy. While Wright and his partners intended Eagle Ranch for people in the "middle," what has happened is that demand for this lifestyle has pushed up prices to the point where seven-figure homes dot the neighborhood. There remain a modest number of "affordable" homes, but even those may be out of reach for locals before long. Fortunately for some, and unfortunately for many, that's the way our economy works. Striking a good balance between unfettered market forces with affordability will always be a challenge.

Wright describes his sense of Eagle Ranch as having "too much complexity. We tried to do too many things at once," he said. With the county, the Town of Eagle, Eagle County and the BLM (Bureau of Land Management) all having a stake in the development, it became complicated and unwieldy. He said he found that "bad boundaries make for bad government." [14] But as you drive through Eagle Ranch into the older part of town, you can see how Wright succeeded in connecting the character of these two parts by using a whole swatch of open space.

Jen Wright took a lifetime of lessons from the mother ship – Vail – and applied them in every down valley neighborhood he helped build. Today, he remains humble and reserved about what he's accomplished. The very opposite of what comes out of the mouth of some politicians.

This story of how a small community was conceived exhibits both unity and diversity. Unity in that the various towns and neighborhoods are connected by their shared love of the mountain lifestyle. Diversity because each is somewhat different in make up from a demographic perspective.

Jim Lamont, a community lobbyist, said, "...for most of its first fifty years, Vail has been a "transformational" community, one that was principally concerned with the quality of life and well-being of its residents; a community that rested on personal relationships and shared goals." [15] With this thought, one could make the argument that the Vail Valley is much more of an evolving organism than a fixed organization.

COMMENTARY – CREATING MORE VIBRANCY

As Eagle County has expanded and become sophisticated, so has the influence of Vail. It took time and experience in creating community, that of the Vail Valley and Eagle County, not just the resort-centric positions of Vail and Beaver Creek.

The Vail Valley Foundation took a leadership position on open space, removing developable land in Edwards and creating the Eagle River Preserve. The ECO bus system, Eagle Air Alliance, Castle Peak Senior Care by Augustana, and regional marketing all reflect achievement by participation county-wide.

We are motivated to improve and redefine in order to maintain a world class community.

Elaine Kelton
Former Owner – RamsHorn Lodge
Former Chair – Vail Symposium

Hopefully, this story has surfaced a few thoughts about the Vail way. To further the thinking, here are several action steps from this chapter worth considering.

Also, the Questions for Dialogue, and the space to write, are intended to stimulate your thinking and generate conversations with friends and colleagues. Talking about your perspectives with others is a good way to learn.

ACTION STEPS:

- Engage others in your ideas; avoid going it alone.
- Think globally – act locally (Rene Dubos)
- Discover what people really need; then find ways to provide that.

QUESTIONS FOR DIALOGUE:

- What does the phrase "the Vail way" mean to you? Can you see it manifested?

  _____

  _____

- What's your reaction to this proverb: "If you want to go fast, go alone. If you want to go far, go together."

  _____

  _____

- How do you define "community"?

  _____

  _____

CHAPTER 4

THE SLIFER LEGACY

*"Can the key leader accept that optimal performance rests,
among other things, on the existence of a powerful shared vision
that evolves through wide participation to which the key leader
contributes, but which the use of authority cannot shape?"*

Robert K. Greenleaf

Gore Creek at dawn

Rod Slifer is a true Coloradoan, born and raised on Colorado's prairie where life was flat and harsh. In Brighton, a farming and ranching town east of Denver, people worked the land and the land gave its reward: sugar beets, pickles, beans, and potatoes. With farming in the family bloodline, Rod was hardened for an entrepreneurial life ahead.

Rod in Vail Ski School uniform

When he stepped into the brighter lights of Boulder at the University of Colorado, he saw how the other half lived. After graduating with a business degree in 1956, he served a stint as a naval supply officer, managing 230 men aboard an aircraft carrier, the USS Bennington, that cruised the Pacific Ocean. Following military service, Rod spent the next two years in Denver working in an office supply business. As he put it, "Selling pencils was a little boring," [1] but his life changed dramatically when he moved to Aspen. This shift to the mountains would be a defining move.

GETTING STARTED

Aspen – Chasing the Mountain Lifestyle

Aspen was the "in" place for skiing in 1960. Vail was still a dream, but Aspen was at the forefront of the skiing craze. Young people were flocking to this former mining town to pursue their own dream – or to find that right mate. Rod showed up in the fall of 1960 and landed a job as a ski instructor with Morrie Shepard, the Aspen ski school director. It was a wild ride, working on the mountain during the day and then busing tables at the Copper Kettle or, later, waiting tables at the Steak Pit. To make ends meet in the summer, he worked for Morrie painting houses. Rod was living the Colorado mountain lifestyle before that phrase came into vogue.

Vail – The Early Days

Morrie Shepard knew Pete Seibert from back home in Sharon, Massachusetts. They skied whatever little bumps or inclines they could find and dreamed of their own ski area. In May 1962, when Pete needed someone to organize Vail's ski school, Morrie was his choice. Even before there were skiers, Morrie hired Rod to be his assistant. When asked why he picked Rod, Morrie replied without missing a beat, "Rod was a hard worker, and he was trustworthy. He also got along with everybody, so I knew he'd fit in."

For extra income, Rod, like most of the other early Vail employees, jumped on the array of odd jobs that popped up like weeds. It was organized chaos, probably a little like the first day of boot camp for every new military recruit. The discipline he learned in the Navy paid off as he tackled administrative duties like keeping time cards, processing bills, and manning "information central" in Fitzhugh and Eileen Scott's house turned Vail Associates (VA) office.

> **SLIFER CHRONOLOGY**
>
> **May 1962**: Hired as assistant ski school director
>
> **March 1963**: Obtained real estate license
>
> **June 1967**: Helped form the Vail InterFaith Chapel
>
> **November 1977**: Elected mayor of Vail
>
> **April 1983**: Married Beth Walker
>
> **July 1991**: Formed Slifer Smith & Frampton
>
> **November 2003**: Elected Mayor of Vail a second time
>
> **December 2014**: Received Lifetime Leadership Torch Award

It was an exciting time: Everyone was focused on getting this embryonic ski area open. Rod remembers the sentiment among so many, saying, "We can do this." Confidence was rampant, even while the construction dust from D-8s and backhoes rained on everything. People worked eighteen-hour days and then crashed in temporary trailers-turned-dorms. There was never a feeling of failure.

As the unofficial office manager, Rod picked up the mail in nearby Minturn and occasionally added a case of beer to fuel a little entertainment at night, including naming ski runs. It was a pioneer's life, and nobody complained. Luckily, the good Lord gave these pioneers a long construction season in 1962 – there was not a flake of snow throughout the fall.

Early Vail Ski School. Rod Slifer is second from the right.
Morrie Shepard is third from the left.

And then with the official opening at hand and no snow and no snowmaking, Bob Parker, VA's publicity guru, called in the Ute Indians. The native occupants of this spacious land performed several of their traditional snow dances. It worked – patience had paid off. Pete and Bob got a little flak from some fundamentalists about using a "heathen" approach, but the heavens delivered – only a few days late.

Real Estate – Seizing the Opportunity

Sometimes opportunity knocks. For Rod, it occurred that first winter Vail was open for business. Pete and George Caulkins had decided to sweeten the Vail Associates, Ltd., investor package with a home site on Mill Creek Circle or Beaver Dam Road, but they needed someone to handle the transactions. Like a committed entrepreneur, Rod raised his hand. He quickly got his real estate license, and even though he wasn't thinking of it at the time, the Slifer real estate realm was born.

It was still early in Vail's existence and everybody was scrambling to make ends meet. Nobody was making a killing, just working like crazy. Rod managed to get by teaching skiing and handling those real estate transactions on Mill Creek Circle. At the end of the third season, Morrie decided to move on from the tiny ski school, and opportunity knocked for Rod once again. Pete turned to Rod to take over, but Rod had on his entrepreneurial hat. Having been part of the Aspen Ski School, where Fred Islem and Freidl Pheiffer owned the ski school outright as an independent business, Rod proposed a similar arrangement. Pete just smiled, admiring Rod's enterprising spirit, and said, "Nice try." [3] By this time, Pete's dream was taking hold, and he wanted, and needed, every dollar VA could find. This door didn't open for Rod, but before long another did.

By the 1965-1966 season, the mountain had caught on. People were raving about the powder skiing in Vail's back bowls. Aspen couldn't match this, and Denver skiers began stopping at Vail. With the mountain growing, Pete wanted the village to keep pace, so he was wheeling and dealing on land. There were a few shops on Bridge Street, and the Lodge at Vail and the Vail Village Inn were open, but the town was still pretty sparse. The Gramshammer's lodge had just opened and there was a growing sense, euphoria almost, that Vail was going to make it. As part of this frenzy, Rod decided to take the leap and buy a small wedge of land on Bridge Street to more firmly establish his real estate business. It was a huge risk, but he saw something others didn't. Maybe he was familiar with that sentiment about entrepreneurs having an underdeveloped sense of fear.

The current Slifer office on Bridge Street.
Just a little fancier than the original.

Before long, Rod built the first phase of the real estate office building that still stands today near the Covered Bridge – even though that bridge wouldn't be covered for years. He partnered with Dick Bailey and Dave Sage, and together they built their business. With overall real estate activity still minuscule, Rod also partnered with Marvel Barnes to start Vail Home Rentals. Marvel was from Minturn and knew where to find the service and maintenance people to staff this infant business.

The early growth just kept building. With more skiers came more homes, restaurants, and retail shops. Throughout the 1960s, Rod and his partners rode the condominium wave, a new form of home ownership at the time. With some significant tax advantages, real estate sales of condos took off. It was the beginning of the first boom; optimism was contagious – it was in the air like a fine mist.

Pete and his colleagues at VA were exhilarated with their progress but burdened with expenses. It was obvious they couldn't continue to handle everything coming at them, like water and sewer services, police functions, parking areas, and all the pressures that crowds bring. Surely someone had anticipated this day, but there was scant attention to the mundane when the excitement of the skiing was so real. Necessity was the main impetus, but many of the natives were restless, including Rod, to have their say. Thus, the idea for a town became a major topic of conversation at Donovan's Copper Bar, the unofficial civic HQ. And a few beers helped in the thinking.

Rod and John Donovan with President Ford

While necessity created the initial Vail municipality, Rod, Pete, and others saw potential in a long-term partnership with the community. The Town of Vail was officially incorporated in August of 1966 and later adopted a home rule charter, giving the residents a greater degree of control over the town's future.

COMMENTARY: GETTING STARTED

I first met Rod when I was involved in a frame shop in the bottom floor of the Slifer Building in 1966. Rod was already well known to even us basement dwellers, but he carried himself in such a friendly demeanor you couldn't help but feel at ease.

Some forty years later I find myself on the top floor of his building and even more enamored with Rod. He has been my mentor, but he feels more like my best friend. He would advocate, "Take care of people and you will earn their respect; listen; be fair-minded; considerate; gracious; be able to laugh at yourself and with others. Enjoy yourself – it's not complicated."

These vignettes always came with a humorous story and were delivered with a twinkle and a smile and a clink of a glass in a friendly toast.

George Lamb: *Senior Broker – Slifer Smith & Frampton*

BUILDING COMMUNITY

Local Government – Becoming a Public Servant

During its formation, the Town of Vail benefited from VA's willingness (and foresight) to gift various parcels of land to the municipality. Over the years, this allowed the town to build parks, maintenance facilities, a library, an ice arena, and other elements of community infrastructure. This gifted land set the tone for a robust collaborative relationship. As opposed to trying to control everything, VA saw the benefit of creating a real community. Terry Minger, Vail's town manager, commented, "What started as a dream soon compelled the need to create a next generation municipal government capable of providing the basics." [4] Rod Slifer was right in the mix during this watershed period. This was probably when his public service calling first took root.

But there may actually have been a glimmer of this direction a few years earlier when Rod, Pete, and Jack Tweedy, VA's attorney, attended a meeting of the Eagle County Commissioners to seek approval of the plat for Vail Village. The commissioners, all hardened ranchers or farmers, liked VA's plan given that mining and agriculture were in decline. But they weren't that familiar with the complexity of land planning – including a plat – and so were not quite sure how to proceed. Pete suggested they refer it to their planning commission. They said, "We don't have one of those." Tweedy said, "Well, why don't you just create one right now?" [5] They knew Pete was too busy, and Tweedy was from Denver, so they said, "We'll do it, but Rod, will you be on the commission?" Within a few months, Rod was chairman, and he has been in the public arena in one capacity or another ever since.

They got their plat approved that day, and it became ever more clear that VA would need to create or attract other entities for the basics of a community, such as a hospital, a school, and a church. Together with all the governmental functions, it was a daunting list, especially given the dearth of cash. So they collaborated with anyone who raised his or her hand – and some were just appointed. A few early examples were the formation of the Vail Recreation District (VRD) and the Vail InterFaith Chapel. Rod was an advocate and board member for both.

The VRD took over Vail's first nine-hole golf course and built tennis courts as well. Of those early days, Rod commented, "The ninth hole was right on the edge of town, and if your approach shot hit the chairlift cable, you got a free drop." [6] The VRD has gone on to manage a whole range of recreational facilities and programs, from tennis to Nordic skiing on the golf course to skateboarding and more. These opportunities are a result of Rod and a host of others stepping up to do what was needed.

In 1968, with Vail only six years old, Pete Seibert called on Rod to assist in buying the Nottingham Ranch – what would one day become Beaver Creek. It took several years and lots of coffee around Willis Nottingham's kitchen table to close the deal. Pete was farsighted, and Rod handled the real estate side of things. Interestingly, the bar in Mirabelle's Restaurant is right about where that kitchen table sat.

His involvement in the 1960s with these various public sector institutions whet Rod's appetite for building a real community. A big step occurred in the mid-1970s when he decided to run for town council. Probably after a beer or two at Donovan's where everyone met to review the day's happenings, John Donovan convinced Rod to run by saying, "If you run, I'll make sure you get elected mayor." Sounds like Irish-Catholic politics, but Terry Minger added, "Rod was exactly the kind of mayor we needed following the go-go years of Ted Kindel and John Dobson. Rod was measured and brought a steady hand to governance." [7]

Rod would serve the community for the next eight years, in what turned out to be the second phase of accelerating growth. Building was so robust it seemed like Vail had more cranes than downtown Denver, which was also booming. Stan Zemler, a later town manager commented on those early pioneers when he said, "Being bold and taking risks is no sure path to popularity. But an inspection of the community's defining moments reveals a pattern. The actions that can now be seen as visionary, ahead of their time, required commitment and resolve." [8] Rod was right there as chief risk-taker.

As more and more skiers discovered Vail, housing was moving west, first to LionsHead and then to Eagle Vail. According to Suzanne Silverthorne, the town's long-standing community affairs person, many locals in the early years "celebrated mountain communities as the last best hope to escape from the urban center and reconnect with the natural world." [9] But too many were escaping causing the community to grow at an alarming rate.

The LionsHead phase definitely compounded the pressures that the municipality had to deal with. In spite of this stress, and in his unassuming way, Rod simply met regularly for coffee with the VA presidents, first Dick Peterson, then Jack Marshall, and later Harry Frampton. These were "no agenda" meetings to just talk things over. What a concept. The relationships were good, born out of an attitude of cooperation. Rod said, "It wasn't that complicated – the ski company and the town had common goals to make Vail better." [10]

The original LionsHead Gondola

Rod and his town council colleagues worked diligently, but not without opposition, in planning and approving the LionsHead parking structure, a library, and developments to both the east and the west of Vail Village. Neighborhoods like Bighorn, Buffher Creek, and Matterhorn all came barreling down the development pike. Demand for housing was substantial, both for visitors in the form of hotels and condos and for workers. The need for apartments for lift operators and front desk people barely outstripped the need for homes for the growing management ranks throughout the community. This rapid growth called for balanced judgment – weighing the merits of needed housing *and* protecting the fragile environment. Rod chaired these discussions.

The town council responded to these mounting demands by taking a risk and doing the right thing. For example, Rod led the effort to institute a controversial 1 percent real estate transfer tax to fund the creation of more parks, including Ford Park. When voters turned down this tax at the ballot, the town council approved it by ordinance after raucous debate and lots of hand-wringing. That took courage. Looking back, that 1 percent has done a lot of good, like acquiring more than one thousand acres of open space and building nearly seventeen miles of bike and pedestrian trails.

Paula Palmateer, who served on the town council with Rod during this time, commented, "Rod was very personable, respectful, and approachable – a good listener – and he was passionate and committed to Vail." [11] Others on the council described Rod as a consensus builder. Bill Wilto said, "He knew when to stand back and when to step in, but always with a velvet touch." [12]

At a time when developers could see there was a buck to be made, Rod made sure that the public was getting a square deal. That meant better planning, including protective covenants and design guidelines, parks, underground parking, and landscaping to beautify the town. Looking back, Rod said, "You could never move this quickly today – there's too much bureaucracy and too many special interests that slow things down. We were pioneers back then!"

CHOOSING GOOD PARTNERS

Beth Walker – When Persistence Paid Off

In 1978, Rod's life took a turn east to Washington, D.C. The Town of Vail needed more affordable housing, so with fellow

---

WORLD ECONOMIC FORUM – DAVOS

In 1983, I traveled with Rod, Pete Seibert, and Rich Caplan, Vail's town manager, to St. Moritz, Switzerland, to cement our newly formed sister-city relationship.

During this visit, we took a side trip to Davos and bumped into the World Economic Forum in progress. Reaching way back in my memory, I realized my high school sweetheart, Nancy Hinz, had mentioned her involvement after college with Dr. Klaus Schwab in forming this now well-respected international gathering of world leaders.

I introduced myself to Dr. Schwab, and when we made the connection to Nancy, we were like long-lost friends. He gave us the full tour, including Henry Kissinger giving a keynote address.

This brief encounter planted the seed to suggest to President Ford that he work with the Vail Valley Foundation to form our own World Forum in partner-ship with the American Enterprise Institute.

Everything happens for a reason!

councilman Chuck Anderson, Rod headed to the nation's capital to lobby Congress and HUD (Housing & Urban Development) for the Pitkin Creek employee housing project. Through mutual acquaintances, and after numerous phone calls, Rod finally got a date with Beth Walker. A native of Jacksonville, Florida, working at the EPA in the Carter administration, Beth was on the rebound and not that interested initially when Rod showed up in a cowboy hat and boots. His persistence, however, resulted in dinner the next five nights and a lifelong partner. But it took five years to convince her to move west. The final straw came as a suggestion from Christy Hill (another Vail pioneer) when she said to Rod, "Send flowers to her office every week, and don't stop until she says yes." [13] After a few months, Beth gave in and joined Rod forming what would become twin pillars in the community.

Slifer Smith & Frampton – Partnering Versus Competing

All the while, Slifer & Company was growing stronger every year, spreading roots like an aspen tree. By the mid-1980s, they had grown to thirty-five brokers in three offices. Beyond the brokerage and the property management arm, Rod was also a partner in several developments including the Cross Roads Shopping Center, the Eagle-Vail Business Center, and the Singletree residential development. And there was plenty of competition from Vail Associates' real estate arm, headed up by Bob Nott, a seasoned executive, plus a handful

THE FIRST MERGER

When Harry Frampton left Vail Associates to start East West Partners, he and Mark Smith saw the opportunity to launch a real estate brokerage to service their development projects in Beaver Creek. Rod got wind of their plans and asked me to undertake a research project to understand more fully how Slifer & Company might better compete.

I was running East West Marketing at the time and was equipped to conduct research for our clients. I spent a few weeks interviewing brokers, studying transaction volume, and assessing the market.

Then, Rod asked me if I could organize a meeting with Harry and Mark to get their reactions to the study. In retrospect, Rod probably knew all along that what he really wanted was an excuse to broach the subject of partnering. He said later, "I didn't want to compete with these guys but join hands."

It was classic Rod Slifer – collaborating with others, building a strong team, being both a player and a coach.

of smaller brokerages around town. Beaver Creek had opened and demand there was starting to recover from the Carter era of high inflation and high interest rates. Both those indicators were so high the experts started calling the combination "the misery index." And while it wasn't quite miserable in the Vail Valley, the community did experience a lull as it worked its way out of the economic doldrums.

In 1991, Rod approached Harry Frampton and Mark Smith about a possible merger. It was a short dance, and the deal was consummated following the story in the adjacent sidebar. It was a good marriage.

Within a year, and thanks to a recovering economy and the active civic involvement of former President Ford, Slifer Smith & Frampton (SSF) hit its stride. With East West Partners developing a string of projects in Beaver Creek under Frampton's guidance, SSF had a strong presence that rivaled Vail Associates Real Estate. They had offices in the Hyatt Regency that gave SSF a great location – something valuable in real estate. Both Mark and Harry speak of Rod as if he were a brother. Mark said, "Working with Rod has clearly been one of the highlights of my career. He is a genuine, straight shooter who loves being with people." [14] Harry added, "He has good instincts and good judgment." [15] Obviously, these qualities are helpful both in business and in the public square.

Mark Smith, Harry Frampton, and Rod Slifer standing

And then within a year of the merger, the last piece of the puzzle presented itself. With Vail Associates having taken over the Arrowhead development and secured the master listing in Cordillera, a new and vast development even further to the west, real estate was becoming a big business. In 1994, recognizing the potential, Craig Cogut and Mark Rowen of Apollo Ski Partners, the controlling shareholder of Vail Resorts, suggested they discuss a merger. Cogut asked, "Why compete when we can do better together?" [16] From that point on the merger with VA Real Estate came down pretty quickly.

By traditional corporate standards, this merger was still relatively small, but to locals it was big news. The new company, Slifer Smith & Frampton/Vail Associates Real Estate, was a mouthful, but its signage and advertising were everywhere. It was a little rocky at first, given this was merging a lot of long-time Vail brokers with the new upstarts in Beaver Creek. When they first brought the two groups together at Garton's Saloon, Mark Smith said, "You could have compared it to a middle school dance with the boys on one side and girls on the other." [17] But once Jim Flaum was on board as president things settled down. Jim was a former Navy flight instructor and a seasoned real estate sales executive who had worked with Harry at VA. There was probably no one better than Flaum, including Rod, to manage the large personalities and demands of one hundred brokers in sixteen offices.

The merger agreement spelled out all the details, including a provision to simplify the name after three years. Of all possible methods, it came down to a coin toss. Rod chose heads, and as was his way, he chose well. Slifer Smith & Frampton became the new corporate name, and VA reverted, in time, to a more silent 50 percent partner in the venture. The rest of this success story is history, albeit still in the making.

Vail's Renaissance – Mayor Again

While Rod's real estate interests were growing, he responded again in 2001 to the call to public service. Before long, he was leading the planning for Vail's "renaissance" during his second term as mayor. With Vail having grown so rapidly in the previous four decades, some of the construction was shortsighted, some actually shoddy. LionsHead was somewhat of a bust – it never felt right when compared to Vail Village.

In the span of a few years, Rod would lead the town council through the tumultuous process of creating the Vail Reinvestment Authority, which allowed future incremental taxes to guarantee the bonds to launch the public improvements. And as in previous phases of Vail's growth, the town partnered with Vail Resorts (the new name for VA), this time to remake the LionsHead into the Arrabelle at Vail Square, which included the renovation of several neighboring lodges and condominiums.

But the renaissance was not limited to LionsHead. During this time, the town council approved the Ritz Carlton Hotel, the Four Seasons Hotel, and the huge Solaris development that replaced the aging Crossroads Shopping Center. And then there was the creation of Donovan Park and Pavilion in West Vail. Beyond Vail, the valley continued to grow with Bachelor Gulch, the big-box complexes in Avon and Gypsum, the expanded Vail-Eagle Airport, plus the more affordable housing development at Eagle Ranch. The political and business leadership required to guide the community took foresight and no small amount of courage. Some may question whether wisdom and enough restraint were used during this period, but the proof is in an improved experience for everyone. For more than fifty years, Rod Slifer has been in the middle of this evolving experience.

Rod retired from public life in 2007, but the die had been cast. His steady hand and his intuitively collaborative style working with other committed leaders and visionaries had created something out of nothing. It was hard work, but looking back he said in his modest way, "This *really is* an amazing story." [18]

Rod Slifer – 2012

COMMENTARY: BUILDING COMMUNITY

While George Lamb was working his way up from the basement in Rod's building, I was a broker with Vail Associates thanks to Harry Frampton getting me into real estate in 1983. The competition between VA and the team of Rod, Harry, and Mark Smith came to a resolution with the merger of the two firms in 1994. Although quite a shock to some, this made great sense as there was land to be developed in Beaver Creek, the formation of Bachelor Gulch, Arrowhead, and expanding the entire ski experience. I was tapped to join the Old Boys' network and come into the Bridge Street Office as Branch Broker.

Rod's example of foresight, fair play, and support was fantastic in helping make this big transition successful for brokers and staff. Everyone benefited then and still does today from his willingness to listen, his wisdom, and good advice. This sets the tone for a wonderful working environment that encourages individual success. Rod's examples of service throughout the years inspires others to give back to this beautiful community and build a strong future for all.

Carroll Tyler
Branch Broker & VP - Marketing
Slifer Smith & Frampton Real Estate

Hopefully this story has surfaced a few thoughts about the Vail way. To further the thinking, here are several action steps from this chapter worth considering.

Also, the Questions for Dialogue, and the space to write, are intended to stimulate your thinking and generate conversations with friends and colleagues. Talking about your perspectives with others is a good way to learn.

ACTION STEPS:

- Be willing to seize opportunities.
- Find partners who share your passion.
- Be of service to others.

QUESTIONS FOR DIALOGUE:

- What's the one big idea you have always wanted to pursue? What's holding you back?

  _____

  _____

- When have you collaborated with others to produce something big? What was that like?

  _____

  _____

Chapter 5

From Ski Area to Multi-National Corporation

"If I had asked people what they wanted, they would have said faster horses."

Henry Ford

Vail's original gondola

The story of how the TransMontagne Rod and Gun Club became Vail Associates, Ltd., that then morphed into Vail Resorts, Inc., is more than a fifty-year story of corporate evolution. It includes the roller coaster ride of several public and private ownership changes, including the toll that these gyrations took on various people. But it's also a story of those who led a progression through prosperous times, recessions, and rejuvenation. It's a classic American entrepreneurial success story – not as big as IBM or Ford Motor – but Vail Associates started similarly with a big idea and very little money. The company was the focus of two Harvard Business School case studies, and the innovations throughout this journey are indicative of the Vail way.

More of Pete Seibert's story is told in Chapter 1, but in his later years, he reflected [1] on the growth that he saw in the Vail Valley in three phases. He said the first phase was the "beyond belief period" when a rough and dusty construction camp turned into a fledgling town. Then came what he called the "sweet and sour" years when the phenomenal growth of both the mountain and the town pushed some pioneers away and yet brought other opportunists. And finally in 2001, he observed that the "future is now," those years when the deeply rooted sense of optimism propelled the community forward into the new millennium. This evolving story is about how the leaders in each era managed change and continued to improve on Pete's dream by keeping his entrepreneurial spirit alive.

SEIBERT ERA CHRONOLOGY

March 1957: Pete and Earl Eaton ski the back bowls

May 1960: Vail Associates formed; Pete Seibert named general partner

December 1962: Vail Mountain opens

November 1969: LionsHead opens

March 1970: Dick Peterson replaces Seibert. Pete becomes board chair

---

BEYOND BELIEF PERIOD

The Birthing: Pete Seibert's Era

There are many keys to this success, but none is more important than a commitment to excellence, to staying the course over more than five decades. From the very beginning, Pete and his colleagues set high standards for guest service with the hope of becoming something special – something different. Their commitment to continually improving the mountain experience required foresight and money. But even more than hard currency, it called for an attitude of courage and the willingness to take risks. You don't become outstanding by sitting back.

Vail's Back Bowls

The story of Vail's founding, of Pete's vision, is reminiscent of pioneers who opened the West. Starting with virtually no money – simply an idea – and enrolling first a few, then hundreds of, entrepreneurs into the Vail vision sounds a bit like a miracle. In many ways, it was a miracle, certainly a tremendous accomplishment of creating something from scratch. Seibert surrounded himself with entrepreneurial-minded people, like Bill Whiteford, Dick Hauserman, Bob Lazier, Rene and Dave Gorsuch, and so many others who functioned like a team – sort of.

The Seibert era saw the establishment of numerous new businesses, new institutions, and new homes to serve the flood of newcomers. It's hard to imagine today pulling off the establishment of a new town without the convenience of regular telephone service, a grocery store, or a church. Remember that President John F. Kennedy had just been elected and the Vietnam War had not yet heated up. Those pioneers did it through passion for the idea – and certainly some help from above. And the 55,000 raving skier days that first year didn't hurt.

Every success brings challenges and failures. As Vail Associates (VA) grew, the demands on Pete and his small team of cohorts, or as Morrie Sheppard called them, "committed amateurs," [2] became somewhat overwhelming. Everything was new, and while they responded heroically in many cases, the sheer volume of management decisions started to weigh heavy. By 1969, the board of VA could see the need for more professional management. And, as many founders do, Pete resisted. But he probably also knew deep down that he needed help.

Transitioning to Professional Managers – Changing the Game

PETERSON ERA CHRONOLOGY

November 1970: Peterson hired as president

December 1970: Hires Jim Bartlett as executive VP

May 1972: Beaver Creek land optioned

November 1972: Colorado voters reject 1976 Winter Olympics

December 1974: Beaver Creek design rethought

April 1975: Contran Corporation makes hostile tender offer

March 1976: LionsHead Gondola accident

March 1977: Goliad Oil (Dick and Harry Bass) acquires VA

May 1977: Peterson and other officers resign

Even though Vail was growing, the company was in trouble. Pete's push for LionsHead had drained precious human and financial resources and put VA in a bind – basically, it was too much too soon. It was time for a change, and most people don't like change. The company's rapid growth called for experienced business management, and neither Pete nor Bob Parker, his marketing director, fit this bill. So, the directors kicked Pete upstairs to chair the board.

If Pete was short in management skills, Dick Peterson had them in spades. As a Harvard Business School grad, Dick knew about systems and finance and organization. The board recruited him from Denver's office of Touche Ross, a well-respected accounting and consulting firm. He was a numbers guy – the cigar chomping kind – and he knew he needed to build a stronger team. He had served several years as an

Air Force officer on a SAC (Strategic Air Command) base where he experienced the value of engaging and trusting the senior enlisted men around him. Military people know that you listen to experience or you get your butt kicked.

Dick's right-hand man was Jim Bartlett, who had also been at Touche Ross, had a Stanford MBA, and was smart and aggressive. As executive vice president of operations, he insisted on having marketing under his purview in order to have some measure of influence over the skier-visit growth that he was accountable for. Bartlett had a very direct style of telling people what he wanted and, at the same time, making them feel ownership of a project.

Everybody on Peterson's team was intelligent and hard-charging. They had to be: Directors, investors, and everybody else was watching closely given the financial stress. This new management team pushed both Pete and Bob into different and more narrow roles, Pete on long-range planning, Bob on publicity, and both on Beaver Creek. There was creative tension, as in a friendly tug-of-war, but in this phase of rapid growth, that tension was needed.

But it wasn't just the mountain; the town was growing up as well. At that time, Terry Minger, then Vail Town manager said, "We were a teenager as a community. Vail started out as sort of a country club and became a company town. Now we are finally moving toward something that resembles a community. Real people live here." [3]

SMILE SCHOOL

One of Dick Peterson's smaller successes, but no less valuable, was to hire the Wilson Learning Corporation to bring a focus to guest service.

In 1975, Larry Wilson and Richard Leider arrived in Vail to start what we all called "smile school." It was an organized program to assist every employee but, most importantly, the front line people (lift operators, ticket sellers, food service workers, and ski school instructors) in how they might create more positive interactions with our guests. The program was based on a concept called "transactional analysis" and rooted in assessments of each employee's "social style." It was very interesting.

As number two in marketing, I was one of a handful of managers selected to carry on this work when Wilson and Leider headed home. I led programs for a couple of years and found the experience of facilitation came naturally to me.

For me, Smile School started a life-long pursuit of personal development.

*"We were a teenager
as a community.*

Land Grants – A Public-Private Collaboration

Vail was growing like crazy; Denver skiers were coming in droves creating traffic and parking problems. A hallmark of Peterson's administration was building on Pete's commitment of collaboration between the ski company and the Town of Vail. As the master developer of Vail and the community's largest employer, VA had power and responsibility...and a lot of land.

Peterson worked with Minger to gift numerous tracks of land for various municipal purposes – open space, parks, stream frontage, parking structures, and other public needs. Of that period, Minger commented, "Dick Peterson was a very smart guy who understood he couldn't go it alone. He needed the town the way a child needs her mother." [4]

Rethinking Beaver Creek – A Second Chance

Righting the ship after the financial drain of LionsHead was only one of Peterson's major challenges. The other was to figure out what to do with VA's multi-million dollar investment in Beaver Creek, Vail's sister mountain ten miles to the west.

Even before Vail opened, Pete Seibert had his eye on Beaver Creek because of its natural mix of ideal ski terrain. But it would have to wait – the financial demands of Vail Mountain were just too great. When Denver began to consider an Olympic bid, Pete started lobbying for Beaver Creek, and in 1971 Denver was selected to host the 1976 Winter Olympics. Beaver Creek was selected right off the drawing boards to be the alpine skiing venue – a huge opportunity. It seemed like a good idea that could put Colorado skiing on the map.

Unbeknownst to many, Bob Parker saw the Olympics as a distraction. He worked for the games as part of the Vail team, but he never believed in their importance. Bob said, "We had enough problems without bringing on more." He felt that World Cup-level races would be more effective. There were others who weren't excited about the Olympics either, especially Dick Lamm, then a Colorado State Senator.

Lamm felt the Olympics would ruin Colorado, and a substantial coalition agreed with him. He led a successful referendum campaign to block state funding for the games, and, within a year, was elected governor. The Olympics went to Innsbruck, Austria. There was rancor on both sides of the issue, but in retrospect it was probably for the best. It's pretty difficult to build infrastructure for the Olympics and then have it also function smoothly as a resort – like building the church for Christmas.

In essence, Beaver Creek was granted a reprieve from the heavy infrastructure demands inherent in creating an Olympic venue from scratch: surges of people, traffic, parking, and competition sites followed by a large void after the events. Places like Squaw Valley have found it difficult to re-establish equilibrium for the future resort in a place conceived for Olympic demands. The decision to bypass the Olympics allowed the necessary time and a careful planning process that led to a sound development plan for Beaver Creek.

Shortly after Lamm's election, Bob Parker received the assignment to rethink Beaver Creek as a twenty-first century resort. Peterson had come to see Bob as a trusted member of the VA team and as the executive with the credibility to get Beaver Creek approved. Parker and Lamm would learn to dance together for many years to come. Reimagining the kind of resort Beaver Creek could become was one thing – financing it was quite another. To pay the Nottingham's their many millions, the company had to sell its Meadow Mountain property at Dowd Junction (then a ski-school teaching area, now a sledding hill) to the U.S. Forest Service. In addition, the company had to engineer a sale/leaseback of the LionsHead Gondola to generate enough cash. It required fast footwork by Andy Norris, another leader on Peterson's team.

Reflecting back forty years later, Peterson said, "My time at VA was mostly marked by progress." [6] He felt best about the continuing commitment to quality, the sense of cooperation, and working with like-minded people throughout the community. The exception to these positives were two things, one mostly irreparable and one challenging but ultimately life altering.

The Gondola Accident – Managing a Crisis

When two cars on the LionsHead Gondola fell in March 1976, it was a tragedy of huge proportions. Four people lost their lives, and the tragedy sent the company into a tailspin. The immediate evacuation of several hundred gondola passengers was handled heroically by the Ski Patrol – and then there was the media frenzy, followed by several lawsuits. The tragedy lived on for many years in the hearts and minds of everyone involved. For Dick Peterson, it remains a blemish.

Chupa Nelson securing a dangling gondola car

The life altering experience for Dick was learning how to handle the stress. Every president of the ski company is in the spotlight. Vail was a small town – not quite a company town any longer – but VA was still by far the largest employer. Peterson admits he was an introvert in a job that demanded a heavy social schedule. No matter where he went – the vegetable aisle at Safeway or the post office – people had a word of advice or criticism, and the latter was not always delivered nicely. Every key decision, such as the amount of trail grooming or price of lift tickets, was reported in the *Vail Trail,* the predecessor to the *Vail Daily.* He was living in a fishbowl. He didn't take the time to get away, particularly after the gondola accident, until Bob Parker urged him to spend some time in the backcountry. Peterson said, "Bob saved my life; I needed solitude and time to reflect." [7] That quiet time out in God's creation away from the din became a spiritual experience.

During this same period and resulting partly from the burdensome gondola litigation, Dick and Harry Bass, brothers on the VA board, took the company private – partly to avoid a hostile takeover by the Contran Corporation. This change in ownership resulted in Dick Peterson and most of his senior management team resigning, except for Bob Parker. It marked the end of one progressive era where professional managers put much of the business infrastructure in place for the company to manage its growing challenges. At the same time, the voices of restraint, to slow down and protect the environment, were starting to rise.

COMMENTARY: BEYOND BELIEF PERIOD

Vail Associates (VA) in the late 1960s was a very small company with an entrepreneurial spirit characterized by Pete Seibert. I remember Bill Brown complaining to me that Pete was "like a butterfly in a bush," always moving from idea to idea – most of them big.

I was the only accountant at the time when the company floated a convertible bond issue to build LionsHead and acquire Meadow Mountain in Minturn. The company was not organized to take on the task of building the gondola, the base and mountain terminals, trails, along with the first condominium project at the base, LionsHead Centre. Don Almond, mountain manager, and Bill Brown summoned the troops consisting of mountain personnel, ski instructors, and others to assign them jobs to accomplish the task. If you were breathing, you had a job. In the end, the gondola opened on time and the lifts ran, and once again Vail was great. However, there was a downside to the event; the company had large cost overruns and the bond prices had plunged; the company was broke and this set in motion the management change from the small, entrepreneurial operation to hiring professional number crunchers.

The transition was not easy; the board of directors ran the company for several months until Clay Simon was appointed president. He was followed rather quickly by Dick Peterson in the early 1970s who brought stability to the company. We survived.

Jen Wright
  Managing Partner – Wright & Co.

THE SWEET AND SOUR YEARS

Still Growing: The Jack Marshall Years

In 1977, Jack Marshall, an architect by training but a developer by trade, was hired as president. His experience included developing the island of Lanai and building the Spanish Bay complex at Pebble Beach and Elkhorn Village in Sun Valley. He was an easy-going guy, almost timid, with a perpetual smile and a *laissez-faire* management style. But this period was a traumatic time for VA, to say the least. With the gondola accident there were victims, litigators, and rescuers who would live with this tragedy for years. Marshall managed the whole process as best he could while trying to rebuild the company and shouldering the burden of many millions in pending lawsuits. It was an extremely demanding time with tight cash and interest rates climbing through the teens.

With Peterson and his chief lieutenants moving on to other resorts, one of Marshall's first tasks was to rebuild the management team. In most departments, he simply promoted the number two person, thinking that the company didn't need any more disruption. It was an opportunity for a lot of people and it worked.

A BAPTISM BY FIRE

When I became VP of marketing in 1977, I was having a blast creating ads and promotions that brought more people to Vail. The marketing team fashioned and promoted the Colorado Card, an effort to bring skiers here during the "shoulder" periods. We also created the initial branding for Beaver Creek, established a sister-city relationship with St. Moritz, and cooked up the Vail Valley Foundation.

I was beginning to see the power of responsibility. I was blessed with a team of creative, energetic people who loved what they were doing. But I struggled with some of the team when follow-through on our agreements was weak. I saw that I couldn't make them take action; I could only take responsibility for my part of the relationship. And, in doing so, I could actually take 100 percent responsibility for myself.

This realization allowed me to move away from the blame game. This was huge for me.

Jack Marshall and Harry Bass on their European tour

The Thirty-eighth President – Beaver Creek's First Citizen

MARSHALL ERA CHRONOLOGY

June 1977: Inaugural Jerry Ford Golf Invitational held

August 1977: Marshall hired as President

August 1978: President Ford acquires lot in Beaver Creek

November 1972: Colorado voters reject 1976 Winter Olympics

September 1978: Vail Associates Foundation formed

December 1980: Beaver Creek opens

April 1982: Marshall resigns

Perhaps Jack Marshall's most innovative move involved President Ford. When Ford lost the White House, Vail gained a "first citizen." In August of 1977, John Purcell, Bob Barrett, and others started the Jerry Ford Invitational Golf Tournament that brought numerous celebrities and Ford friends to the valley. It was a major happening. Bob Hope cracked jokes, Willie Nelson sang, and Jack Nicklaus won the fairly sizable purse but gave it all back to the Vail Valley Medical Center.

In the midst of VA's turmoil and angst, Marshall negotiated a wonderful arrangement with President Ford. He traded Ford's condo at the Lodge Towers in

Vail for a lot in Beaver Creek that would make the Ford's one of the first residents. The kicker was VA got fifteen days of Ford's time each year for the next fifteen years. Marshall's initiative launched the Vail Associates Foundation, which is described in more detail in Chapter 7.

President Ford and his architects and builder,
Mitch Hoyt, reviewing the president's home site in Beaver Creek

Building Beaver Creek – Making It Come Alive

Marshall's other huge task was to prepare VA to open Beaver Creek. Harry Bass, as the new chair, saw Beaver Creek as an opportunity to make his mark. With Jack Zerhen, VA's staff architect, in the lead, they put together a team of architects whose goal was to design the Beaver Creek Village that reflected the style and grace they saw in European mountain villages. They focused on the future buildings within the village such as the Village Hall (now known as Ford Hall), the quaint Poste Montane

Lodge, the Plaza Lodge, a performing arts center (now the Vilar Center), and the primary hotel (now the Park Hyatt).

By mutually critiquing their collective design work in creative, collaborative on-site work sessions, these architects assured that the scale, interest, and vitality of the pedestrian spaces and buildings were achieved. Other architects worked on the mid-mountain restaurant named Spruce Saddle and the important employee housing facilities near the entry to the resort. At the same time, graphic designers worked on directional signage and the artist renderings that introduced the resort to investors, the local public, and approving authorities at the federal, state, and local levels. It was an incredibly creative and exciting time when all these design professionals focused on creating a new village and ski mountain from scratch.

1979 work session of Beaver Creek architects with village model

All the while, Marshall worked with Bob Parker in the arduous negotiating process with the U.S. Forest Service, the EPA, and Governor Lamm's administration to resolve the myriad environmental and development issues in a constructive and cooperative manner. To get the critical Forest Service Use Permit for Beaver Creek Mountain, the state had to be satisfied first. Given that Lamm was elected by trying to block the development, this was a daunting task.

In retrospect, this was a time when Marshall relied on all of Bob Parker's experience, leadership, and patience. Bob's approach was largely "come let us reason together." He had credibility with Lamm's people and with the Sierra Club, due to his long-standing environmental views and positions. Bob was walking a fine line between Marshall and Bass and the "greens." He was a naturalist who clearly loved the outdoors, so it was hard for the opposition to discredit him. Every time they threw a new objection at him, his pragmatism and patience found a way to satisfy their demand *and* keep the process moving forward.

For example, when Lamm's administration demanded limiting the number of cars in Beaver Creek Village, Parker and his planners designed a bus transportation system from base parking lots. It was expensive but worked. As Parker said years later, "We were broad-minded enough to recognize the right of the public to participate and the right of environmental groups to be involved, and we were willing to sit down and work things out." Jack Marshall had the leadership courage to let Bob run with VA's biggest challenge.

Another important aspect of Marshall's leadership was to bring in the necessary expertise to implement the plans. This expertise included real-estate deal making through Charlie Gardner, a six-foot-nine former NBA player who crafted joint-venture relationships with investors and developers for the critical initial phase of the village lodging and retail. And Charlie had a great sense of humor that kept the negotiations friendly.

Marshall knew he needed to build integrated teams, so he tapped Roger Lessman, a former missile engineer, to head up Beaver Creek Mountain. Lessman was a big, strapping guy with a calming presence. He was a master at collaborating with diverse stakeholders – as in launching a missile – and holding them accountable. In fewer than twenty-four months, Lessman's teams had built lifts, trails, a huge snowmaking system, the mid-mountain restaurant called Spruce Saddle, plus all the ancillary infrastructure including utilities, roads, and employee housing. Opening Beaver Creek took a little longer than launching Vail because by the 1980s the regulatory hoops were much more complex. In fact, the December 1980 issue of *Sports Illustrated* billed Beaver Creek as "The Last Great Resort."

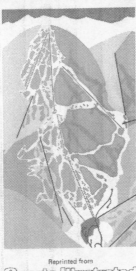

BEAVER CREEK

Reprinted from
Sports Illustrated
December 15, 1980

*Sports Illustrated article reprint – December 15, 1980
the same day Beaver Creek cut its opening day ribbon*

Marshall also brought in Brian Rapp, who structured the operating entities for the village including the Beaver Creek Resort Company. Kevin Conwick, VA's attorney at Holme Roberts & Owen, lobbied the State of Colorado and pushed through special legislation creating a new "service corporation" allowing for the Beaver Creek Resort Company. It was, and still is, like a private government. It was another remarkable innovation.

The outcome of this arduous governmental approval process was a series of land use and environmental requirements that would guide future development throughout the Colorado high country. They addressed air quality, water quality for the namesake Beaver Creek, the number of residences and lodging rooms that could be built, and the visual implications of new ski trails on the mountain and buildings within the village. The combination of these requirements and the environmental vision of Marshall and Parker, plus the whole VA team, led to a development that fit its setting and was environmentally responsible. Beaver Creek subsequently received acclaim in national media including *Sports Illustrated* and *Good Morning America*. The whole collaborative process was indicative of an evolving Vail way. These "intrapreneurs" had a vision and the capacity to make it happen.

The initial Beaver Creek team. Bob Parker is holding the shovel with Harry Bass, chair of Vail Associates. President Ford is to Bass' right with Jack Marshall to his right.

In December 1980, Beaver Creek opened, and Dick Lamm had been converted – partly. At the opening ceremonies, Lamm called Beaver Creek "the Cadillac of ski resorts" and praised the model design and planning that had gone into it. It was political grandstanding, but he couldn't resist the invitation.

Looking back, Beaver Creek was considered by most observers as a success – pretty much as planned. VA stayed the course even during the several economic downturns. But some will argue that it's still not Vail. They point out the key difference is what Pete wrestled with at the outset of Vail – the level of control. Is it better to relinquish some things to other business owners and essentially form a municipality or maintain tight control and create more of a company town? VA kept a tight hand on Beaver Creek, and it can be seen and felt. Some say that's actually better – others say it's too contrived.

FRAMPTON ERA CHRONOLOGY

August 1982: Frampton became president of VA.

June 1983: Vail Associates Foundation became Vail Valley Foundation

March 1983: Vail and Beaver Creek hosted the first American Ski Classic

August 1983: Beaver Creek Club formed; Beano's Cabin followed three years later

March 1984: American Express conceived SaddleRidge retreat

February 1985: First detachable quad chairlifts purchased

June 1985: 1989 World Alpine Ski Championships awarded

September 1985: Gillett Holdings acquires Vail Associates

January 1986: Frampton resigned; formed East West Partners

Advancing Beaver Creek: The Frampton Era

With Beaver Creek barely open, Marshall decided to move on. Harry Bass conducted a nationwide search that brought Harry Frampton to town. At first, Harry's South Carolina drawl seemed odd and out of place, but before long everyone could see that he knew what he was doing. As a new CEO faced with double-digit inflation and interest rates (known to many as Carter's Misery Index), Frampton embarked on a wholesale reorganization of the company. Real estate sales were dead in the water, and a huge excavated hole in the ground for the future Hyatt hotel made the resort pretty unappealing. Some heads rolled and lots of consolidations occurred, including combining the Vail and Beaver Creek marketing groups and the two accounting departments. Those early years of the Frampton era were a real eye-opener for many who experienced what it was like to work for a leader who integrated character with competence.

Quads – A Whole New Technology

While Frampton and his real estate team were scrambling to right the ship in Beaver Creek, largely as a result of the sagging economy, others were focused on improving the Vail Mountain experience – after all, that was the company's primary cash engine. With Larry Lichliter in the lead, Harry and a few others flew off to Austria to check out these innovative four-person (quad), detachable chairlifts. No ski resort in the U.S. had anything like these; almost everyone was stuck in the Riblet double-chairlift past.

In 1983, the group visited Lech, Austria, where they met the imposing and charismatic owner of Doppelmayr Garaventa Group. His first name was Arthur, but everyone called him Mr. Doppelmayr. It took only a few minutes at the base of that lift in OberLech to see what a masterpiece of engineering Doppelmayr had created. A trip to their factory in Wolfurt sealed the deal, and Vail Mountain was on the threshold of a transformation. Four new high-speed, detachable quads nearly eliminated lift lines and set the tone for upgrading the skiing experience in the Vail Valley. When the competitors saw the impact, many of them jumped on board the detachable bandwagon.

The Beaver Creek Club – Creating the Social Fabric

With real estate in the weeds, Frampton initiated several projects intended to re-invigorate Beaver Creek and show the market a fresh face. He bulldozed the old "hair-bag Hilton" and created an entry statement for this "Cadillac" of resorts. He accelerated the completion of Village Hall, deflating the temporary tennis bubble that has served as the "base lodge." But one of his most lasting innovations was the creation of the Beaver Creek Club.

Working with real estate wizards Mark Smith and Ross Bowker, whom he had brought with him from Hilton Head, Frampton introduced a new idea to mountain resorts. Shortly after his arrival in Vail, Frampton took a tour of the leading resorts throughout the Rockies. Sun Valley was on the tour, and when he saw the Trail Creek Cabin, built in 1937, the light bulbs went off. "We've got to do something like this," he said, and many years later added, "This experience reminds me that you don't have to invent everything yourself." [9]

The Beaver Creek Club was born that day as a private membership organization with access to skiing and golf, with clubhouses for both, linked to selected real estate purchases. It was immediately attractive. Unlike the classic day-skier lodge experience, this nicely appointed club appealed to the well-heeled second-home owner. This innovation spurred Mike Shannon, the next CEO, to later create Beano's Cabin, an on-mountain restaurant serving lunch to club members and dinner via sleigh rides to the general public. It was a game changer. The club movement spread to similar arrangements at the Arrowhead Alpine Club, the Bachelor Gulch Club, the Game Creek Club, the Arrabelle Club, and finally, the Vail Mountain Club – all wildly successful. Of course, Vail pioneers know that the concept really started with the Camp Robbers Club in Game Creek Bowl back in 1964.

This notion of special benefits in a club setting, together with the Vail Valley Foundation's Friends of Vail program, anchored by the Eagle Medallion (a transferrable all-facility pass), was at the forefront of accelerating the Vail Valley's ascendance to world-class status.

CONSEQUENCES

By 1984, personal computers were becoming available, but not necessarily affordable. Frampton thought his management committee should join this revolution. So, he proposed that all of his direct reports buy a Compaq personal computer. The deal was that the company paid half and you paid half, but in two years, it was yours. They were dubbed "luggable" because they resembled one of those portable Singer sewing machines. Harry's concept probably accelerated our comfort level with computers by at least five years. The digital revolution had started, and we were prepared.

Once Frampton's two-year period was up, and I was comfortable with that Compaq Luggable, the next generation laptop was out and I was hooked.

A few years later, I gave the luggable to my seven-year-old son, Conor. He proceeded to take it apart and reassemble it several times. And he's never looked back.

He became the go-to guy at every school he attended while managing to "go" to places in the school's computer system he shouldn't have. The school district's head of technology said, "When you graduate, come see me – you've got a job."

Conor is now a lead software developer for Salesforce.com, a Silicon Valley success story. You just can't know the down-stream consequences of your decisions.

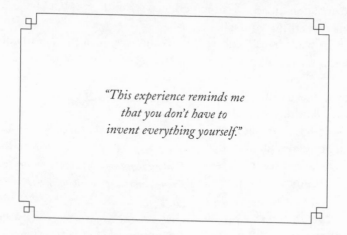

*"This experience reminds me
that you don't have to
invent everything yourself."*

SaddleRidge Retreat – Credibility Grows

In March 1986 during the American Ski Classic and shortly after Frampton had resigned from VA, he struck gold for his new venture, East West Partners – although it took several years for him to cash in. American Express was the main sponsor of this expanding event, and Harry met Jim Robinson, CEO of American Express, and Peter Cohen, president of their Shearson Lehman subsidiary. After seeing the excitement of the event, plus the beauty of Beaver Creek, they said, "We should build a retreat here for our executives." [10] Frampton sensing a deal, said, "Why don't we come back to New York and show you a few ideas." [11] After giving a high five to Jack Zehren, his architect, they brainstormed designs.

Two weeks later, Frampton and Zehren showed up at the Amex Tower in Manhattan with a roll of blueprints and no small amount of enthusiasm and a little bit of angst. After laying out their plans, the two Amex guys said, "It's not big enough." With their tails between their legs, Frampton and Zehren went back to the drawing boards. The second trip to New York was better but still not quite right. In the end, SaddleRidge was built and remains a classic. Zehren engaged the temperamental New York designer, Naomi Leff, to handle the interiors, and the collection she gathered of original Buffalo Bill artifacts helped make the retreat special.

COMMENTARY: SWEET AND SOUR YEARS (FRAMPTON ERA)

I arrived at the company during a period when we operated without a CEO for the better part of a year. During that time, Vail Associates struggled to decide whether we were primarily a real estate development company or a ski company. Opening Beaver Creek in 1980 had resulted in taking on a huge number of employees primarily focused on land planning, design, construction and everything else needed to create a whole new community. Even the finance group spent much of its time and efforts on real estate related activities. A new CEO was hired with an extensive real estate development background. He brought in an experienced real estate team, but they were fighting quite a storm during this period of record high interest rates, the S&L loan crisis, the federal RTC program and an extended period of correcting in real estate values. Despite this headwind, the new group managed to complete a few successful real estate projects in Beaver Creek. But it became increasingly important to focus on competitive advantages in the ski business.

The challenge was to improve the ski experience in a period when the infrastructure of both the mountain and the community were being stressed. Extensive investment was made in snowmaking and lift expansion, including the introduction of much higher capacity detachable quad chairlifts in 1985. Vail added 4 such chairs that first year and continued to replace the antiquated fixed grip chairlifts for years to come. The impact was dramatic as we increase our uphill capacity by more than 50% and dramatically improved the skier experience in the process. The "build it and they will come" adage worked in this situation, as skier visits increased by a similar rate over the next several years.

Gerry Flynn
President – Polar Star Properties, Inc.
Former CFO – Vail Resorts

GOING BIG

Connecting to the World – The Gillett-Shannon Era

In 1985, VA's world turned upside down yet again. The Bass Family Trust, the actual majority owner of the company's stock, decided to divest. Harry Bass' children were not happy with the VA investment because they weren't seeing any benefits (read cash), so they overruled their father and put the company up for sale. Investment bankers from Denver were hired, resulting in the sale to George Gillett. This change launched a new era in the life of the company – new energy, new capital, and new management.

George Gillett – Guest Oriented

GILLETT-SHANNON ERA CHRONOLOGY

April 1986: Gillett hired Mike Shannon as president

December 1988: China Bowl opened

February 1989: World Alpine Ski Championships held

February 1989: Gillett invited Pete Seibert to return to Vail

November 1989: Hyatt Regency Beaver Creek opened

December 1989: Vail-Eagle Airport opened to direct flights from Dallas

June 1992: Gillett lost VA to Apollo Ski Partners.

George was a very happy man – he was always smiling. Acquiring Vail Associates was a dream come true because he loved skiing, and, as a salesman at heart, he loved the challenge of building the Vail brand. He had an office, but more often than not he was out on the mountain. Within a short time, he dubbed himself director of guest satisfaction, meeting employees and riding lifts with skiers. He brought Disney people to Vail in an effort to improve guest service levels and achieve a seamless experience. His infectious personality spread enthusiasm everywhere.

Gillett's focus on improving the skiing experience was textbook marketing – be customer oriented. This philosophy was ingrained during his years with

McKinsey and later with sports teams like the Harlem Globetrotters and the Miami Dolphins. He was simpatico with Sarge Brown who preached like a Baptist that you need to know the mountain. And so, he was out there reflecting delight as bright as the Colorado sunshine. He could be on the mountain because he had his trusted president, Mike Shannon, in the office "keeping the trains running on time."

Mike was young – only 28 when he arrived – but bright and wise beyond his years. He had an MBA from Kellogg and he knew numbers. And he was like George in that he was smiling all the time, which may have been a reflection of being in the mountains versus the big city. He had been Gillett's banker at First Chicago working on George's various holdings, including his growing group of network television affiliates. He even lived in George's basement in Nashville for a short period. George had almost adopted Mike.

The Rolling Option – Energizing Real Estate

Shannon knew he had to jump-start real estate if he wanted to have Gillett's investment make sense. Every previous VA administration had used real estate to fuel expansion of the mountain.

In order to energize Beaver Creek development, Shannon negotiated a "rolling option" with Harry Frampton that would result in a hotel – in time. Because it would take several years to plan and finance a hotel, Shannon made a favorable deal with Frampton's East West Partners on land in the eastern portion of the Beaver Creek village. Once one project was selling, the next piece of land was made available. And things rolled along very nicely. Shannon's entrepreneurial bent allowed Frampton time to successfully build and sell several condominium projects while securing financing for a Hyatt Regency hotel. Because Gillett gave Shannon the freedom to innovate, he got his hotel, and Beaver Creek emerged from the doldrums. Years later, Shannon commented that "returning to the entrepreneurial spirit of the founders was a huge influence." [12] That dimension of the Vail way was continuing to evolve.

China Bowl – Even More Terrain

Vail Mountain was already vast, but George and Mike saw the possibilities to the east. Among the many positives that Vail offered, perhaps the most distinguishing were the back bowls. On a fresh powder day, it's hard to beat. The only problem was that you had to get up early to find any untracked snow. George understood the importance of enhancing your most important feature, so developing China Bowl was an easy decision. But it wasn't that easy to implement.

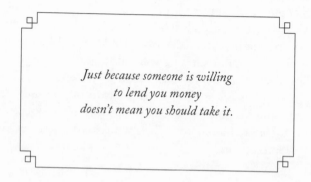

*Just because someone is willing
to lend you money
doesn't mean you should take it.*

In the early days, getting Forest Service approval was somewhat straightforward, but now with the EPA and the Sierra Club at the table, the process was daunting and expensive. It was both good and bad. Everyone wanted to do it right, but the public process was stupefying. Some people just looked at VA as the big corporate exploiter of our fragile environment. But the truth is, they cared every bit as much as the tree-huggers. With a protracted planning and approval process, it took years and millions to make China Bowl a reality. Thank God that George had developed patience along the way.

Between 1986 and 1992, various Gillett-Shannon teams advanced the Vail Valley to new levels of success and recognition. They were innovators committed to excellence and high quality. The professional management trend that Dick Peterson started was taken even further with leaders who understood how to grow an already-profitable business. They emphasized a family orientation through innovations like Fort Whipper Snapper, Jack Rabbit Alley, and Bear Cave, inspired by their relationship with Disney president Frank Wells.

Unfortunately, this era came to a close in 1991 when George found himself overextended in his television ventures with junk bonds. He was forced to sell his Vail interest. He commented at the time, "Just because someone is willing to lend you money doesn't mean you should take it."[13] It was a sad day for Gillett fans, but like most aspects of life, including corporate life, one chapter ends and another begins. He and Mike had set in motion a myriad of initiatives that improved the quality of the guest experience. And, unbeknownst to them and everyone else, their chapter in VA's journey was just the beginning of explosive growth.

The Apollo Era – Leveraging Vail

The buyer of Gillett's interest was Leon Black, a Wall Street investment banker who had started Apollo Advisors following years at the junk bond firm of Drexel Burnham Lambert. To take over the reins in 1992, Apollo promoted Andy Daly, who was then president of the Beaver Creek Resort Company, to be the next CEO of Vail Associates. Over a fifteen-year period, Andy had worked his way up the ranks at Copper Mountain from head of the Ski Patrol to president and then on to Beaver Creek. Again to Gillett's credit, he attracted talented people. Daly was a well-schooled ski mountain operator.

Arrowhead and Bachelor Gulch – Stretching Beaver Creek

One of Apollo's first moves was to acquire Arrowhead Mountain from Isom Fares. Many VA executives, starting with Jack Marshall, didn't think much of Arrowhead from a skiing perspective because it was too low – just below the normal snow line. But with snowmaking and careful grooming, Arrowhead proved to be a good addition. Then, with the opening of Bachelor Gulch, Beaver Creek stretched into three interconnected skiing experiences. "Down valley," as locals called it, was starting to become viable. The Town of Avon at the base of Beaver Creek was beginning to come out of its doldrums with basic services like grocery stores and gas stations. The claim that the Vail Valley was more than Vail was becoming real.

Keystone and Breckenridge – Expanding Beyond the Vail Valley

In August of 1996, Apollo revealed its plan that had been in the works back-stage for several years. Leon Black's guys convinced Ralston Purina, the pet food manufacturer from St. Louis, to sell its skiing interests in Keystone and Breckenridge to VA creating Vail Resorts, Inc. (VR). It was big news in the mountains, less so on Wall Street. In Colorado, the anti-trust critics were up in arms, but on Wall Street they were scratching their heads. The merger would lessen competition, some said, and give Vail a powerful lock on the Front Range market. In New York, the critics couldn't understand why smart money would buy into a seasonal business, one that was capital intensive and yet chasing after a market that was flat. As it turns out, Leon Black's team, including Marc Rowan, Rob Katz, and Craig Cogut were envisioning what others didn't see.

The IPO – A Different Focus

To pull this off, Apollo needed leaders with public company experience who could execute an IPO. In 1997, they tapped Adam Aron, an executive with an impressive resume from stints at United Airlines, Hyatt Hotels, and Norwegian Cruise Lines. Over the next few years, Aron brought in other executives and lawyers in marketing, finance, and public affairs who would help him prepare the company to go public. And his wisdom was evident in keeping Andy Daly as president, essentially as COO, to manage the

THE DALY-ARON ERA CHRONOLOGY

June 1992: Apollo appointed Andy Daly as president

January 1994: Arrowhead Mountain acquired

June 1995: Bachelor Gulch opened

August 1996: Adam Aron appointed CEO and chair

December 1996: Adventure Ridge opened atop a new LionsHead Gondola

January 1997: Keystone and Breckenridge acquired

February 1997: Vail Resorts launched through an IPO

July 1998: RockResorts acquired

October 1998: Terrorists destroy Two Elk and several chairlifts

May 1998: Joint Venture with Gart Bros. Sporting established

January 1999: Blue Sky opened

February 1999: World Alpine Ski Championships hosted again

March 2002: Heavenly Valley acquired

May 2004: Vail renaissance began with Antlers Hotel expansion

February 2005: Arrabelle at Vail Square broke ground

May 2006: Adam Aron resigned

growing ski operation. Andy knew mountains – Adam knew big corporate life.

Within a few short years, VA went from a successful, mid-sized local company to a big, regional company, although still small compared to the Fortune 500 behemoths. With the public company complexities, together with the expanding responsibilities as stewards of vast tracts of public land, Vail Resorts was becoming a different kind of company. While the implications were many, two major shifts involved more focus on short-term cash flow and less on innovation. The changes were noticeable, especially to long-time locals.

One shift was in people. Aron brought in some smart people, but they weren't locals or, for that matter, even mountain people. All of a sudden, strangers were running the place. Some newbies kept their primary homes elsewhere and flew into Vail to conduct business. It was more difficult for locals to get meetings, and when they did get them, they were short so the new guys could quickly move on to the next thing. Everybody was in a hurry, and it was disconcerting to many. Locals would ask, "What do these hot shots know about what made Vail great?" The corporate newbies would say, "These locals are just ski bums." There was probably just a little truth in both points. And then there were the Apollo overseers in Manhattan shouting directions from afar.

While the people shift had emotional implications, another shift had huge business ramifications. When the IPO was announced in late 1997, the whispers in Vail were rampant. Was it a good investment or would Wall Street suppress the value because of skiing's seasonality? Could weather-dependent "snow farmers" play at this higher level? But Leon Black and his shrewd partners had a plan.

The plan was to diversify – expand and grow in every direction. The proceeds from the public offering generated a boatload of cash, and Aron put it to good use. The initial strategy was to capture more of each guest's expenditures, what some VR executives called "more of their wallet." In the resort world, that meant owning hotels, restaurants, golf courses, ski shops, and transportation. They even bought the high-end collection of hotels known as RockResorts. According to Andy Daly, "We really bought the name since these hotels founded in the 1930s by the Rockefeller family had really declined." [14] If Vail Resorts wasn't in a particular retail or service business, it might be the landlord for others who were. Before long, it became apparent to local businesspeople that Vail Resorts was becoming their competitor. There was a fox in the henhouse.

The focus quickly went from the traditional ski industry philosophy of long-term asset appreciation to short-term quarterly earnings. The influence of the complex SEC guidelines was onerous. Now the stock price was the barometer of health, and initially the ticker tape on Vail displayed wild swings. The entrepreneurial drive initiated by Vail's pioneers was still present, but now it was manifested in some new and expansive ways. While the game had changed, many people realized that having a strong mountain operator was actually a good thing. Vail Resorts now had an even stronger balance sheet reflecting the ability to continue investing in the mountain, innovating and improving the primary experience. And they did. Not only did the stock price grow, albeit slowly at first, this process of continually adapting to changes was supporting a hallmark of the Vail way.

Blue Sky Basin – Completing Pete's Dream

In the early years, Pete and Bob Parker called it SuperVail because of the scope of terrain that would be added to Vail Mountain; the engineers labeled it Category III. But because it was labeled by the Forest Service then as "future development", VA was forced to jump through a whole range of hoops that would take years and many millions. Andy Daly had the overall responsibility to wade through an incredible bureaucratic maze at every level, with several environmental groups and anti-growth factions. Once the approvals were received, then a long and arduous appeals process kicked in. Each step along the way, VR exhibited professionalism and patience.

*Pam Horan-Kates and Don Simonton of the Colorado Ski Museum
with Pete Seibert's original scale model showing Blue Sky Basin*

Among the many stumbling blocks, the biggest was the small, but endangered, Canadian Lynx, whose habitat was reported to be largely in the Blue Sky area. Much work was poured into proving the dangers that this unnecessary expansion would bring. After years of wrangling and posturing, the courts rejected the appeals and paved the way for VA to proceed. Blue Sky added roughly six hundred acres, and because it was north-facing and tree-covered, it provided great ski terrain and made Vail Mountain that much better. Then, on October 18, 1998, tragedy struck.

Terrorists Strike – Two Elk Lodge Destroyed

Eco-terrorists from the Earth Liberation Front took things into their own hands and set fire to three on-mountain buildings, including the expansive Two Elk Lodge, as well as four chairlifts. When Daly got the call from Paul Testwuide to look out his window, it was a heart-wrenching moment. After all the negotiating and all the appeals, these terrorists simply flashed their middle finger in disrespect at our legal processes. It was an unnecessary catastrophe.

But Daly rallied the troops to say they would not be bullied; instead they would rebuild – ultimately at a cost of more than $16 million. Eventually, all those who perpetrated the crime were caught, except for one who committed suicide, and Pete's dream was completed. Blue Sky, a vast addition to Vail's powder skiing terrain, now stands as another hallmark of what makes Vail special. And a demonstration of perseverance.

Fire at Two Elk

Daly didn't stop with re-building Two Elk; he and his team built Adventure Ridge, a whole complex of facilities and activities that would attract guests up the mountain in all seasons. Using the LionsHead Gondola terminal and its restaurant as a base, they added ice skating, tubing, and a wedding deck, all intended to expand the mountain-top experience. While skiing has always been the driver, summer business was never too far from everyone's mind. Adventure Ridge was enough of an attraction to jump-start another revenue source. Daly had the privilege of working again with Pete Seibert to launch the Game Creek Club, Vail's response to the down-valley club movement. While Daly's stint in the CEO's chair was somewhat short-lived, his world, and that of many others in Vail, was turned upside down by Leon Black's moves over the next few years.

High Tech Arrives

A good example of the adaptive mindset was in technology. One of the "outsiders" that Daly brought in was Charlie L'Esperance. Charlie came with a master's degree from Cornell and twelve years of leadership experience at Marriott. He was a technologist with a strategic bent. His job was to prepare for the complexities of a public company from a tech perspective. There were numerous compliance-oriented upgrades that were needed, but the bigger challenge was supporting a new direction coming from the new board and executive team. They had a vision that included integrated new products and customer services, economies of scale, and centralized management. However, Vail Resorts' technology at the time consisted of a very long list of non-integrated systems from many different vendors. To achieve the company's vision, Charlie quickly realized that the required technology didn't exist – it would have to be invented. He recruited a team of talented young software developers – not hard to do when the job was in Vail. They proceeded to work with the operations staff to develop a fully integrated suite of software applications that revolutionized ski resort operations. They essentially changed the game!

Members of Charlie's team:
Andy Shenberger, Mike Hibbs, and Eric Phannenstial

For example, the sticky printed tickets applied to those little metal hangers were definitely old school. Computerized passes were developed with digital photos, bar codes, and magnetic stripes. With this new technology, passes could be purchased and renewed online rather than waiting in long lines. Also, the ski pass could be used for "resort charges" throughout the ski operation. And with bar code scanning of tickets and passes, controls were greatly improved, and management had better information for decision making.

This new technology was extremely valuable, so much so that in 2001 a separate company called Resort Technology Partners (RTP) was created. The plan with RTP was to license the software to other resorts, recoup costs, and generate incremental revenue. Eventually, RTP grew to have hundreds of ski resort and theme park customers around the world. The entrepreneurial spirit was alive and well. Of the RTP experience, Charlie said, "We were very fortunate to have a visionary, supportive CEO and CFO, Gerry Flynn, some of the industry's best resort operations managers. We also had a very talented, committed technology team, led by Bob Hansen. Living in the Vail Valley, they all worked hard and played hard. These factors created a unique environment for technology development and innovation, which continues today within the current Vail Resorts organization." [15] A more recent application of this technology is linked to the creation of the Epic Pass and the related Epic Mix.

The Apollo era under Aron's leadership forever expanded Pete's dream to one focused beyond the Vail Valley. As a public company navigating the new and byzantine Sarbanes-Oxley regulations and needing to satisfy Wall Street's appetite for growth, moving beyond Vail was inevitable. While some would criticize and bemoan the shift, it resulted in a stronger company more capable of reinvesting and innovating.

Adam Aron's tenure continued through 2005, allowing him to participate in the planning for what became known as Vail's "new dawn." This renaissance included a whole host of public and private efforts that would modernize Vail. Under Aron's leadership, Vail Resorts continued to be the market-share leader, and the company's properties enjoyed strong ratings by prestigious third parties as the undisputed quality leader. He continued the long tradition of leaders of the ski company of looking ahead, innovating, paying attention to the customer, and collaborating with the community.

And let it not be forgotten, there was this other little thing during Aron's era – the 1999 World Championships. Another huge boost in international markets!

Going Really Big: The Rob Katz Era

Rob Katz was an East Coast guy – "was" being the operative word. He grew up in New Rochelle, New York, went to college at the University of Pennsylvania, and ended up in Manhattan, eventually landing at Drexel Burnham. After Michael Milken, the junk-bond king, took Drexel Burnham down, several senior people, including Leon Black, formed Apollo Global Management. Rob joined Apollo in 1990 and learned the ropes the Wall Street way.

Rob Katz

He moved his family to Colorado following the September 11 tragedy, leaving the rat race behind. He remained heavily involved with Apollo, serving on the Vail Resorts Board of Directors, and the healthy, laid-back lifestyle in Boulder seemed preferable to the urban pressures of New York.

The friendlier people of Colorado resonated with Rob's more gregarious personality. He started smiling more. The change allowed Rob time to reflect on what was important and how he wanted to lead in business following the go-go years on Wall Street.

In February 2006, the Vail Resorts board asked Rob to step up from lead director to become CEO. It was a big step but one that he was well suited for and well prepared for. However, one of his first moves reignited the "us versus them" acrimony in the Vail Valley.

THE KATZ ERA CHRONOLOGY

May 1997: *Joined Vail Resorts board*

February 2006: *Appointed chairman, president, and CEO*

August 2006: *Headquarters moved to Broomfield*

April 2008: *Epic Pass announced*

March 2009: *Kirkwood and Northstar acquired*

May 2012: *Mt. Brighton in Michigan and Afton Alps in Minnesota acquired*

May 2013: *Canyons Resort acquired*

November 2014: *Park City acquired*

February 2015: *World Alpine Ski Championships held*

March 2015: *Perisher Resort in Australia acquired*

Broomfield – Leaving the Nest

In 2006, Katz announced that the company headquarters was moving to Broomfield, not far from his home in Boulder. Many locals saw this as purely self-serving. What had been whispers around the time of the IPO now became shouts of angst and bewilderment, particularly among those in corporate administration but also from community business owners. People working directly on one of the mountains or in a hotel were less affected than those in marketing, accounting, or HR. The company was generous with those they asked to move. Some found it terribly disruptive; others saw it as an opportunity. From a pure business growth perspective, the move made sense. It would allow the company to better manage its growing empire and give it access to a much larger talent pool. On the other hand, it would foster a different kind of company, which is exactly what Rob felt was needed.

The Vail Valley's economic development people were lamenting the loss of hundreds of good-paying jobs. Some commented that they had been trying to get to the mountains for years and weren't interested in returning to the urban life, even though Boulder is not too urban. But for Katz and his team, Colorado's Front Range was better positioned to support the acquisition and growth strategy about to unfold.

The Epic Pass – A Game Changer

In April of 2008, amid early slowdowns and the looming economic turmoil around the country, Katz announced the Epic Pass. The innovations that had stopped around the time of the Arrabelle development were kick-started by this "epic" thinking. It was a somewhat radical departure from previous season-pass policies where pricing and holiday restrictions were designed to move skiers off peak periods. The Epic Pass tossed that thinking aside.

First, it would be unrestricted, that is, good during the holidays – a popular move among locals. Second, it was less expensive than even the merchants' pass offered through local business organizations – also a popular decision. Finally, it was good at all Vail Resorts ski mountains. It was a blockbuster concept. As Katz said, "It got people committed to skiing before the season started." [16] It was so popular and brought in so much pre-season cash, it reduced somewhat the company's typical fall borrowing needs. The Epic Pass was doing what every business school teaches – enhance value and build customer loyalty. It was an enhanced business model giving VR a major competitive advantage.

Now, skiers were able to take advantage of the Epic Pass' interchangeability and ski five mountains. And that was about to get even better. In addition to Heavenly Valley ski area in South Lake Tahoe acquired during Adam Aron's rein, Katz acquired the Kirkwood and Northstar resorts, also in the Lake Tahoe region. This move gave Vail Resorts the best skiing in Colorado and some of the best in California. It set the stage to acquire "feeder resorts" in several metropolitan areas and in Europe and Japan. And now Park City in Utah is in the fold. John Garnsey, who helped implement Katz' Epic Pass, commented, "Rob's strategy was brilliant. Expanding the number of resorts and feeder ski areas within Vail

Resorts' orbit simply enhanced the value of the pass – and the value of VR stock." [17] It's been a game changer, causing the rest of the ski industry to scratch its head. On the flip side, some locals blame the Epic Pass for excess crowding, especially on I-70 on high-traffic days.

Hotels and Retail – Diversification Brings Even More Value

If Vail Resorts wasn't already in the dominant position for mountain destinations, it definitely was now. It had a growing market share from a more firmly committed customer, and its financial position was stronger. Beyond RockResorts properties, the company was acquiring additional hotels and moving others into management contracts. They continued to be involved in both horizontal real estate (land) and vertical development (buildings). Both were profitable. And EverVail, the village development west of LionsHead, promises to be the third major portal to Vail Mountain. It's a huge undertaking that has been years in planning, even as VR seeks joint-venture partners to help develop that village.

Beyond skiing, VR is investing heavily in summer attractions, like alpine slides, zip lines, and hiking and biking trails – all accessible via the Epic Pass. Add VR's involvement in retail, primarily through their joint venture with the Gart family in their Specialty Sports stores, and you have a diversified enterprise touching the guest at multiple points. As Rob sees it, "Our core is mountain resorts, but what drives our business is vacation travel. Our product is the great outdoors." [18] Mark Gasta, the vice president of HR – better known as the chief people officer – expanded on this sentiment when he said, "What we're trying to do is re-imagine the mountain experience. We're becoming the first global mountain vacation company." [19] It seems this patience for a big, long-term vision is consistent with a long-standing Vail way approach.

The Leadership Summit – It's a People Business

As Rob Katz settled into his expansive, entrepreneurial role, he saw how vast the company had become. Perhaps because of his more relaxed pace, or maybe it was the Boulder water, he realized his role and the entire mission of Vail Resorts was about people. From his Wall Street experience, he said, "I learned it's not just being smart, but getting anything done involves building relationships." [20] He began reading everything on leadership – Jim Collins, Stephen Covey, Bill George, and others. Some said he became a leadership junkie.

In 2011, Katz established VR's Leadership Summit. He would bring 400 of the company's leaders to Keystone for several days of listening, thinking, and sharing leadership perspectives. They would talk about values, like service, safety, doing good, and, perhaps most important, having fun. It was a big deal. He was focused on his people so they could be focused on customers. Of his leadership approach, Katz commented, "By building trust, I've gotten people to work together." [21] He did this by periodically bringing his direct reports together for a retreat. They'd get real with what was really going, on and this made all the difference. Katz said, "Leadership starts with taking responsibility for yourself." [22]

In 2013, during a presentation at the University of Denver's "Voices of Experience," Rob described in some detail the shift in his thinking from the Wall Street way. In New York, the saying was, "if you want a friend, get a dog." It was pretty much about the bottom line. While he learned to understand risk and how to make decisions, there wasn't a focus on people. At Vail Resorts, Katz said, "I came to see my role as guiding and assisting my direct reports." [23] He described his focus as being on the person – the whole person. He wanted to know how they were doing with their goals, but he also urged them to find balance outside of work. While a focus on people had always been part of the Vail Way, Katz was now confirming that with his actions. He said, "We're very business focused, but sometimes we take ourselves too seriously. We need to rest – to take care of ourselves – but not coast." [24]

There is much more to be written about the Katz era, like shifting out of the real estate business, or like his pledge to safeguard the natural environments where Vail Resorts operates. Almost everyone at VR understands that the environment is a cornerstone of the guest experience – everything from waste management to water conservation to energy efficiency. The company's investment in facility upgrades and the general commitment to quality and excellent guest service is definitely in keeping with the Vail way. The financial success of the company allows for continued capital investment in its resorts that will go a long way to keeping it at the top of the heap and providing what Katz refers to as "real experiences in the great outdoors." [25]

Over these fifty-some years, a great deal of continuous improvement and collaboration, both on the mountain and in the community, has occurred. Every CEO has moved the ball. When Pete Seibert passed away in the summer of 2002, the Ford Amphitheater was filled to overflowing. It was emotional – but beautiful. Many spoke of Pete's passion for skiing and his love of Vail. He was dearly loved. His son Pete (known to locals as "Circle") summed up his father's philosophy when he said, "It's not about what you accumulate; it's about what you accomplish." [26]

What Pete Seibert started, Rob Katz is continuing to build.

COMMENTARY: THE FUTURE IS NOW

Vail Associates enjoyed tremendous financial success during the Gillett-Shannon years. The company they inherited had plenty of talent and had embarked on some aggressive expansion plans, but the real estate debacle of the early 1980's had taken its toll and the planned expansion of Beaver Creek Village had come to a screeching halt. The new focus would be growing cash flow from skiing. We would give land away to the right developer if we thought they could successfully deliver live beds in the form of a hotel like the Hyatt and the various fractional ownership properties. Gillett essentially valued the real estate assets at zero in his acquisition, but knew it would be critical to achieving the growth they needed in the ski business. Over the succeeding six years (1986 through 1992), the company had grown resort cash flow from $6 million to $35 million.

It was ironic that this period of growth came to dramatic close when the company was forced to file for Chapter 11 bankruptcy protection in May 1992. Gillett Holdings (VA's parent company) had defaulted on its debt obligations used to finance several TV stations, and it threatened to bring down the entire enterprise. Mike Shannon and I had to make the very difficult decision to stop sending our ski season profits to a sinking ship. We held $35 million in cash reserves on the day we filed for Chapter 11 protection. We emerged as a separate company again 4 ½ months later. It was difficult to comprehend by much of our management and staff how such success could culminate with a bankruptcy filing.

Gerry Flynn
President – Polar Star Properties, Inc.
Former CFO – Vail Resorts

Hopefully this story has surfaced a few thoughts about the Vail way. To further the thinking, here are several action steps from this chapter worth considering.

Also, the Questions for Dialogue, and the space to write, are intended to stimulate your thinking and generate conversations with friends and colleagues. Talking about your perspectives with others is a good way to learn.

ACTION STEPS:

- Engage visionary leaders, and encourage them to innovate.
- Shoot high, learn from your mistakes, and stay the course.
- Focus on your customers, and keep investing in what they want.

QUESTIONS FOR DIALOGUE:

- When did you take a risk that really paid off? What was that like?

  _____

- What's the most innovative leadership process you know of? What has it produced?

  _____

- What does "first quality" look like to you? Can you think of an example?

  _____

- What does "disruptive innovation" mean to you? If you've seen it in action, what did you notice?

  _____

Chapter 6

The European Influence

*"Whatever you can do, or dream you can, begin it;
boldness has genius, power and magic in it. Begin it now."*

Johann Goethe

Vail Village Streetscape

The European influence on Vail started long before Pete Seibert saw the Gore Valley. Many of the founders experienced Europe during and after World War II. Pete went to hotel school in Switzerland, and Bob Parker trained military personnel in Austria for years following the war. In the late 1970s, Vail Associates executives traveled to Europe to study alpine villages and apply "old world" thinking in Beaver Creek. In the 1980s, the Town of Vail established a sister-city relationship with St. Moritz to glean what it could from this centuries-old resort. Beaver Creek did something similar with the Lech/Zurs complex in Austria in 2002. The influences in architecture and guest service can be felt throughout the Vail Valley, but more important than these tangible aspects are the people – the Europeans – who brought a passion for the mountains that has made a big difference.

THE PEOPLE

Skiers – Bringing the Alpine Perspective

First, there were the European ski instructors. In the 1960s, skiing in America was fledgling and struggling to get off the ground, especially in the West. But skiing had been the winter sport of choice for many years in Europe's nordic and alpine countries. Europe's ski racers dominated the competitive scene with many champions returning home to run ski schools, like Pepi's friend and teammate from the Austrian National Team, Toni Sailer, who ran the ski school in Kitzbuhel with the eminence of a national hero.

Roger Staub – Ski School Director

In 1965, Pete Seibert recruited Roger Staub, the 1960 Olympic Giant Slalom Gold Medalist, to head the Vail Ski School. Roger was from Arosa in Switzerland and brought a huge smile and a flair for powder skiing in Vail's Back Bowls. Unfortunately, Roger died in a hang gliding accident in Verbier in 1970. The news brought great sadness to Vail, for he was dearly loved.

And there were many others from Europe; Ludi Kurz and Johnny Mueller from Austria; Pia Riva from Italy; Pentti Tofferi from Finland; Malin Johnstotter from Sweden; Karl Hochtl from Germany; Hans Oberlohr from Austria; Diana Mathias from Great Britain; Erich Windish from Germany ; and Frank Biancia from France. And there were many more, including lots of Americans like Joanie Hanna, but really too numerous to mention here. Each in their own way, they brought some of Europe to Vail. It was people like these who conveyed their love of the mountains – an exuberance really – a passion for the freedom of being out in God's creation. In many respects, the Vail way is an attitude – an outlook – as much as it is a way of leading.

Restauranteurs – Bringing a Continental Grace

Pepi and Sheika Gramshammer were some of the first Europeans as described in Chapter 3. And right behind them came the Stauffer brothers, who left an Austrian mark in hotels and restaurants – Joe at the Lodge at Vail and later at the Vail Village Inn, Herman in the Lancelot restaurant, and Gottfried in Ambrosia. Other European restauranteurs included Pepi Langagger at the Blue Cow in Vail and then the Golden Eagle in Beaver Creek. Peter Stadler has run Up the Creek with flair and consistency for almost thirty years. Luc and Liz Meyer brought French cuisine to the Left Bank. And there are many other European restauranteurs who influenced their American friends with a "linen, crystal, and china" style that experienced travelers expected. Joe Stauffer described the difference between European and American attitudes about food this way; "We think of it as dining; with the other it's just eating." [1]

In the 1960s and 1970s when Vail and other Rocky Mountain ski resorts were just getting off the ground, there was this feeling that weekend skiing was like a winter picnic. Destination ski vacations were just starting to be promoted by the airlines. In the on-mountain restaurants, you saw paper plates and plastic cups. Catsup and mustard were on those long, folding tables. Everything felt temporary. With European influence things started to change. The Cook Shack, our first on-mountain sit-down restaurant at Mid-Vail, was an early stab at European elegance. It was constantly booked with

DINNER IN ST. MORITZ

In 1985, Pam and I co-hosted with Pepi and Sheika Gramshammer a "Vail Ambassadors" trip to Europe as part of our campaign for the 1989 World Championships.

One of the stops was in St. Moritz, our sister-city. They rolled out the red carpet and we had a blast. Beyond the socializing, we had a chance to experience Swiss hospitality up close. The atmosphere in almost every restaurant was classy – with fine appointments on display. The adjacent photo was taken at the Chesa Veglia, a centuries-old house that heavy stone walls had helped preserve. The table service was exquisite, with linen tablecloths and starched napkins. And the food was unbelievable. To me, this was the way a world-class resort should look and feel.

I came back to Vail singing Europe's praises and promoting wherever and whenever I could the quality we had experienced.

discriminating skiers. It set a tone, and today, Vail Resorts has replicated that feeling at the Game Creek Club, at the 10th at Mid-Vail, and in other facilities throughout both Vail and Beaver Creek.

Bob Parker, standing, with Elizabeth Juen,
Pam, and me in St. Moritz

The Faesslers – Cementing the Bavarian Style

While the Faesslers weren't the first Europeans to land in Vail, they are arguably some of the most influential. They raised the bar on guest service through their brand of old world hospitality. It started shortly after World War II.

The rolling hills south of Munich comprised rich farmland but this area was ravished from the war. Outside the town of Kempton near Obersdorf, the Faessler family farmhouse was turned into a tiny guest house as a means of survival. German couples fleeing the devastated cities found a Sound of Music-like splendor in the Bavarian Alps. As the word spread, they added more rooms, then a wing, and finally several wings. Over twenty years, Karl and Gretl Faessler had built the Sonnenalp Resort into a five-star resort and one of Europe's leading hotels. They understood guest service and how to deliver it by doing it themselves. They had also built a profitable business, realizing occupancy rates that became the envy of every German hotelier.

The Sonnenalp Resort in Bavaria

THE EUROPEAN CHRONOLOGY

1962: Joe Stauffer beame GM of the Lodge at Vail. Sigi Fowler was sales manager

1964: The Gramshammer's built their gasthof

1966: Roger Staub appointed ski school director

1970: Karl Faessler bought the old Wedel Inn. In 1979 also bought the Kiandra–Talisman Lodge

1978: VA incorporated European village design into Beaver Creek

1986: The Bavaria Haus opened

2005: Arrabelle transformed LionsHead with European feeling

In the mid-1960s, Karl travelled throughout Canada and New England in search of hotel investments. Nothing seemed to exhibit the quality he was looking for until he got to Denver and a friend said, "You need to see Vail." [2] As he walked down Bridge Street, he felt at home. It was still early in Vail's development, but it reminded him of alpine villages back home.

With the help of Marta Cadmus, they looked at the Wedel Inn on the north side of the Covered Bridge. It was basically a well-located twenty-five room model quickly built in 1964 using mostly discarded building materials. But Karl could see the potential. He negotiated a four-week option from Peter Cramarus and hurried home to review the idea with Gretl; she had the eye for guest service and he needed her to buy in for the acquisition.

They closed on the property in August of 1979 and in quick order renovated it top-to-bottom instituting their brand of guest service. They set a tasteful, high-quality tone that others would notice – and in time – follow.

In Vail's early years, some critics found the various European touches to be phony, referring to Vail as "plastic Bavaria." But Vail was establishing its brand, and it felt good to more and more visitors. People were treated differently and they liked it. A Vail way was starting to take root.

The two Faessler sons, Johannes and Michael, were soon sent to the University of Denver's Hotel Management School, and they both could sense the opportunities in Vail. Michael was two years older than Johannes, and so upon graduation, he was given the opportunity to run the renamed Wedel Inn, the Austria Haus. When Johannes completed his studies he took over in Vail, and Michael returned to Bavaria to run the hotel there.

In the mid-1990s with Johannes in the lead, the Faesslers bought the Kiandra-Talisman Lodge, and with patience and foresight, they took a re-development proposal through the Town of Vail's complex and demanding approval process. Ultimately they build the Bavaria Haus in the family tradition of old world hotels. It has won many awards and people who have been fortunate to stay there know what it means to be pampered.

European "dining" at the Bavaria Haus

Prior to the Faesslers' arrival in Vail, most of the hotels and restaurants were typical American minimalist in style. Buildings had been constructed quickly and mostly inexpensively; after all, no one had any money. An example of European hospitality came in what hotel people call "the top of the table." What they're referring to is how a dining table is set – what it feels like. Rather than checkered table cloths and inexpensive flatware, the European approach is white linen table cloths, crystal glassware, and silver. Typically, a flower arrangement would add color, and the whole presentation was classy. This tone and style extended into the lobby, guest rooms, and even hallways. It was different – it was inviting!

THE ARCHITECTURE

Alpine Villages – Built to Last

There's something about European alpine villages that captured Pete Seibert and so many other Vail founders. First, everything is built with stone, accented with stucco. Not only was stone readily available but also it withstood the weather over the centuries. It seems like every building is a different color; bright yellow, deep red, and everything in between. Windows are typically shuttered, with flower boxes alive with more color. The streets are narrow since they were built for horses and oxen. The whole feeling is intimate and inviting.

In 1963, FitzHugh Scott became Vail's first architect. Fitz, as everyone called him, had travelled throughout Europe and interpreted what Pete wanted. He created design guidelines and built one of Vail's first homes to demonstrate what he preferred. He made Bridge Street narrow and designed curves into it to create interest and surprise. The Faesslers describe the alpine style as "organic" [3] reflecting nature and a more laid-back approach. This European style has been maintained over the years, and now even LionsHead with the Arrabelle complex, reflects this feeling. People like it. It feels right.

Arrabelle at Vail Square

The design of Beaver Creek had considerable influence from Europe. In 1980, Jack Marshall, VA's president, Harry Bass, the new owner of VA, and Bob Parker visited leading alpine resorts as well as the quaint villages in Europe, like Kitzbuhel and Val D'sere, and came back with a ton of ideas, photos, and a shared vision. Jack Zehren, the newly hired staff architect, conducted a comprehensive analysis of European mountain communities and created a distinctive village master plan and an architectural motif for Beaver Creek.

Beaver Creek Village

Their goal was to create a village at the base of Beaver Creek Mountain that provided the charm and human scale they'd seen in Europe. They envisioned architecture that blended a classic alpine heritage with the Western influences of the rural Colorado mountains. To convey this shared vision, Zehren put together sketches, models, and design guidelines that depicted the intimate feeling and "sense of place" they wanted, while keeping some balance with the large scale building density needed to make the numbers work. Some may argue with the end product, but when you walk through the Beaver Creek plaza today, it feels pretty special.

Flowers accent Vail Village

The European influence in the Vail Valley is manifested in a patient outlook derived from a long-term perspective. While some might argue that America long ago left Europe in the rear view mirror, worldly people – well-traveled people – know that Europe is still pretty special. They've been at it a lot longer. In fine European hotels, it's easy to see that the concierge's are usually older; they are people who have made this their profession. Guest service is honorable work. The same is true in restaurants where waiters are professionals who have made this their life's work. We Americans still have a lot to learn in this regard, but the guidance offered by our European friends has rubbed off.

COMMENTARY: THE EUROPEAN INFLUENCE

I came to Vail for the first time in 1979 at 18 years old on my first trip to the US.

After spending the summer that first year and many weekends and school breaks during my years at the University of Denver from 1981- 1984, I found Vail to be an extraordinary place of opportunity for a young man having grown up in a Bavarian mountain resort town as part of multi-generation hotelier family.

From the very beginning, Vail seemed such a logical and "easy" place in which to succeed. Clearly, the natural setting and the perfect mountain resort climate was a big part. But Vail also looked and felt just enough like home that I immediately felt a sense of belonging and a feeling that the customs I knew from my home country were welcome and would fit. Most of the businesses were owned and operated by "pioneering spirits" – many from Europe but seemingly all of them full of positive energy and a vison to create something special. It seemed as though many had come to Vail and found opportunity to realize dreams not possible in their birth homes.

Few businesses were operated at a high level of sophistication in the early 80's, which gave me as a "just-out-of-school new-comer" outlook. With little experience but deep knowledge of what "very good" looks and feels like, I immediately had confidence that I could succeed in Vail. There was so much positive "vibe" around that the thought of anything but future success was completely drowned out. Wherever one looked, there was another example of a European that had more or less accidentally ended up in Vail and successfully put down their roots inventing their future in Vail.

Johannes Faessler
Owner: Sonnenalp Hotel – Vail

Hopefully this story has surfaced a few thoughts about the Vail way. To further the thinking, here are several action steps from this chapter worth considering.

Also, the Questions for Dialogue, and the space to write, are intended to stimulate your thinking and generate conversations with friends and colleagues. Talking about your perspectives with others is a good way to learn.

ACTION STEPS:

- Think long-term; build things that last.
- Bring passion to whatever you do, or find something else.
- Welcome diversity; it makes life more interesting.

QUESTIONS FOR DIALOGUE:

- What does serving as a leader really mean to you? How might you foster this approach in your organization or community?

  _____

  _____

- Describe the leadership approach of someone you know who fits this serving mold.

  _____

  _____

- Can we effectively lead by serving?

  _____

  _____

CHAPTER 7

THE VAIL VALLEY FOUNDATION

FROM MY PERSPECTIVE

"Those who say it cannot be done should not interrupt the people doing it."

Chinese Proverb

The Gore Range from Piney Lake

Some people credit me with coming up with the foundation, but it was really Jack Marshall's idea. He had in mind a community organization that was robust enough to engage President Ford.

Marshall became president in 1977 when Harry Bass took control of Vail Associates. He was an architect by training but a developer by trade. He'd come to Vail by way of the Pebble Beach Company, so he knew resorts. One of Jack's first moves was to make an arrangement with President Ford who had lost the White House the year before. The deal gave VA access to Ford's time for fifteen years. Jack asked me to figure out how to use those days most effectively. He said, "Go out to Pebble Beach and learn how they've organized the Bing Crosby National Pro-Am. Maybe that's a model we can follow." [1] Going to Pebble Beach was tough duty.

In Carmel, we learned about the Pebble Beach Foundation, a nonprofit, charitable community organization that hosted several events beyond the Bing Crosby. Upon returning, we pulled together the marketing team and brainstormed the possibilities. That was a blast – to think about how to involve a former president was awesome. We had lots of ideas, but it would take several years for the full plan to evolve. Our first move was to propose that the Vail Associates Foundation be the organizing vehicle, primarily to maintain some measure of control. President Ford agreed to serve on the board, and we were off and running. Right from the start we decided that the foundation's vision would include three areas: athletic events (e.g., ski racing and mountain biking), educational endeavors, and cultural activities.

CHRONOLOGY

June 1978: *Vail Associates Foundation formed*

January 1981: *Jerry Ford Celebrity Cup served as Beaver Creek's opening event*

January 1982: *Legends of Skiing added to the Ford Cup*

March 1983: *World Cup added, creating the American Ski Classic*

June 1983: *AEI World Forum launched*

June 1985: *1989 World Alpine Ski Championships awarded*

July 1985: *Gerald R. Ford Amphitheater started*

February 1999: *World Alpine Ski Championships hosted*

July 2009: *Edwards Preserve opened*

February 2015: *World Alpine Ski Championships hosted*

SKI RACING

The Jerry Ford Celebrity Cup – An Amazing Start

At the beginning, the foundation was a Vail Associates program. Jeanne Reid worked with me to run the foundation as another facet of the VA marketing department alongside advertising, sales, and public relations. As the company moved toward the opening of Beaver Creek, we proposed to President Ford a counterpart to his already-successful golf tournament, dubbed the Jerry Ford Celebrity Cup. He was a pretty decent skier and loved the idea.

The Ford Cup, as it became known later, was essentially the grand opening event for Beaver Creek in January 1981. Like the golf tournament, it drew tons of celebrities, and, similar to having PGA golfers, Ford asked Pepi Gramshammer to invite skiing professionals and former World Cup and Olympic skiers to captain the teams. It was a fantastic party that ended up on both NBC's *Today Show* and ABC's *Good Morning America* at almost the same hour the following Monday morning. For a brand new resort, it was a home run. Everyone was ecstatic. Jack Marshall wrote me a letter saying the Ford Cup was the best event he'd ever been part of. I thought he was exaggerating a bit, but I nevertheless was pleased, even a bit proud. In retrospect, it wasn't me, but rather the former leader of the free world that launched this success story.

The former president training for the Jerry Ford Celebrity Cup

A year later, Marshall decided to step down, and Bass brought Harry Frampton to town. As the new CEO, Frampton reorganized the company and asked me to manage a consolidated marketing department. However, within a year, I proposed that I give up this combined marketing role and take on the foundation full time. I saw events, especially if television was involved, as a good way to leverage our tiny marketing budget. Frampton said, "I think you're crazy," [2] but he gave me a year of cover from VA. We were "profitable" almost immediately. I was still an employee of VA but under a contract to run the foundation. This little detail becomes important as the story unfolds.

We moved into separate office space and began the process of growing the "business." Even though the foundation was a nonprofit with tax-exempt status, I saw it differently. The lawyers didn't approve of my use of words like "partners" and "profit" and "sponsors" – since that wasn't the common way of describing a classic 501(c)(3). But I was a business-oriented guy and saw myself as an entrepreneur wanting to run it like a business. I was clear that if there wasn't surplus cash on hand, we were in the weeds. We needed partnerships with other entities, and certainly collaboration with the community, to have an impact.

The Legends – The Race Becomes Serious Fun

While the educational and cultural side of the foundation was starting to develop, we were more focused on expanding the Ford Cup. In 1982, Pepi Gramshammer suggested we add the Legends of Skiing to the event by creating a specific race just for the former Olympic and World Cup racers – basically all of his friends. It was an immediate hit – and a television program. Most of the racers thought this race would be mostly a social occasion, but when Otto Tschudi, a former Norwegian racer, showed up in the starting gates with a skin-tight racing suit, the tone changed. It was still mostly for bragging rights, but once a racer has winning in his or her blood, the competitive juices remain. It was a blast!

Martina Fortkord, Ylva Nowen and Karen Stemmle
on the podium in the 2013 Legends of Skiing race

And some of the fun involved major cash prizes. Moose Barrows, an Olympic skier from Steamboat and friend of everyone, brought the idea of a "Calcutta" to the Ford Cup. Here's how it worked.

Teams were formed of locals, sponsors, celebrities, and legends. Each team was then auctioned off, typically for several thousand dollars – sometimes for more than $10,000 in the case of Jean-Claude Killy, the French champion, or Stein Ericksen, the Norwegian hero. The top three finishing teams would divvy up the pot with something like $25,000 going to whomever had bought that first place team, with 20 percent off the top going to the Vail Valley Medical Center. It added a little financial incentive to the fun. Not quite Las Vegas but close.

THE VAIL VALLEY MONIKER

Just before we left for Interlaken, Harry Frampton met me for coffee at the Rucksack and asked me to think about how we might connect Vail and Beaver Creek from a marketing perspective.

On the long flight to Frankfurt, the thought jumped into mind to ask the other Bill Brown, the trail map artist, to create a new rendering depicting the "Vail Valley." When I got back, I called Brown and instructed him to take a little liberty and show the two mountains a "little" closer together. It was amazing how he just rearranged the landscape, and bingo, it looked like one valley.

To this day, Frampton credits me with coming up with the Vail Valley concept. In truth, on that flight, I remembered that the Vail Valley Medical Center was already using this phrase, so it just made sense.

As the community grew, the name seemed to stick, in part, because the foundation inserted "Valley" into its name.

The slightly modified geography of the Vail Valley

At the closing banquet, the winners were to be honored and checks distributed. But Will McFarland and Fred Green, two of the local hosts, changed everything. When the third-place team was called to the stage, Fred made the gracious offer to give *all* their winnings to the Vail Valley Medical Center. It was about $10,000. From the back of the room, McFarland shouted out, "I'll match that." The applause was huge, but that wasn't the end. The second placed team came to the stage to receive their $20,000, and they too gave their winnings to the hospital, and someone else yelled, "I'll match that." There was electricity in the room. You could feel it. The same sequence played out with the first-place team with yet another match. In the space of about ten minutes, more than $120,000 was raised for the hospital. The atmosphere was jubilant. This spontaneous fundraising was yet another wonderful example of the "whole village" concept.

The American Ski Classic – Adding a World Cup

Following this success, the next logical step was to add an event with the current world-class skiers from the World Cup circuit. This would be more complicated given that the sanctioning body was the FIS (the French acronym for the Federation de Internationale Ski) and becoming a stop on the World Cup tour was highly political in a long-standing, good-old-boys network. But we realized we'd get nothing if we didn't ask.

So Byron Brown and I went off to Interlaken, Switzerland, for the FIS Calendar Conference. Byron was then on the board of Ski Club Vail, the organization the FIS would consider the local hosting entity. As the Calendar Conference progressed, we could see the schedule for the 1982-1983 season unfolding with no place for us – a new venue. We were locked out by the traditional sites. Then at the last minute, Serge Lange, the feisty, mercurial French journalist whose tight grip on the World Cup was legendary, directed a quick question to Byron: "Would Vail host a Women's

GS on the second Wednesday in March?" Without hesitation Byron said, "Yes, absolutely." Although we hadn't actually named it as such, at that moment, the American Ski Classic was born.

But that's not the end of the story. That night as the conference wound down there was an evening cruise for about a hundred people on a beautiful alpine lake. As we cruised, I noticed over at a corner table a small huddle consisting of Marc Holdler, the president of the FIS (really the godfather of ski racing), Dr. Bud Little, the vice president of the U.S. Ski Association, and two executives from Aspen. It looked pretty serious, like they were cutting some kind of deal. I was standing with Graham Anderson, another U.S. skiing official, and asked, "What do you think they're talking about?" He said, "Probably Aspen's candidacy for the World Championships." [3]

I was incredulous and astonished that our primary competitor was taking this bold step. Once Graham explained the scope and breadth of international exposure that the World Championships represented, I was even more staggered. All I could say was, "Damn. I can't believe it. If they ever back out, call me, would you?" [4]

Fast forward to March and the inaugural American Ski Classic. With celebrities in the Ford Cup, famous ski racers in the Legends, and the current best women skiers, you had the makings of a great party. Add an hour of television on NBC, and we felt we'd arrived. All of this attention, accentuated by sunshine and Colorado's fabulous snow, left me and many others pretty euphoric. Then, a few weeks later, Graham Anderson called. "Aspen has backed out of the World Championships bid. Would Vail jump in?" he asked. My response was, "Give us forty-eight hours."

This started a whirlwind of meetings and phone calls. Harry Frampton saw the possibilities; Harry Bass wasn't so sure. He wanted to see a full budget – by the next day since he was leaving town. We produced a quick budget, but the euphoria of the Ski Classic was more than enough to get a green light. The problem was that the FIS decision for the 1987 championships was about a month off and thousands of miles away in Sydney, Australia. This then began one of the most fun and creative exercises of my life.

Once we realized what we were up against, including other major resorts from Europe and Scandinavia, plus a timetable that made you shake your head, we pulled together a campaign team from throughout the community. Everyone jumped in. We produced brochures, an exhibit, a slide show with music, plus the formal FIS prospectus – all in three languages. We got a letter from President Ford, and he got one from President Reagan. All of this was produced in three weeks because we had shipping to Australia to deal with. And then there were travel arrangements and visas for the team: Pepi and Sheika Gramshammer, John Garnsey, Ed Livran, Bill Brown, and several others. We put together an entertainment plan that included an event at the famous Sydney Opera House. It was fast and furious and it all came together because we cut people loose and let them be creative.

We got everything and everybody there in time, but, in the end, we came in second to Crans Montana, a Swiss resort. We were disappointed but not surprised. Many of the FIS delegates gave us kudos and great encouragement to come back in two years for the next bid, this time for the 1989 championships.

The 1989 World Championships – Gaining International Recognition

Whether it's true or not, George Gillett commented early on that one of the main benefits he saw in buying Vail Associates (VA) was the coming World Championships. He could see the potential, particularly in the television coverage. At the time, Aspen was still the more known entity, especially in Europe, resulting from their hosting of the World Championships in 1950.

Vail's event was a huge success and a wonderful celebration that Pete Seibert was proud of. Men and women from more than twenty nations competed in Downhill, Slalom and Giant Slalom at venues split between Vail and Beaver Creek. A thousand journalists descended upon the Vail Valley and experienced American hospitality and Colorado's powder. The Opening Ceremonies took place in twenty-five degrees below zero, but everyone was warmed-up by a John Denver concert at Dobson Arena. And President Ford was

THE MEN'S DOWNHILL

This is the big one. Every race is important, but the Downhill is what really draws the attention.

It was Saturday, February 13, 1989, and the Men's Downhill was set to start at 11:00 a.m., 7:00 p.m. in much of Europe.

The problem was that it had snowed all night, dumping three feet of God's finest. The entire racing entourage was in Beaver Creek ready to go and awaiting word from the FIS officials as to the plan. All of Bill Brown's crew knew there was no way to get the course ready with that much snow. So, by 10:00 a.m. the race was cancelled.

Then I saw a marketing guy's dream come true. Standing at the finish line with snow up to his waist, the announcer for ORF, the European TV network says, "The Downhill has been cancelled; there's too much snow." Because it was prime time in Europe, the television audience was probably ten million skiing fanatics.

Once that sank in, I decided to take the rest of the day off.

everywhere. The whole community got behind the effort. There was a great deal of renovation and face-lifting that occurred, plus new improvements like the phone company running fiber-optic cable throughout the valley. The economic impact was significant, and, to cap it off, the event produced a profit. Pretty much a home run.

There is more to this story about our multi-year campaign for the World Championships that's in Chapter 2. It talks about how Pepi Gramshammer and I cooked up the Vail Ambassadors that resulted in the creation of the Friends of Vail, now the foundation's core funding source.

EDUCATION AND LEARNING

The World Forum – Our Response to Davos

With the athletic side of the foundation moving nicely, an educational opportunity presented itself as if in a dream. In the winter of 1983, I traveled to St. Moritz as part of a delegation to advance our sister-city relationship with this world-renowned resort. Many of us were aware that we needed to upgrade Vail's guest service, and the Swiss, we felt, had a pretty good handle on this perspective, as did the Austrians and Germans. After our sister-city schmoozing was handled, we slipped over to Davos, which was about thirty miles away, to check out this resort. There we came across the World Economic Forum, seen even then as one of the most prominent gatherings in the world. This happenstance encounter was the seed for the next dimension of the foundation.

We returned to Vail and suggested to President Ford that we create something like the World Economic Forum. The Davos event gathered world leaders and multi-national CEOs. It was an international confab of the highest order. Ford readily agreed and sent me to the American Enterprise Institute (AEI) in Washington, where he served as the honorary chair, to begin developing the idea. AEI was the pinnacle of conservative think tanks alongside the Brookings Institution. When the Democrats were out of office, many landed at Brookings; with the Republicans out with Ford's loss to Jimmy Carter, AEI's roster had lots of familiar names, like Henry Kissinger, Alan Greenspan, Dick Cheney, Jack Kemp, and many others.

By the summer of 1982, we had organized the first World Forum with most of the heavy lifting of program content handled by AEI. We decided to make the focus business and economics. Our role as host was mostly logistics, but with an event chaired by a former president, that became a major undertaking. Ford invited the heads of state from the G-7 nations with whom he had served: Giscard D'Estaing of France, Helmut Schmidt of Germany, James Callahan of Great Britain, Malcolm Fraser from Australia, and Pierre Trudeau of Canada. The fifty or so leaders who came included AEI's stable of experts, plus multi-national CEOs that read like a *Who's Who* list of blue-chip companies. It was an august gathering!

Class reunion: Giscard, Callaghan, Ford, Fraser and Schmidt stroll down memory lane at the World Forum in Colorado

Ford with world leaders from Time Magazine, *September 12, 1983*

By the second year, the World Forum was a hot ticket. Marvin Esch, a former Congressman from Michigan, who led the AEI team said, "When you put persons with the experience, knowledge, and capability in a room together, focusing on important questions, something is going to happen and it's going to be good." [5] Many of the same people came back, augmented by even more international leaders. ABC came to interview Ford and several other former heads of state for *This Sunday with David Brinkley*. This hour-long television show from the lawn at the Charter at Beaver Creek was yet another example of recognition that was the result of Jack Marshall's idea. This collaboration with AEI continued for the next twenty-five years. Interestingly, it also was the seed for the creation of what would become the Vail Leadership Institute, but that's another story covered in Chapter 10.

The Ford Amphitheater – Growing Arts & Culture

From the outset, the Vail Valley Foundation's mission included "education, athletics, and culture." With the World Forum in place, the

American Ski Classic set, and the World Alpine Ski Championships coming, that left culture, which to most people meant the arts. Here again, things just fell into place like we had a helping hand from above.

In the early 1980s, John Dobson, Vail's second mayor, and Fred Meyer, a retired lawyer, conceived of an outdoor amphitheater. They hired renowned architect George Eisenstadt to create a first-class arts center. A design was settled on and fundraising began. It was tough going because of the national economy, but they raised enough to lay the concrete slab for the seats. And then the money stopped. Most people don't realize that those orange seats that we sit on today were the originals put in by Dobson and Meyer. But they sat for several years overrun by tumble weeds and wild grass – they almost disappeared.

But Dobson and Meyer were committed to the project. They came to the foundation and asked if we could take over the project, assuming that President Ford, who was on the board, would lend his support. Ford agreed and the third leg of the mission came into view. We launched a new fundraising campaign and, with Ford's name on the building, began to build momentum raising $2.2 million. But it wasn't a slam dunk. It took several years and lots of creative deal-making with builders, architects, suppliers, and community leaders to complete the project. Shortly after the facility was completed, the Bravo Colorado Music Festival was born, and the community had yet another world-class dimension. The amphitheater has become the focal point of Vail's cultural offerings in the summer.

Ford Amphitheater

This progress all happened in just a few years through collaboration or, as some would prefer, teamwork. The quote that advocates "it takes a village" is apt. Even though the Vail Valley Foundation was a Colorado nonprofit, it operated like a business. Our shareholders were thought of as stakeholders because they represented the whole community. While some argued for tight control by Vail Associates, in the end, wiser heads prevailed, and the foundation began to put some distance between itself and its parent. After all, people knew instinctively that the community – that is, sponsors, donors, hotels, and suppliers – would give support to an independent nonprofit entity, whereas they would not give similarly to "the company."

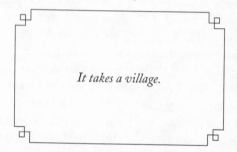

It takes a village.

It was a team approach. The foundation's leaders brought together lots of engaged people from diverse interests. It started with the local community, including commercial interests, residents, and government. On the skiing front, it included the sanctioning bodies like Ski Club Vail, the U.S. Ski Association, and the U.S. Ski Team. It included television, their representative agencies, print media, and, of course, sponsors who paid the freight.

The same was true for the World Forum. The partnership with AEI was central to the program's success. At every step, VA pitched in with transportation, food, and access to on-mountain facilities. No one entity could pull off a complex event like this, with participants from around the world.

The American Ski Classic and the World Championships Organizing Committees included volunteers from every point on the compass for every conceivable function. People pulled together because it was exciting and fun, but more importantly, because it was a unifying cause bigger than anyone.

I left the foundation in 1986 when "the powers" decided I was getting "too big for my britches," maybe a little too independent. They were probably right. In retrospect, it was a blessing even though I couldn't see it that way for about six months.

At first I saw being let go as a failure. Then I realized that the good Lord was simply closing one door and opening another. If J.K. Rowling's book, *Very Good Lives*, had been available back then, I would have been reminded that failures are simply stepping stones – stones of a foundation – on which to build a life. The big lesson for me was realizing that I needed to work more cooperatively with those on the team. It was an opportunity to re-direct the focus of my work and live in integrity with my values.

There is much more to the Vail Valley Foundation story, but my observations would be from afar and thus probably not fully informed. But just consider that in the last thirty years the foundation has produced the Vail International Dance Festival, originally inspired by the Bolshoi Academy of Moscow, run two additional World Alpine Ski Championships, advanced the GoPro Mountain Games, created a twelve-acre park in Edwards called the Preserve, brought the Vilar Center for the Performing Arts under its wings, renovated and improved the Ford Amphitheater, expanded its K-12 educational programming by merging with the Youth Foundation, and helped promote the World Energy Forum. It's gone from a staff of ten when I was there to more than seventy today. The Vail Valley Foundation is a pretty amazing accomplishment!

Much good has been done by all the subsequent leaders, specifically, Bob Knous, John Garnsey, and Ceil Folz, each of whom served as president of the foundation. And to Harry Frampton who has chaired the board over all these years. Kudos to all!

COMMENTARY

As I reflect back, the day I accepted a position with the Foundation was life changing. Convinced by friends and colleagues this fledging organization had amazing upside, I took the plunge.

I was so fortunate to work in an organization poised to be a difference maker for the Vail Valley.

The brainchild of Vail Associates and supported by President Ford, the Foundation evolved from a marketing-based entity into a diverse and complex organization designed to enhance the lives of all living and vacationing in our valley.

You may have been a participant, volunteer, spectator, or your business may have been enhanced by incremental guest visits or the results from short- and long-term TV and media. The world's best dancers may have entertained you or the Magic Bus may have helped your child integrate into a new culture. We have all benefited from the Foundation's events, programs, and facilities.

The future looks to be as exciting as the past with the Foundation exploring new athletic events, helping to fill the slow seasons, and developing new educational programs that stimulate the minds of guests and locals alike as well as young children who need it most. Truly exciting times are ahead.

John Garnsey
Retired President – Global Mountain Development: Vail Resorts, Inc.
Former President – Vail Valley Foundation

Hopefully this story has surfaced a few thoughts about the Vail way. To further the thinking, here are several action steps from this chapter worth considering.

Also, the Questions for Dialogue, and the space to write, are intended to stimulate your thinking and generate conversations with friends and colleagues. Talking about your perspectives with others is a good way to learn.

ACTION STEPS:

- Engage with others – perhaps the whole community.
- Recognize you can do more collectively than you can individually.
- Go big or go home!

QUESTIONS FOR DIALOGUE:

- What are your best examples of collaboration? What resulted?
  _____
  _____

- What stands in your way of working more closely with others?
  _____
  _____

CHAPTER 8

ENVISIONING A SCIENCE SCHOOL

*"If one advances confidently in the direction of his dreams,
and endeavors to live the life which he has imagined,
(s)he will meet with a success unexpected in common hours."*

Henry David Thoreau

Hiking through the Aspens along Buck Creek

How does one evolve into a leader who claims as her purpose "to give voice to place?" [1] How does that happen? For Kim Langmaid, she followed a passion for the natural world, starting along the beaver ponds near Vail Village and maturing, most recently, along Buck Creek in Avon. Kim's story typifies a Vail way of doing things.

Kim Langmaid, Ph.D.

THE SEED

Beaver Dam Road – Where a Vision was Shaped

Growing up in Vail with a family connected to the burgeoning ski resort was exciting, inspiring, and at the same time, limiting. Kim's parents, Charlie and Lynne, moved to Vail in 1969 when she was three. They lived in the apartment in the house of Jack Tweedy, a Vail founder and its first attorney, on Mill Creek Circle. Back then, everybody helped newcomers.

Her grandparents, Bunny and Joe Langmaid, instilled in Kim an early interest in the natural world. At every opportunity, they encouraged Kim to learn more and to explore the wonders of the forests and wildlife around their neighborhood along Beaver Dam Road in Vail Village. As a young girl, Kim spent time building forts in the forest and snow, collecting tadpoles from nearby ponds, and learning the names of birds and wildflowers. These early childhood experiences were imprinted on Kim.

Kim's dad worked at Vail Ski Rentals and later opened Charlie's Gondola Ski Shop in LionsHead, responding to the growing number of skiers who had discovered Vail. Kim's early educational experiences eventually felt confining and insular. Pre-school was under the Rams Horn Lodge, kindergarten in the Vail Chapel, and early grades were above the tiny clinic that is now the Vail Valley Medical Center. Then it was on to Meadow Mountain Elementary in Eagle Vail and later to Vail Mountain School when it was located in modular trailers at the base of Meadow Mountain near Minturn, where Peter Abuisi was teaching English and History before becoming Headmaster.

KIM'S CHRONOLOGY

July 1969: Kim's family moved to Vail from Marblehead, Massachusetts

March 1988: Hired at the Vail Nature Center

May 1995: Attended Teton Science School

September 1998: Launched Gore Range Natural Science School

July 2001: Opened Nature Discovery Center at Eagles Nest

July 2003: Oscar Tang donated land in Avon

June 2006: Kim earned her PhD in environmental studies

August 2011: Walking Mountain Science Center opened

"To give voice to place"

Kim Langmaid

By 1982, Vail was definitely too small for a teenager, and Kim was eager to expand her horizons and meet new people. So she went off to boarding school at the Fountain Valley School in Colorado Springs. Looking back she commented, "This is where my passion for education and learning was ignited." [2] She was exposed to students and teachers from around the world, to interesting field studies, and generally to a world beyond the mountains.

Then it was on to college at Lewis & Clark in Portland, but the rainy weather brought her back to Colorado State University with a start in forestry and then a quick shift to biology. She wanted to understand how natural systems worked rather than how to cut down trees. This was when a seed of sustainability and stewardship took root that would influence and help shape her passion for the environment.

Kim's jobs following college were all out in nature, including working with Colorado Llama Trekking and several roles at the Vail Nature Center. From helping as a naturalist giving tours to serving as director, she became familiar with every flower and tree. Terry Minger was town manager at the time and said of Kim, "She was always happiest in nature. Her passion and dedication helped create the community's nature center out of whole cloth." [3]

Her vision for the community started to take shape around the time the Vail Recreation District (VRD) was considering building a par-three course at the east end of the Vail Golf Club. Looking back, she felt she was a little naïve but nevertheless had the guts to stand up at a town council meeting and speak against VRD's plan, a bold move especially since VRD was her employer. The urge to preserve versus developing every square inch was growing.

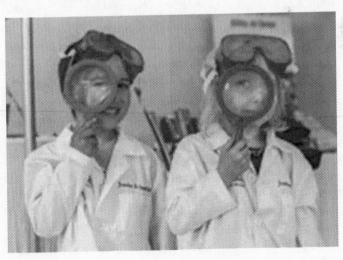

Kids at Walking Mountains

The Vail Nature Center gave Kim the opportunity to get more involved in community environmental activities like the Eagle River Watershed Plan. This involvement became a turning point because Kim's supervisors gave her increasing responsibilities and opportunities for leadership in the Vail community. This was Kim's sweet spot – this was where she belonged – at least for the moment.

A Science School – Learning from the Best

It was around this time in 1995 that Kim realized there was a huge unmet need for environmental education, and the tiny Vail Nature Center was just scratching the surface. She decided to go to graduate school to explore and develop her growing passion for environmental education. So, she went to an advanced program at Teton Science School in Jackson Hole, Wyoming, for two years and while there earned her master's degree in environmental studies through Prescott College. She also learned the nuts and bolts of running a science school – curriculum planning, fundraising, and outdoor program administration. All the while, she was giving shape to the dream of starting a similar nonprofit educational organization in Vail.

Like most visionaries, she started talking to people – science teachers, the Board of Education, County Commissioners, U.S. Forest Service representatives, and various community leaders. In less than a year she had a curriculum written for the Gore Range Natural Science School (GRNSS known locally as "grins") and was ready to offer the first programs to elementary school kids. In September 1998, the Red Sandstone Elementary fifth-grade class was the first group to participate and learn hands-on about the local forest. Things were starting to roll.

Kim's motivation for the Science School was "to inspire people to take responsibility and become stewards of this place." [4] And while there seemed to be broad-based funding support early on, the first major donation came from Harry Frampton, then chair of the Vail Valley Foundation board. It was just in time to make payroll for the first programs. Then they received a grant from the Berger Fund in Denver whose sole purpose was to connect kids with nature.

Next young Ryan Souto enrolled in a four-week program and was so excited that he got his dad, Rick, to serve on the GRNSS board, and he in turn convinced Slifer Smith & Frampton to adopt the organization and help it with fundraising initiatives and events. Kim got the school district and the Town of Red Cliff to lease and reopen the old Red Cliff School and made it workable. The historic old brick school building, which served as the original Battle Mountain High School, had been closed when the school district consolidated because more and more students were living in the Eagle River Valley.

By 2001, most of the Eagle Valley schools were participating, and a new partnership with Vail Resorts and the U.S. Forest Service allowed GRNSS to expand and operate the Nature Discovery Center at Eagles Nest on Vail Mountain. Kim's vision was unfolding.

Colorado Mountain College students on a Walking Mountains hike

It was a challenging time leading a fledgling nonprofit with very thin revenues and growing expenses. But Kim was committed, and by participating in the Colorado Nonprofit Leadership and Management Program that was focused on training nonprofit executives, Kim gained a network of connections that opened many doors. The early years of the Science School were precarious. She didn't pay herself for the first eighteen months and paid her personal bills by working for Axel Wilhelmsen at his store Gore Range Mountain Works in Vail Village. It was an exciting yet stressful time for Kim – she was a social entrepreneur long before the term became popular.

The Science School was at a point where it needed more financial support, but as is often the case with start-ups, people questioned giving money to an organization they weren't sure would survive. Jack Shea, one of

Kim's mentors from the Teton Science School, came to a GRNSS strategic planning retreat and said to the group, "Look at what you've done already – you can take it further. There's an economic component and an educational component that would be really good for the community." [5] Oscar Tang, a long-time supporter of education in the valley, was in a breakout group that day focused on a permanent home, and Kim thinks that may have been the time when the idea was planted in Oscar to get even more involved.

COMMENTARY: THE SEED

I've come to understand that in this world there are both entrepreneurs and entrepreneur caregivers. I've always been very good at the care giving part, perhaps because I have incredible respect and admiration for the absolute fearlessness that it takes to be a real entrepreneur.

In the case of Walking Mountains, Kim Langmaid was the entrepreneur and I was one of the caregivers, in fact, there were many of us who played that important role over the years. We all had a wonderful symbiotic relationship with Kim. The more we were able to help germinate and nurture the seed that Kim planted, the happier we all were.

As I think back on my Walking Mountains experience and other "start-up" experiences I have been privileged to be a part of, I realize that it is the entrepreneur's unwavering focus on and belief in the goal that makes all the difference. In Kim's case it was all about inspiring stewardship, and after one meeting with her I was hooked by her vision— no arm-twisting necessary. I am convinced that Kim was able to attract her large corps of very loyal, capable and dedicated helpers because her focus and belief were so evident.

Alan Danson
Walking Mountains Board Member

THE SEED IS WATERED

Leadership – Walking with Others

To sharpen her skills, Kim enrolled in Leadership Vail Valley, an early program of the nascent Vail Leadership Institute. She had in-depth conversations with thought-leaders and mentors, people like Peter Senge, author of the *Fifth Discipline,* and Dr. David Burger, an adjunct professor from the Center for Creative Leadership. They challenged her with questions that were enriching and provoking. The leadership group visited the Aspen Center for Environmental Studies where Kim was inspired by yet another visionary environmental education facility that had been founded by Elizabeth Paepke in 1968. Elizabeth and Walter Paepke were also instrumental in establishing the Aspen Music Festival, the Aspen Institute, and the Aspen Design Conference, what has become known as the Aspen Ideas Festival.

When Oscar Tang's Buck Creek parcel in Avon was identified as a possible permanent location for GRNSS, Kim wrote to Oscar in New York City saying, "Wouldn't that land be good for a school?" A real highlight of Kim's dream came true when Oscar responded, "I'd be willing to donate the land, and I'll give

---

KIM MEETS MICHIE

In 2001, during the Leadership Vail Valley program, Kim met Michie Slaughter, a Cordillera homeowner who was involved with the Kauffman Foundation of Kansas City. Kauffman was the largest foundation in the country dedicated to entrepreneurial education.

Slaughter was speaking to the leadership group, and, in a breakout session, he asked Kim what she needed right then to move the Science School forward. She said, "$50,000 would make all the difference." A few weeks later a check arrived. It was a key moment that moved the school to the next level.

Shortly thereafter, Kim was connected with Tony Mayer, also involved with Kauffman and a second homeowner in Vail. Tony and his wife Barbie were very committed to science education, and they got personally involved.

The momentum was beginning to build – the school was becoming an early-stage enterprise.

you four years to raise the additional capital." [6] That started the ball rolling for a permanent location.

Dan Carroll, a retired organizational consultant for Booz Allen Hamilton, helped expand the board. Mimi and Woody Stockwell served as mentors, and Buck Elliott, Kathy Borgen, Bill Jensen, Rich Rogel, Susan Pollack, and many other community-minded leaders helped move the vision forward.

The real breakthrough for GRNSS came courtesy of Kathy Borgen, when she helped Kim recruit Alan Danson to the board in late 2001. Alan was a venture capital investor and entrepreneurial manager who served on Kathy's husband's Founders Fund board. He was initially pressed into service as chair of the development committee and then became board chair when Dan Carroll retired.

Alan recalled that he had just finished an intense four years with a very demanding startup when Kathy called. He needed something to occupy him, and GRNSS was just the thing. Kim laughingly recalled that Alan was so intense at the beginning that he worked more hours as a volunteer than did most of the staff. "He jumped in with both feet and helped us professionalize the organization and raise the money we needed to progress," [7] she said.

Once the decision was taken in 2005 to build a campus on the land that Oscar Tang had offered to donate, Alan was asked to co-chair the campaign with Kathy Borgen. Alan and Oscar were good friends who skied together in the Streeter Group. Alan remembers Oscar coming to him with a big grin on his face after deciding to donate the land and saying, "Ok Alan, my job is done, now yours begins, don't let me down". [7] Alan also remembers that the next five years represented the most intense effort of his career. These people, and many others who were willing to step forward with money and talent, are indicative of the Vail way.

All during this incubating stage, Kim was challenged in ways she never contemplated. As the pressure and responsibilities mounted, she remembered how supportive her parents were in saying, "You can do whatever you put your mind to." [8] She believed in herself and knew that anything was possible; all it took was making a commitment and sticking with it. Periodically she would reflect on Goethe's famous quote that said, "Whatever you can do, or dream you can, begin it. Boldness has genius, power, and magic in it. Begin it now!" [9]

Passing the Baton

But she also remembered the Leadership Vail Valley counsel to be aware of the "founder's syndrome" that causes many organizations to fail because the founder holds on too tightly. She decided to introduce new leadership to GRNSS.

Several years earlier, she had met Markian Feduschak who had been running Outward Bound programs in Leadville. His response to the opportunity to run GRNSS became a real turning point for Kim. So after six years at the helm and recently married, she was exhausted and was ready for a change. Markian was someone she respected and could entrust with the vision. Markian said, "What I saw in Kim was not only a great vision but also a great drive. She just exuded great energy." [10] His steadiness, passion for natural science, and his strong background in leadership gave Kim the freedom to let go and move on. Being a lifelong learner, Kim wanted to go back to school for her Ph.D. in environmental studies.

Once Markian was on board and settled in, Kim enrolled in the low-residency doctoral program at Antioch University of New Hampshire. Antioch was known for its interdisciplinary studies, weaving together social science and natural science, and was a place where her burning interest in understanding the relationship between humans and nature could flourish. It was a pretty intense five years but very exciting.

While Kim was earning her doctorate, she was also developing a new graduate program for the Science School in partnership with Colorado State University. At the same time, she also served as interim program coordinator of the new Ph.D. program in sustainability education at Prescott College. She was super busy, but so were Markian and the whole GRNSS team as they contemplated a permanent campus.

COMMENTARY: THE SEED IS WATERED

I first met Kim in the late 1990's when the buzz started about Gore Range Natural Science School. It was a fascinating story about a determined young woman, a native of Vail, who wanted to build an environmental science school. This school would serve the local schoolchildren and visitors to Vail, and the Eagle River Valley, so they would learn about, and appreciate this very special place.

From the get-go, her entrepreneurial spirit, tenacity and persuasiveness allowed her to share her dream with other like-minded people who love this place. In many ways, Kim "sees" thing from a 30,000-foot view. Far-seeing, intuitively, and way ahead of the game, she "knew" that Eagle County residents and visitors alike would support and embrace an environmental/science education center.

But that didn't mean that beginning the process and getting it rolling was easy. Skeptics, who supported the idea, but were far from sure that it could be done abounded. Many different constituencies formed the mix. However, Kim was able to unite these disparate groups because she spoke on two levels: one, practical conversation on benefits to the community, and on the other, her deep love and attachment to the natural world, which resonated with those to whom, she spoke.

The topic of accessibility promoted spirited discussion in the early years. Where should we plant the seed of our dreams? And, if we build it, will they come? Although a remote campus like the Teton Science School seemed very attractive, we had to ask ourselves to whom do we want to learn about vision of the wonder of the natural world? We wrangled a bit, but ultimately settled on the idea that we must build close to I-70 to serve the school children and other who travel that road.

Once we decided the location, there was not turning back. Several times in subsequent years, we struggled to make payroll, but somehow we always made it. Kim didn't panic, and neither did we. Some of her board members backed-up the dream with a line of credit, but we never had to use it. We were on our way.

Kathy Borgen
Walking Mountain Board Member

THE PLANT EMERGES

Walking Mountains – The Full Vision Takes Shape

As part of the capital campaign planning process, the team at GRNSS came up with a new name, "Walking Mountains Science Center," to guide the organization into the future. The mission became "to awaken a sense of wonder and inspire environmental stewardship and sustainability." It may have seemed an odd choice, but the new name took hold as the capital campaign developed. Kim says "walking mountains" is an idea inspired by place-based education. When you live in a place long enough and know it well, you observe that even the mountains are changing, or walking. With a new name settled on, the board of directors focused on raising the many millions needed to construct a new facility. Alan Danson, a local attorney and education nut, became a huge champion of the project and introduced many of his friends who joined the effort. The first leadership gift came when Jay Precourt, an original Vail pioneer, indicated he wanted to contribute to the campaign. When word reached Kim, she cried out, "Oh my God." The rest of the story is history as another $9 million was raised to build the campus that far exceeded everyone's expectations. Following the grand opening, Kim commented, "A great thing about Vail is the people here who can help make dreams come true. They invest in visions to enrich our mountain community, get involved, and help make them happen. It's a wonderful aspect of the Vail Valley." [11]

The Walking Mountains Science Center in Avon

But Kim was not done. When Walking Mountains was fairly stable, and more than she ever expected, she was hired in 2011 as the first Colorado Director of the National Forest Foundation, the nonprofit affiliate of the U.S. Forest Service that exists to perpetuate values that the forests represent. In this position, her job was to get people involved in the restoration of forest lands across Colorado. This job included restoring the Upper South Platte watershed that was damaged as a result of the devastating Hayman Wildfire of 2002. Vail Resorts was the lead private financial contributor to that restoration project that protected drinking water for Denver and other cities along the Front Range. Restoration also included trail maintenance, repairing terrain around abandoned logging roads, culvert repairs, and a whole variety of small projects that brought the forest back to its original state. Kim also worked with the Eagle-Holy Cross Ranger District to develop a vision and plan for the ecological restoration of Camp Hale, a special place where much of the Vail story has its roots.

What is needed long-term, according to Kim, is the development of a local "sustainability and stewardship economy" that would include a variety of local businesses, nonprofits, and groups of various types who understand that environmental sustainability and stewardship have economic potential and long-term benefits for future generations. Organizations that depend on lumber for furniture, for example, or educators and social entrepreneurs who see the forest as a learning laboratory and want to bring it back to a more wild state – they are people who want to heal the land. The biomass plant in Gypsum, Colorado, is a good example of what can happen when entrepreneurs get engaged. Many of these possibilities have a stewardship dimension where we take care of the natural resource that is so attractive to visitors from around the world. For example, if we don't provide active stewardship for the beautiful Eagle River Preserve in Edwards, the thistles and weeds will take over. Stewardship is central to the Vail way.

Although it was important work, Kim decided that working with the National Forest Foundation was not the best long-term fit for her career. She felt drawn to continuing to make a difference in her home community rather than spending her time and energy working on forest projects that spanned across the state of Colorado from Fort Collins to Colorado Springs to Durango. On top of that, the Foundation's relationship with the huge government bureaucracy of the U.S. Forest Service was too much for Kim. Despite household expenses and college debt, she had the guts to pull the plug on a well-paying job. It just wasn't the right fit.

So Kim moved on from the National Forest Foundation and signed up for the Vail Leadership Institute's (VLI) Exploring Entrepreneurship program and embarked on a four-month course to craft her next chapter.

Near the end of the program, Kim negotiated with the board of the Eagle Valley Alliance for Sustainability to take over their chief executive's role. Within months, she saw the potential of this environmental-sustainability and stewardship-oriented organization, and she successfully merged it with Walking Mountains.

She has come full circle and is now a senior vice president at the place she first envisioned. Kim has also been instrumental in developing the new bachelor's degree in sustainability studies at Colorado Mountain College. She served on the committee to develop the curriculum and secure approvals from the Higher Learning Commission. She continues to teach courses for Colorado Mountain College in systems thinking, fostering sustainable behaviors, social entrepreneurship, and sustainability leadership. And recently, as part of the 2015 FIS Alpine World Ski Championships Environment Committee, Kim has helped develop a new vision with the "Actively Green" initiative involving local businesses, organizations, and governments to create a "sustainable destination" in partnership with the global nonprofit Sustainable Travel International.

So that's Kim's story to date. It's the story of fulfilling a vision. And her story begs the question, what does the community want to become in its second fifty years? The dust is settling from the first generation of Vail Valley pioneers and the younger, emerging leaders, like Kim, are stepping up to create new visions and to have their say. Kim believes that "whether it's education, rejuvenation, health and wellness, environmental sustainability, or stewardship – whatever you want to call it – we ought to be thinking triple bottom-line – people and planet along with profit." [12] She feels we ought to do a better job of re-envisioning and re-developing our communities so they are more sustainable for the long haul. She says, "We need place-based planners and community-minded thinkers who contemplate longer-term perspectives for the benefit of future generations living amidst a changing climate. We need entrepreneurs who can see the potential of environmental sustainability and stewardship as integral to our economy." [13]

Kim is very optimistic about the community's future. She senses that people really want to help grow the community in a good way – they just need to become more aware of where the opportunities lie. She sees her role in the Vail community as "giving voice to place" while helping facilitate positive change. She'd rather channel good change than fight development.

One of her favorite quotes, taken from a Vail Symposium poster that hung in her family's living room while she was growing up, is the famous saying from Heraclitus, "Nothing endures but change." As Terry Minger so aptly said recently, "Vail should be ever grateful that Kim chose to stay here and share her love of the environment with us all." [14]

With a passion to help others incubate their ideas and their lives, we can be thankful that one strong visionary is giving that voice to the Vail Valley. What is remarkable is Kim's tenacity to that purpose.

COMMENTARY: THE PLANT EMERGES

At about the same time that the decision was made to build a new campus, the board members finally listened to Kim who had been telling them regularly the counsel she received from Leadership Vail Valley to be aware of the "founder's syndrome" that causes many organizations to fail because the founder holds on too tightly. The board decided to form a search committee and seek a new director for GRNSS.

Kim already knew Markian Feduschak who had been running Outward Bound programs in Leadville, and he quickly became the leading candidate. His hiring became a real turning point for Kim. After six years at the helm and recently married, she was exhausted and was ready for a change. Markian was someone she respected and could entrust with the vision. His steadiness, passion for natural science, and his strong background in leadership gave Kim the freedom to let go and move on. Being a lifelong learner, Kim wanted to go back to school for her Ph.D. in environmental studies.

Alan Danson
Walking Mountains Board Member

Hopefully this story has surfaced a few thoughts about the Vail way. To further the thinking, here are several action steps from this chapter worth considering.

Also, the Questions for Dialogue, and the space to write, are intended to stimulate your thinking and generate conversations with friends and colleagues. Talking about your perspectives with others is a good way to learn.

ACTION STEPS:

- Follow your dream. It worked for Kim.
- You don't have to go it alone; find others who share your passion.

QUESTIONS FOR DIALOGUE:

- What is your dream? And what are you doing about it?

  _____

  _____

- What talents and gifts do you bring to this vision?

  _____

  _____

- In order to achieve your vision, what must you let go of or release, and what must you embrace.

  _____

  _____

- What is the change you want to see in the world?

  _____

  _____

CHAPTER 9

DESTINATION MEDICINE

"Everybody can be great, because anybody can serve.
You don't have to have a college degree to serve.
You don't have to know about Plato and Aristotle to serve.
You don't have to know Einstein's Theory of Relativity to serve.
You only need a heart full of grace and a soul generated by love."

Dr. Martin Luther King, Jr.

The Gore Range

What started in a back room of a restaurant in 1962 has become a world-class medical facility. Today the Vail Valley Medical Center has an annual budget of $240 million and is an independent, nonprofit "business" with facilities spread over seven campuses. It's just another testament to Vail's entrepreneurial way.

MODEST BEGINNINGS

The Vail Clinic – Winter Doctors

Even before hiring the first full-time doctor, Pete Seibert engaged several "winter doctors" who splinted broken bones and stitched up lacerations in the basement kitchen of the Red Lion restaurant. One Mexican family required more.

Victor de la Lama, an architect from Mexico City, had been skiing in Aspen for years. In January of 1963, Vail's first ski season, his family decided to check out this new ski resort. Unfortunately, the day was marred by a torn ACL of Victor's eldest son. It was a bit traumatic with no real medical facilities on hand, so the family headed to Denver. But before they left, Victor said to Pete Seibert, "We loved the skiing, but we won't be back until you have a hospital."[1]

To Pete's credit, that incident put in motion the creation of what would become a robust medical capability.

CHRONOLOGY

December 1962: First doctor's office located in the Red Lion restaurant

September 1965: Tom Steinberg opened small clinic in the Mill Creek Court

January 1967: The Vail Clinic opened on West Meadow Drive

October 1971: Dr. Jack Eck joined Vail Mountain Medical

August 1980: The clinic became the Vail Valley Medical Center

June 1987: Major hospital expansion occurred, including the Howard Head Sports Medicine Clinic

June 1987: The Steadman Clinic moved to Vail; opened a research lab

August 1997: Hospital expanded again with twenty additional beds

June 2001: Shaw Cancer Center opened; Jack's Place built in 2006

June 2012: Surgery center opened on the Edwards campus

February 2015: VVMC and Town of Vail announced redevelopment plan

June 2015: Castle Peak Senior Care Center broke ground

While these "winter doctors" filled the gap for a few years, everybody knew they needed something a bit more permanent – so they advertised. Among the 135 applicants, Tom Steinberg stood out when he took the initiative to make his case. A brother-in-law of Steinberg's happened to know John Murchison, the Texan oil man and early Vail hospital advocate, and when Murchison was in New York City on business, Steinberg took the forty-five minute train ride to the city to introduce himself. That led to an interview with Pete in Vail that sealed the deal.

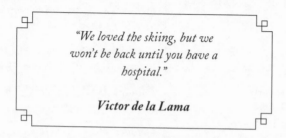

"We loved the skiing, but we won't be back until you have a hospital."

Victor de la Lama

Tom Steinberg's determination and work ethic had been honed, first on the family farm in Iowa and later on the battlefields of Germany in World War II. Once the future doctor saw the horror of the Dachau concentration camp, it would forever influence his perspective on serving those in need. Even though he wouldn't talk about the Holocaust for the next forty years, it was deeply embedded. And like the other Vail founders, Steinberg knew what hard work was like. After working as an "industrial doctor" for Ford Motor Company for ten years, he brought his considerable experience as a general practitioner to the mountains.

In the summer of 1965, the same year President Johnson committed the first 3,500 Marines to the Vietnam War, Dr. Steinberg, and his ever-energetic wife, Flo, left the pressures of urban life in New Jersey and moved to Vail. He set up shop at the Vail Clinic in the first floor of the Mill Creek Court building. It was sparse; Steinberg said, "We were providing frontier medicine in a dog-house office." [2] While Murchison bought an X-ray machine, Steinberg contributed his own medical equipment and exam tables. In those early days, Steinberg was a one-man band serving as doctor, coroner, and ambulance driver in his own 1957 Chevy station wagon. It was a little like the Wild West – and an early demonstration of Vail's entrepreneurial way.

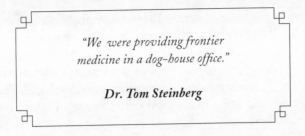

*"We were providing frontier
medicine in a dog-house office."*

Dr. Tom Steinberg

Before long, John Murchison and Gordon Brittan, another early hospital champion working with Vail Associates, who had gifted a parcel of land, launched the Vail Clinic. Like every other aspect of the burgeoning resort, community leaders were simply trying to keep up with demand. First it was minor medical procedures, but before long they were delivering babies. What started as a two-story clinic and doctor's office became, over the years, a hodgepodge of buildings. Today, the Vail Valley Medical Center is a multifaceted, extensive collection of medical services and facilities throughout Eagle County and even stretching into neighboring Summit County. It's a huge community-service business, especially for a nonprofit, but it has all the typical corporate challenges of strong personalities, tight budgets, and complex decision making. Balancing patient care with economics was, and always will be, no easy matter.

Dr. Steinberg in 1995

If Tom Steinberg didn't have enough to handle in those early years, he served several terms – a total of eighteen years – on the Vail Town Council. These were exciting years but contentious in many ways. He served as mayor *pro tempore* during the years of planning and construction of LionsHead. Beyond classic medicine, Steinberg saw the need for mental health, so he helped establish the local chapter of Alcoholics Anonymous. And he was an early and consistent advocate for the environment, and still serves today at 92 on the board of the Eagle Valley Land Trust. While Pete Seibert was the primary business entrepreneur, Tom Steinberg was a community entrepreneur.

Enter Jack Eck – Trained in the Heat of War

Even though he wasn't the first doctor, Dr. Eck is still one of the most beloved. He's cared for thousands of locals and visitors – on the mountain, at the hospital, or on nearby ranches. His thorough but gentle manner may be what makes him special among the many talented physicians, nurses, and caregivers who have chosen the Vail Valley as home.

Dr. Jack Eck at Jack's Place

THE DOCTOR'S TOUCH

Dr. Eck had a special touch, and sometimes that meant the lack of a touch.

In the case of our daughter Brooke's bout with a mysterious illness, one exam with Dr. Eck amounted to nearly an hour of questions about what she felt, what she had been eating, how she was exercising, and so on. He never touched her, but was making an experienced diagnosis.

While Jack left the exam room, Pam and I were praying like crazy for a recovery, especially from her hugely swollen glands and high fever. As the last step in Dr. Eck's exam, he asked Pam, "What does Mom think? Should we check her into the hospital?"

Pam looked surprised at the return of normal color to Brooke's face and neck and said, "I think she's going to be fine."

It seemed like a miracle. Maybe it was the "touch" of a special caregiver paired with the touch of a hand from above.

174

Dr. Eck first came through Vail in January of 1971 following service as a flight surgeon with the 101st Airborne Division in Vietnam. It was the great skiing that attracted him, but it was the opportunity to practice medicine given to him in June of that year by Dr. Steinberg that kept him here.

Jack Eck grew up in Shavertown, an eastern Pennsylvania coal mining town to parents of German heritage. It was a hardscrabble beginning in a family that worked their way up. It was this no-nonsense work ethic that inspired Jack to start college as a biology student, then a pre-med major at Muhlenberg College in Allentown. With the Vietnam War heating up, Jack was drafted in 1964, but was given a deferment for medical school at Temple University in Philadelphia.

As with so many others who served in that challenging conflict, Jack was thrust into a new warfare strategy that the Pentagon called "air mobility." Helicopters would insert soldiers near a rice paddy or into an open field where Viet Cong or North Vietnamese regulars were often concealed in the incredibly dense foliage. Very often, these airborne troops found themselves under immediate attack. It could be deafening, horrific, and bloody. Jack's job as a flight surgeon was to attend to the most severely wounded with the hope that they would make it back to base for more comprehensive medical attention. He said, "Field medicine made me a better diagnostician." [3] It probably also developed that sense of humility that is part of Jack's demeanor.

For those who served in Vietnam, it was a powerful experience, indelible in many ways. For Jack it was traumatic; in fact, he probably experienced what has become known now as PTSD (post-traumatic stress disorder). In addition to so many bloody bodies, he saw officers who yelled to get things moving but who were largely ineffective. He met others for whom he would have taken a bullet. The military experience can be defining in so many ways; just as it influenced Vail's entrepreneurial founders coming out of World War II, the Vietnam conflict influenced Dr. Eck's generation. It taught them what service meant – it gave real meaning to the freedoms that are often taken for granted.

COMMENTARY- MODEST BEGINNINGS

The Vail Clinic opened in the Mill Creek Court Building in 1965 with Tom Steinberg as Vail's first physician. From this modest beginning the Vail Clinic moved to its present location on West Meadow Drive in 1967. That original building was small but met all the basic medical needs of the community.

In 1980 the hospital's updated wing was added and the Vail Clinic became the Vail Valley Medical Center. With the baby boom in the early 80's the hospital expanded its maternity services to accommodate Vail's new babies. In addition VVMC now had the capacity to expand its surgical facilities and provide a much larger array of services for its patients.

In the early 1980's the hospital experienced a severe financial crisis due to insufficient cash flow that threatened to close the facility. The Vail community rallied to this need and generously raised enough funds to keep the doors open.

1990 was a transformational year for VVMC. Howard Head made a generous gift to create a new Howard Head Sports Medicine Center in Vail. That same year VVMC leaders teamed up with George Gillett to bring Drs. Richard Steadman and Richard Hawkins to Vail where they established their orthopedic clinic. Thus began Vail's trajectory into a worldwide center of orthopedics and sports medicine.

Art Kelton
Chairman – Vail Valley Medical Center Board

GOING WORLD CLASS

The Steadman Clinic – Orthopedic Super Stars

Vail's medical community took a huge leap forward in 1987 when George Gillett, then principal owner of Vail Associates, together with Cindy Nelson, an Olympic skier, had the brilliant idea of bringing Dr. Richard Steadman and his cutting-edge clinic to Vail. Steadman had been operating out of South Lake Tahoe, reconstructing knees of skiers, many of whom were U.S. Ski Team racers.

Richard Steadman was an innovator. Born, raised, and educated in Texas, Steadman retained many of the qualities Texans are known for: perseverance and compassion wedded to an entrepreneurial, risk-taking spirit. His primary interests were his patients and research. The micro-fracture procedures that Dr. Steadman and his colleagues developed to repair damaged cartilage and encourage its re-growth are only part of the story. He felt strongly that beginning post-operative rehabilitation, what he called the "healing response," immediately following surgery was a better way than waiting, but he needed scientifically validated research to prove it. It took courage to pursue this theory because no one else was doing orthopaedics this way. He stood to be ridiculed by the medical community.

Working with Dr. Gene "Topper" Hagerman and John Atkins, they revolutionized the post-surgical rehabilitation process. Steadman would work his microscopic magic with great skill, and then get his patients moving almost immediately – no waiting for stiffness to set in. Hagerman, with a Ph.D. in sports physiology, would then guide the patient through a rigorous routine to strengthen the knee. While Steadman's expertise was guiding the whole process, it was a team approach that Hagerman described as "the physician-patient-physical therapist triad all working together that was the key to a successful outcome."

The stories of famous athletes recovering from serious injuries are legend, owing much to their determination and commitment to get back to their sport. (See Cindy Nelson's story in Chapter 11.) When you walk the halls of the Steadman Clinic, it's amazing to see the plethora of hockey, football, baseball, and soccer jerseys of athletes they have treated. But one of Steadman's goals was also to help non-athletes stay active longer, and he met that goal by treating more than 12,000 patients during his time in Vail. Steadman has become a role model to many in health care by showing that "compassion and a deep desire to push the limits of what's possible for patients after major surgery makes a difference." [5]

Steadman Philippon Research Institute

The Steadman Clinic is one entity, but its research institute is quite another. When Gillett convinced Steadman to move to Vail, the expanded research component sealed the deal. Steadman saw the opportunity to advance orthopedics to a new level, focusing on joint preservation versus replacement. Gillett's gift of several million dollars allowed the building of two additional operating rooms and a state-of-the-art research facility inside an expanding medical center. The high-tech equipment allowed doctors and researchers to test procedures on cadavers flown in daily from distant morgues. That may sound gruesome, but it provided hands-on, applicable research experience.

Dr. Marc Philippon & Dr. Richard Steadman

Many people have questioned why Dr. Steadman needed an independent, nonprofit organization for this research, but with the huge costs of scientific instrumentation and research complexity, together with the need for peer-review validation, it makes sense. Steadman knew intuitively that his mirco-fracture procedures worked – he could see it in his athlete patients' performances. But in the scientific world, you've got to prove it.

For the past five years, the Steadman-Philippon Research Institute (SPRI) has sponsored eight to ten new orthopedic surgeons to perfect their skills and research capabilities in Vail. Among various research orientations, the institute focuses its evidence-based research and education on biomedical engineering, imaging research, and regenerative medicine. At the end of their year, these "fellows" present their research findings and what they've learned and taken from this unique experience in Colorado's high country. One young physician who was serving as a U.S. Navy doctor said, "This was clearly the capstone of my medical training." [6]

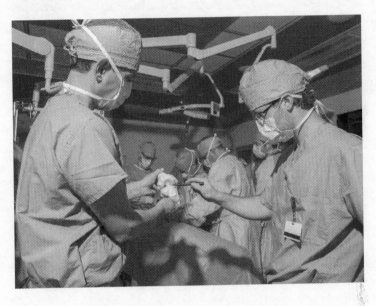

Steadman Fellows in the Operating Room

Major kudos go to George Gillett for seeing the possibilities and investing in research that would prove the merits of joint preservation. And to Dr. Steadman for seizing the opportunity to keep active people active. Their collective vision launched the initial aspect of "destination medicine." These doctors work like crazy; when they're not operating, they are conducting research and then writing up their results in papers to be presented at major medical conferences – all to expand the acceptance of re-generative procedures. This approach to health care – rejuvenation really – is indicative of the Vail way by helping people maintain an active lifestyle. Of the Steadman influence, Dr. Eck said, "Dr. Steadman moved the VVMC from a small seasonal clinic to a year-round, full-service hospital. He brought a large following and a huge infusion of new business. He advanced Vail's reputation beyond skiing." [7]

Ford Frick, a Denver-based economist commented in an economic impact study, "As resort communities mature, health care services will be a critical component of local services, and few areas can compete with the diversity and depth of medical services offered by the Vail Valley Medical Center. The Steadman clinic's operations diversify the local economy, providing market opportunities beyond skiing, real estate, and recreation – an enviable market position." [8]

COMMENTARY – MODEST BEGINNINGS

The Vail Clinic opened in the Mill Creek Court Building in 1965 with Tom Steinberg as Vail's first physician. From this modest beginning the Vail Clinic moved to its present location on West Meadow Drive in 1967. That original building was small but met all the basic medical needs of the community.

In 1980 the hospital's updated wing was added and the Vail Clinic became the Vail Valley Medical Center. With the baby boom in the early 80's the hospital expanded its maternity services to accommodate Vail's new babies. In addition VVMC now had the capacity to expand its surgical facilities and provide a much larger array of services for its patients.

In the early 1980's the hospital experienced a severe financial crisis due to insufficient cash flow that threatened to close the facility. The Vail community rallied to this need and generously raised enough funds to keep the doors open.

1990 was a transformational year for VVMC. Howard Head made a generous gift to create a new Howard Head Sports Medicine Center in Vail. That same year VVMC leaders teamed up with George Gillett to bring Drs. Richard Steadman and Richard Hawkins to Vail where they established their orthopedic clinic. Thus began Vail's trajectory into a worldwide center of orthopedics and sports medicine.

Art Kelton
Chairman – Vail Valley Medical Center Board

TWENTY-FIRST CENTURY CARE

The Vail Valley Medical Center 3.0 –

If 2.0 was VVMC's middle years from 1980 to 2005, then 3.0 started when the hospital leadership knew it had to expand in response to mounting demand in a growing community. They also had to fix the dysfunction that had permeated the hospital as a result of turnover at the top. The return of Doris Kirchner as a health care professional in 2009 was just what the doctor ordered. She has made a huge difference.

Doris Kirchner – CEO of VVMC

Kirchner is a nurse by training but a leader at heart. She came to Vail from Canon City, Colorado, and worked as chief nurse for several years for several different CEOs at VVMC. Tiring of turnover in the hospital's leadership, Doris left Vail in 1994 and before long connected with Mike Shannon, George Gillett's CEO at Vail Associates, who was then launching KSL Resorts (Kravis, Shannon, and Lichliter) to acquire golf resort properties. While she claimed to know little about the resort business, she later realized that being "hospitable" applies to both the medical and resort fields.

Following several years of helping with the accelerating growth at KSL, in 2007 Doris decided it was time to move on just when VVMC was experiencing yet another round of leadership challenges. Before long, she was on the board, then interim CEO, and, finally, she became president of VVMC in 2010. Of all these machinations, Dr. Eck commented, "Doris had a history with VVMC in the ER and the OR, and she knew many of the players. She studied Toyota's 'lean principles' and implemented them working closely with Charlie Crevling, the CFO. In a word, she brought much needed stability." [9]

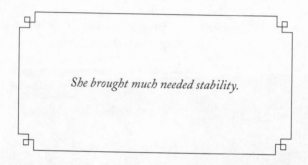

She brought much needed stability.

Destination Medicine – Taking Advantage of Technology

The incredible success of the Steadman Clinic became the first major dimension of destination medicine, the practice of bringing people to Vail for first-class orthopaedic care. For this dimension to grow, the hospital needed to grow. So a series of complex discussions ensued about how to fix the aging appendages at the hospital, and at the same time, create even better facilities. At first, a coalition between the Town of Vail, VVMC, and the Steadman Clinic developed an approach that would result in a much bigger hospital and a new town hall (given that this new complex would extend onto town property). Everyone was excited about this prospect, even though it would be expensive given the need to carefully phase the construction to keep the hospital fully functional during development. Then "ObamaCare" (the name given the Affordable Care Act) became a reality in 2010.

To say the least, President Obama's landmark legislation changed the game – in so many ways. The impact that this new law would have on the whole medical world was unclear. Of particular concern to the Steadman Clinic, and everyone else for that matter, was the economic implication, particularly the more stringent reimbursement policies that were sure to come. This uncertainty caused the Steadman Clinic to pull out of the three-way deal and sent VVMC back to the drawing boards. This decision sent no small amount of rancor throughout the community.

What remained after all this back-and-forth was the need to continue to serve the ever-expanding healthcare requirements of an evolving community, one with a growing population and an increasing number of aging baby boomers. What services and facilities would be needed for the next fifty years, and how could VVMC become financially sustainable given these economic and demographic shifts? Among many conclusions, destination medicine became a rallying cry. But what did that notion really mean?

Like many entrepreneurial endeavors, the process of growing a leg of the economy involves patience and resources – certainly money and the right people – but also a vision. As Mike Shannon, chair of the Vail Health Services board tells it, this next wave in medicine was propelled forward in 1997 with the successful sequencing of the genome. This scientific breakthrough led to a whole host of possibilities in health care. When Shannon attended a "future of medicine" seminar at Mayo Clinic in Rochester, Minnesota, and first heard about these possibilities, the ideas started flowing. From his experience with Mayo, plus involvement at the Eisenhower Medical Center and with relationships in Vail, an opportunity began to take shape. The key would be the expanded use of the stem cells in re-generative medicine. And much like what Dr. Steadman realized for his micro-fracture procedures, research to support the medical finding would be necessary. But first, the hospital needed to get a new plan approved.

VVMC's new look

After what seemed like an endless amount of effort, negotiations, and bureaucratic hoops, VVMC and the Town of Vail reached agreement in 2015 on how the hospital would expand in Vail, with the Steadman Clinic and the Steadman Phillipon Research Institute as a major partner. At first glance, the improvements spread over several years would fix the hodge-podge of appendages added over the last fifty years as demand grew. Among a host of improvements, the main entrance would be moved away from its current residential street and underground parking would be added. A substantial expansion to the emergency room would allow doctors more room to perform their magic. And a new heliport would be connected directly to the hospital, shaving critical minutes in those most urgent situations. While these much needed improvements would bring VVMC fully into the twenty-first century, the major addition would be a huge expansion of research space.

All of these improvements would certainly benefit locals and visitors needing medical attention, but the research facilities are the key to making VVMC financially viable and sustainable. What Shannon and his astute colleagues – many of whom are successful business people – have concluded is that by partnering with entities like the Mayo Clinic, several research universities, and high profile doctors and scientists, Vail can become a major crossroads of this re-generative movement. Already, VVMC is attracting doctors, chemists, biologists, and research scientists to begin building this capability. And much like what the Steadman and Vail-Summit Orthopedic doctors have done, this opportunity will attract patients who want the best care possible. Shannon said, "We know that patients will follow the best doctors." [10] It's an economic engine that portends great things.

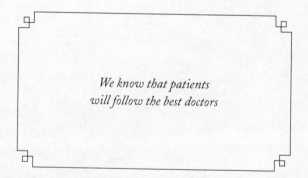

We know that patients will follow the best doctors

An ancillary dimension of this deepening movement is the popping-up of for-profit enterprises around orthopaedics. For example, Reinhold Schmieding set up a small operation in Vail for his company Arthrex, Inc., that makes orthopaedic surgical supplies for arthroscopic and minimally invasive procedures. Schmieding's involvement in Vail led to his company helping to establish the Feagin Leadership Forum at Duke University. Every other year Duke medical students come to Vail at the invitation of Dr. John Feagin to advance their leadership perspectives. Dr. Feagin said, "Our relationship with Arthrex and leading industry initiatives has led to expanded opportunities and vision both at Vail Valley Medical Center, the Vail community, and the efforts to improve leadership learning opportunities at the Duke School of Medicine. The privilege to work and share with the Vail Leadership Institute has been a special part of my journey." [11]

The hospital's new expansion plan is good news, particularly given that Kirchner and her team have improved the culture and the financial situation at VVMC such that community trust is growing. When one thinks about the complexity of the healthcare business; the growing competition from Valley View Hospital of Glenwood Springs, Centura Health, and Kaiser Permanente; the many interlocking relationships; the multiple independent doctor groups; and the evolving and unclear economic models, it's amazing what has been accomplished. Today, the main campus of VVMC is a Level III trauma center with fifty-eight beds served by almost 300 physicians. It has several specialty clinics for cardiology, endocrinology, and plastic surgery; three urgent care facilities; and a state-of-the-art cancer center. The hospital also houses the Howard Head Sports Medicine Clinic providing outstanding physical therapy. Plenty of credit can be spread around, but Kirchner claims, "From my chair, none of this would have been possible without help from above." [12]

When you combine Vail's high alpine climate with enthusiastic, concierge-oriented, health care professionals and a new focus on re-generative medicine, you get a holistic environment where healing becomes more natural. Shannon added, "A generation of professional athletes and grateful patients owe their livelihood and mobility to his successful, pioneering, and exceptional delivery of innovative orthopedic healthcare." [13] It's the Vail way.

Castle Peak Senior Care – Taking Care of Our Own

Yet another dimension of the Vail Valley's healthcare system is the newly conceived senior-care facility that broke ground in mid-2015. Similar to how VVMC evolved in response to a need, the Castle Peak facility grew out of engaged citizens realizing that many local residents did not want to live out their final years somewhere else. Even though the Vail Valley is young by most community standards, the founders and first generation "Vail-ites" are in their seventies or eighties, some in their nineties. They have called this valley home for decades, and most have little interest in pulling up stakes to live among strangers. The Castle Peak center in Eagle will respond to several stages of aging: independent living, assisted living, and skilled nursing or memory care.

Castle Peak rendering in Eagle

Many people and entities should be credited with responding to this need. The primary advocate was Eagle County, which acquired the land, funded the various studies, and engaged Augustana Care from Minneapolis to lead the design and fundraising, and which will operate the center. But the fundraising champion was Merv Lapin.

Merv Lapin came to Vail in 1966 after earning his MBA from Harvard. He built a robust life starting as a night auditor at the Vail Village Inn, then founded Vail's first securities brokerage, followed by some visionary real-estate investments. He says, "Everything I do is really with a long-term vision." [14] Over the years, he made enough money to allow him to invest in various community projects that focused on children. Starting in 1975 and running for thirty-eight years, Lapin headed the local hockey program and took teams in alternating years to Eastern Europe or China. In addition to giving his time, he donated funds to worthy causes. Most recently, he pledged a generous gift to Castle Peak and led the campaign to raise $4.6 million to complete the facility. Like many of Vail's founders, Lapin gave back generously from his financial gain to an unmet community need.

The Shaw – Cancer Treatment Near Home

When Dr. Eck retired from his medical practice in 2012, he stayed connected to the medical world by becoming a development officer for VVMC. But that wasn't his first fundraising foray.

His first fundraising was in 1972 when he secured an anonymous gift for the hospital's first ICU equipment. He did it by simply sharing the need with a patient and friend. Later, when many of his patients were struggling with cancer, he saw the need for greater local capability for cancer treatment. A series of conversations with Art Kelton and Hal Shaw, both of whom served at the time on a VVMC board, ultimately led to the Shaw's making a lead gift that helped build the Cancer Center.

Jack's Place at the Shaw Cancer Center

The Shaw, as it is frequently called, is just another example of entrepreneurs responding to a demonstrated need. Later, as a result of working with Susie Donohue, Mary Randall, Rob Ford and others on the Shaw Outreach Team, Jack's Place was built adjacent to the cancer center, allowing families of cancer patients to stay close to their loved ones during treatment. The Shaw is a key component of Vail's evolving healthcare system. The need was obvious, but it required servant-leaders to act.

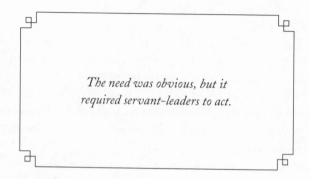

The need was obvious, but it required servant-leaders to act.

Colorado Mountain Medical Doctors – Serving Beyond the Vail Valley

In 1967, when the Colorado Medical Board dictated that doctors could not work directly for hospitals, Tom Steinberg formed Vail Medical Professional Corporation as a separate entity. In 1972, the group became Colorado Mountain Medical and now includes primary care physicians, specialists, and other practitioners emphasizing wellness and preventative medicine. Several of these doctors, including Kent Petrie, organize volunteer medical mission trips to Africa and Central America each year. They take nurses, psychologists, dentists, and a whole host of support people. Most of them know they are fortunate to call the Vail Valley home, so sharing that blessing with those in need is a labor of love.

A good example is the African mission led for the past five years by Dr. Janet Engle, a pediatric physician serving in VVMC's facility in Eagle. In 2015, Dr. Engle took twenty-two people from her church, Calvary Chapel, to Kenya to not only provide examinations and distribute medicine but also to spread love. Mike McClinton, who traveled with Dr. Engle said, "Dr. Engle is a saint and exemplifies 'servant-leadership'. In the most remote wilderness of Kenya, I saw her treat hundreds of Massai with the same love and care as she does my daughters in her Eagle office. Janet is an inspiration!" [15]

This story extends a long span like a bridge from frontier health care to destination medicine – from very modest beginnings to a world-class medical infrastructure involving many organizations across multiple campuses. It happened because of entrepreneurs of various stripes – physicians, business people, public servants – who were dedicated, service-oriented people wanting to meet the growing needs of a nascent community. They did it by collaborating with one another. They did it by taking risks and innovating.

The Vail Valley Medical Center, as an organization independent of many health care conglomerates, is an integral part of the community. Kathy Langenwalter, a cancer survivor who benefitted from local care at the Shaw, said, "What's nice is that the hospital has become as important as the other community assets. You get treated differently when you're dealing with people who know you from day-to-day living. Having that personal attention is really something special." [16]

Much like the evolution of skiing on Vail Mountain, the story of the hospital, a cornerstone of a healthy community, points to a Vail way of doing things.

Commentary:

During the decade from 2005 to 2015, the Vail Valley Medical Center grew in both size and maturity. Physical growth included new Urgent Care Centers in Avon and Gypsum, a new HealthCare Center in Eagle, and a major new Surgery Center in Edwards. Also, thanks to a group of hard-working volunteers call the "Shaw Outreach Team", a cancer caring house called "Jack's Place" was built for those in need of lodging during cancer treatment at The Shaw.

The hospital also grew – and matured – in other ways. Professional governance was implemented, thanks in large part to Ron Davis, who was board chair for most of this time period. Ron also created a new Vail Health Services Board to help with strategic planning and growth. Hospital leadership improved under Doris Kirchner and her team. Hospital Administration, working with the medical and nursing staff, deployed new computer technology, including electronic medical records. They also implemented the LEAN Quality Healthcare Model, improving quality and patient safety.

The local community increased its involvement and support of the hospital, forming a strong and very active Volunteer Corps. Similarly, this decade saw a growing and increasingly productive relationship between VVMC and the its local partners, like Howard Head Sports Medicine, Vail Summit Orthopedics, and the world-renown Steadman Clinic and Steadman Philippon Research Institute.

Charlie L'Esperance
VVMC/VHS Board Member & Trustee 2006–15
VVMC Board Chairperson 2012–13
Former CEO – Resort Technology Partners

Hopefully this story has surfaced a few thoughts about the Vail way. To further the thinking, here are several action steps from this chapter worth considering.

Also, the Questions for Dialogue, and the space to write, are intended to stimulate your thinking and generate conversations with friends and colleagues. Talking about your perspectives with others is a good way to learn.

ACTION STEPS:

- Be of service to others – as doctors are.
- Build relationships by asking questions.
- Mentor someone.

QUESTIONS FOR DIALOGUE:

- When was the last time you felt you were serving others? What was that like?

  _____

- Where can you be of service in your community?

  _____

- Name three mentors who have touched your life. What qualities did they demonstrate that made their help effective? Have you thanked them?

  _____

- Do you believe service requires a work ethic just as entrepreneurship does?

  _____

  _____

Chapter 10

Cultivating Leaders

From My Perspective

"Do you want to be a positive influence in the world? First, get your own life in order. Ground yourself in the single principle so that your behavior is wholesome and effective. If you do that, you will earn respect and powerful influence. Your behavior influences others through a ripple effect. A ripple effect works because everyone influences everyone else. Powerful people are powerful influences. If your life works, you influence your family. If your family works, your family influences your community. If your community works, your community influences the nation. If your nation works, your nation influences your world."

John Heider

The symbol of leadership emanating out from within – and from this community

I have been leading most of my life. It wasn't something I sought, although I did keep raising my hand.

My first role was at Redford High School where I was elected vice president of our Key Club and represented the school at the national convention in Long Beach, California. Then in college I was elected secretary of my Delta Chi fraternity chapter, followed by service as a naval officer. In Vail, I led teams at Vail Associates (VA), the Vail Resort Association (VRA), the Vail Valley Foundation, East West Marketing, the Beaver Creek Arts Foundation, Vail Christian High School, and finally the Vail Leadership Institute. Until this latter involvement, I hadn't really given much thought to how I was doing it – I just seemed to stumble along.

CONNECTING THE DOTS

The Vail Leadership Institute – A Learning Organization

The Institute came about from a long-standing interest in creating a "learning economy" in the Vail Valley. I initially thought that the Vail Valley Foundation might take on this role, but it wasn't to be – at least not during my tenure.

In 1996, Buck Elliott, a long-time Vail visionary, and I reconnected at a Vail Symposium event featuring Richard Leider, someone I had met when he delivered a "smile school" program for VA's guest service people. We both loved Leider's message of "purpose" and decided to get serious about bringing that message to Vail.

Art Currier, me, and Buck Elliott

193

In 1997, in order to launch an institute, Buck Elliott and I hooked up with Art Currier, whom I had met in the ski business, and we travelled to Minneapolis to test our preliminary concept with Leider. He was very supportive and encouraging and toward the end of our time together asked a question that stopped me in my tracks. He asked, "What is your leadership perspective?" [1] We all scratched our heads, especially me, not really knowing what our perspective included. We all knew right away that we would need to figure that out. We had our own experiences but hadn't articulated an approach. About this time I remember hearing this phrase somewhere that became somewhat of the driving passion - blend leading thinkers with thinking leaders.

From that day forward, and for the next ten years, we would work at defining a philosophy that we felt was needed and a perspective that we thought we knew something about. It would be a journey that continues to this day.

Our visioning group at Trappeur's Cabin

Leider's first recommendation was to meet Frederic Hudson, a delightful, sage psychologist-thinker-coach. After starting the Fielding Institute, a college exclusively offering doctoral degrees in psychology, he launched his own institute for executive coaching. Hudson's philosophy was based on what he called a Cycle of Renewal that described how leaders are ever evolving through various phases and stages of life, taking one both on the inside, in the heart, and then outside, in the head. Sometimes you're in a phase when things are going well, when you're meeting your objectives and really producing the desired results. Other times you're in the "doldrums" when things seem out of sync or when you've got to let go of the past. And sometimes you simply need time to reflect. As an evolving leader, I began to see how much I didn't know, and so I re-committed myself to an earlier decision – a process of lifelong learning. With Hudson's guidance, I became an executive coach and learned the incredible power of questions.

INSTITUTE CHRONOLOGY

August 1996: *Concept paper reviewed with Richard Leider*

June 1998: *Exploring Potential Forum held in Beaver Creek*

June 1999: *The Town of Vail sponsored study of the Vail Renaissance Center*

September 1999: *Leadership Vail Valley program launched*

September 2002: *Exploring Leadership created*

June 2003: *Changing the Game Forum is organized*

September 2006: *Foundations of Leadership launched*

June 2008: *First RoundTable of Leaders formed*

October 2012: *The Vail Way conference hosted*

April 2013: *Entrepreneurs BaseCamp opened*

August 2015: *Vail Centre for Higher Learning announced*

Frederic Hudson at Allie's Cabin in Beaver Creek

During this journey, Stephen Covey, the author of **The 7 *Habits of Highly Effective People***, also had a significant impact. So did Joe Jaworski, John Gardner, and Robert Greenleaf, the author of numerous books and essays on servant-leadership. And in his work as general editor of *The Leadership Bible*, Sid Buzzell used a three-phased organizing structure that ultimately led to the adoption of the water drop as our logo. This image symbolized leadership emanating out from the center – from our inside – and interestingly to me as a community-builder, from this small, but potentially influential mountain valley.

It wasn't until later that thought-leaders like Henri Nouwen, Ken Blanchard, John Heider, Bob Vanourek, Max DePree, Larry Donnithorne, and Parker Palmer became influences. As I read the work of these masters, I began blending and synthesizing their philosophies with the influences I gleaned from a whole raft of biographies of exemplary leaders like Mother Teresa, Mahatma Gandhi, Theodore Roosevelt, Nelson Mandela, Eleanor Roosevelt, Abraham Lincoln, Ronald Reagan, and others. When I stumbled across Jesus' words, "…first cleanse the inside…that the outside may be clean as well," [2] we labeled our perspective "inside first." It was then that we felt we were beginning to "connect the dots."

In the literature on leadership, a focus on the inside was becoming more and more common. It was being referenced in a variety of articles and books from Peter Senge's essay *"The Ecology of Leadership"* to Bill George's book *True North Groups*. Sometimes you'd see it referenced as "inside-out" thinking, sometimes as the "inner life." A special issue of the **Harvard Business Review**, entitled *"Why Knowing Yourself is the Best Strategy Now,"* talked about leadership being personal and put its focus on the inside. The inside is about heart – it's where character is built. Parker Palmer's perspective on the word heart is:

> *"In ancient times it meant that center in the human self where everything came together – where will and intellect and values and feeling and intuition and vision all converged. It meant the source of one's integrity."* [3]

This perspective assumed that in order to grow as a leader, one must first grow as a person. As a beginning point, this involves understanding our essence, integrating heart, mind and spirit, and then, with a focused inside and a commitment to serving others, we can attempt to lead. I realized that people could sense my essence and could choose, voluntarily, to follow. Reflecting back, I speculated that this perspective may have somehow been embedded in many of Vail's founders – perhaps it was an early Vail way of thinking.

A graphic illustration we adopted to describe the Inside First philosophy was a set of building blocks. It has values and beliefs as the foundation, then character as an inside realm that drives how we behave, then skills as the primary outside activity, and last, relationships at the top as a facet permeating every dimension of leadership. Within these major domains or realms, a set of principles and leading practices began to emerge. These principles touch on both hard and soft skills; and Bob Vanourek reminds us how Carl Sandberg felt Abraham Lincoln referred to them as "steel and velvet." [4] All of this sounded like a reasonable perspective, but then we knew we had to test-drive this thinking.

Commentary: Connecting the Dots

I have had the great fortune to work with, collaborate with, and reinforce John and Buck in the launch and development of the Institute. From the very beginning, when we shook hands and agreed to help other leaders, little did we anticipate that we would also personally grow in so many ways.

In the early years, the three of us were not always in agreement though we shared many core values. In Frederic Hudson's vernacular, we moved the "boulders" that blocked us. We gained respect for the importance of what we each stood for and the significance of operating from our Inside First framework.

We used Bob Vanourek's Alignment Model that works to align everyone around "purpose" whether it be one's personal reason for being or that of a company or an organization. We were then able to use this process to ensure that the entire Board of Trustees was aligned around not only purpose, but also values, vision, goals, strategies, etc. This uncovered the relevance of spirituality (as clearly distinguished from religion) to the work of the Institute. It took many significant conversations before everyone was aligned around the significance of this value.

In the end, we are thrilled that so much has been gained by the many individuals, teams, organizations, and companies that have become aligned around their purpose.

Art Currier
Founder – Vail Leadership Institute
CEO – Currier Designs, Inc.

EARLY PROGRAMS

Leadership Vail Valley – Testing Inside First

Following several preliminary speaker events, including an initial visioning retreat held at Trappeur's Cabin in Beaver Creek, we launched Leadership Vail Valley in 2000. It was a five-month program that started with a two-day retreat and then met monthly for half days thereafter. For many of the participants from all over the Vail Valley, it was the first time they had ever examined the deeper questions of values, purpose, and a vision for their future. For some, it was life changing. For Tom Moorhead, then Vail Town Attorney, it gave him the opportunity to envision a future that ultimately led him to being selected as a chief judge in Colorado's Fifth Judicial District. Of his experience, Moorhead commented, "The program started me on a new path by providing the opportunity of working with other leaders in the community. I responded positively to developing my life in a more purposeful manner. 'Life changing' may be overused, but in my case it was true." [5]

MY VISION

For years, I have thought that the Vail Valley could become a truly vibrant, model community. To achieve this, I felt we would need a strong, diverse economy, great facilities, a great education system, and excellent, forward-thinking leaders.

Being a year-round community, I felt Vail would benefit from more than just skiing, golf, and the performing arts. With a campus of excellent facilities – hotels, clubs, huts, ranches, as well as the surrounding White River National Forest – I envisioned that we could build a learning economy, not unlike Santa Fe or Boulder or even Boston. It might include several institutes or centers, perhaps the University of Vail, maybe one or two technical schools.

The learning would embrace resilience, renewal, and rejuvenation, both of the body and the soul. After all, people have been coming to the mountains for millennia to restore themselves.

This vision isn't something that can be achieved immediately, but having a sense of what this place might be like in twenty or thirty years was, I felt, worth shooting for.

In 2000, as we were digesting what we'd learned, Art Currier and I had lunch with Bob Buckman, a Beaver Creek home-owner. Bob was an entrepreneur from Memphis who, through Buckman Labs, had developed a keen interest in leadership manifested in what he called "knowledge management." He thought we were on to something, and before the lunch was over he committed $100,000 to our work. He was keen on developing a new kind of leader. That was a gift of confidence!

A major takeaway from Leadership Vail Valley was the use of dialogue. During these early years, we were introduced to the practice of dialogue by a wise woman from Santa Fe named Suzanne Maxwell. She taught us how to have "respectful conversations" by listening first. This approach was counterintuitive to the classic communications technique of "effective speaking."

Dialogue was a way of communicating based on uncovering truth versus telling or teaching what was "right." This methodology became central to Inside First and led to the use of "story" as the way to build trust within a peer group. Before long, our retreats would begin with the request of participants to simply "tell us your story." This practice made all the difference. With just a few basic guidelines like "where are you from, what were some defining moments for you, and what have you learned along the way," people would pour out information about themselves that, by their own admission, they normally didn't share.

What this approach did was allow the group members to get to know one another at a deeper level than is typical among work groups or teams. It built on the notion that we trust the people we know the most. With the retreat behind them, the group's monthly meetings became a thoughtful "uncovering" of what was important to each person. What were they really dealing with at the office or at home? Conversations were guided by a trained facilitator from the institute who allowed people to get real. Everyone could see that this was different – this was powerful stuff.

Buck Elliott's leadership group

While Leadership Vail Valley was populated primarily with senior executives from businesses, government, and nonprofits, we felt the need to offer something for emerging leaders. Thus we created Exploring Leadership. It was for those roughly twenty-eight to thirty-five who were in their first or second job and were facing real-life challenges like paying the mortgage and possibly wrestling with marriage. It used the same Inside First philosophy but was focused over a three-day weekend retreat. One of the sponsors of this program was the Vail Valley Tourism and Convention Bureau (VVTCB). Over a three-year period, with hundreds of participants, one trend among many jumped out. Every manager sent from the VVTCB was truly outstanding. Each was a strong, self-assured individual who impressed me. After a while I said to myself, "What's going on over there?"

After only a little reflection, I realized the common thread was Frank Johnson. As president of this community organization, he was guiding and coaching these people in a very effective manner. He had drunk the Kool-Aid and was passing it on to his people. Johnson commented, "The young staff members that I encouraged to participate were really being asked to think about themselves and their future in a whole new way. The structure of the retreat, and the level of intimacy they reached with other members of their peer group, who were all sharing the same kind of life decisions, was a key to their focus for the next years of their lives." [6]

The Center for Corporate Change – Addressing Business Ethics

One of my most poignant experiences of how the inside first approach manifested itself occurred in 2004. We were in the post-Enron funk, scratching our heads, wondering how a member of Enron's Board of Directors could actually say something like, "I move for a suspension of our Code of Ethics." [7] What?

Something was terribly wrong, so we convened a group of both active and recently retired seasoned business executives and college professors with the intent of trying to "change the game." Because of the high-powered people that this initiative attracted, I saw this as a possible source of long-term sustainability for the Institute. And it seemed that a focus on corporate ethics was consistent with our direction as an organization. In fact, during the early stages of this initiative, we modified our purpose statement to read: to cultivate effective, ethical leaders. It seemed this was the right path with the right people.

The concept became known as the Center for Corporate Change, and it resulted in research on the root causes of malfeasance, publications articulating the results, a major annual conference, and smaller programs for corporate Boards of Directors. It seemed to be well thought out and attracted many thoughtful, seasoned leaders.

My Bolt of Lightning

About eighteen months into the Center for Corporate Change, I had what I called my "bolt-of-lightning" experience. It was 2:30 in the morning and I received the words "declare your faith – stay the course." That was it. So, I walked around the house for a couple of hours thinking about that and asking God for clarity. What did that mean?

Before long I concluded that "declare" meant for me to write, and so I started working on a book, which I published a year later.

The "stay the course" part was less clear and remained so for about a year. Then I got a second word from above. This one was, "Go through the open door." So, that's what I do. I don't push my agenda. I don't worry or agonize over projects. I remain responsible for the things I commit to, but mostly I look for the open doors.

About eighteen months into this effort, a light bulb went on for me that signaled "we're on the wrong track." What had occurred to me was that the approach we were advocating was not going to work because it was all about the head – devoid of much heart. I could just sense it in the conversations. These were all good people – successful, prominent people – but their focus was on compliance through the rules and regulations coming out under the new Sarbanes-Oxley law. There was talk about how boards could be guided to work within these rules and sometimes how to get around them. The solutions seemed more evasive and less about any fundamentally changed approach.

The clear message I was getting was that the old method of figuring out how to get leaders to comply with the new rules would ultimately lead back to the same problematic behavior that got us into the current ethics mess. The lawyers and accountants would devise creative ways to avoid the real issue. What was needed was different behavior. And the best way to change behavior was through a change of heart, a fundamental change in the way leaders were thinking and acting. We knew that new rules wouldn't really change things. Deep down, we knew that apart from a change of heart, reforms were futile.

> *The best way to change behavior was through a change of heart, a fundamental change in the way leaders were thinking and acting. We knew that new rules wouldn't really change things. Deep down, we knew that apart from a change of heart, reforms were futile.*

I had come to this conclusion through a deep personal exploration of my evolving spiritual perspective. I was reading books by Bill George, Peter Vaill, Henri Nouwen and other thought-leaders who touched on the spiritual dimension in a way that said to me a change of heart was needed. And so I decided to proactively raise the issue with our key people that we must get the heart into the conversation. I said, "We've got to find a way to introduce the spiritual into the process as a way to get past the ego-centric behavior and really change the game." [8]

The result was not surprising. Most of the prominent business and academic leaders said, "It won't work. You can't go down that road because it's religious, and it won't go anywhere." [9] Of course, the classic church-and-state arguments were raised as well as the typical anti-religious sentiments. My efforts to convince these guys, and it was all guys, that the spiritual dimension was different went nowhere. The approach I was recommending came in the form of questions about how one's spiritual perspective informed decision making, rather than proselytizing some "right" answer or some doctrine. But the wall of separation was too high with this group, and I met very significant resistance. But, in my heart I sensed this was the way I was being called.

It should be said that the other factor at play was that this corporate change effort was running out of money. The participation was flat, and few new people were joining the nascent movement. Our efforts to build support from likely sponsors, such as the accounting firms and foundations, fell largely on deaf ears. I was running into closed doors.

So, I decided to fight for what I thought was right. I advocated that we shut down the operation, lay off the staff, cut back all unnecessary expenses, and basically start over. Half of the board agreed with me, while the other half wanted to continue the corporate change effort, largely as originally conceived. Having been one of the founders of the Institute, I led the organization into a twelve-month reassessment. We tested our evolving thinking through focus groups and new trial programs. We embarked on a comprehensive alignment planning process that resulted in an updated curriculum and a new business model. Given that our "corporate change" trustees were all friends or close acquaintances, we gave a helping hand by lending our nonprofit status to the group while they pursued their own tax-exemption. But in a little more than a year, they were out of business. We re-built the Institute into a sustainable organization based, in part, on the principles of integrating head and heart.

Inherent in this period of partial hibernation, we spent a fair amount of time in winter reflecting and reassessing how we might conduct our evolving programs. What I found was that I needed to develop a more mature spiritual perspective, a connection with my creator that would work with secular audiences. I needed to keep learning – reading, journaling my thoughts, and spending more time in reflection – sometimes even in solitude. Given my own inclinations toward the head activities (after all, I was a business guy), I realized I needed to build up my own heart. One of the most powerful activities that helped with this re-focus was participating in a small, weekly men's group.

Around this time, I realized I needed to redefine my purpose to incorporate this evolving thinking. My purpose for years had been to "build community." I had been building things my whole life – structures, organizations, teams – and so the community was simply an extension of this passion.

But when our pastor stated he wanted to build a Christian high school, things took a major turn. I became the chairman and suddenly I was thrust directly into a serious spiritual role. I started reading the Bible carefully and seeing that relevant scripture was incorporated into the high school curriculum, the hiring of teachers, and the building of our initial campus. And I began to pray and felt a renewed sense of meaning. This is when my purpose morphed into "building spirit-filled community."

This whole personal evolution showed me the value of bringing the heart into the conversation and into the process of leading. Everything made more sense when the good and positive thinking of scripture was added to the mix. I was still fundamentally an action-oriented marketing guy, but now my sensitivity to people, my understanding of the creator's love, and my willingness to slow down and incorporate the attributes of the heart had transformed me. It's never been the same since!

The Leaders Journal – Expressing My Perspective

It was 2005 when I got a "bolt of lightning" to write a book. Having no experience in writing, other than thousands of memos over the years, I wasn't sure how it would go. As part of my spiritual journey, I had been working my way through Henry Blackaby's journal called *Experiencing God*. It was a daily journal that used scripture as the lead, followed by Blackaby's commentary, and then room for you to record your own thoughts and reactions. I thought, "Maybe that's a format I could follow." So, I just started – and it flowed.

I decided to draw from a massive quotes file I had been keeping for years that was organized around the key principles of Inside First – integrity, commitment, vision, communication, trust, etc. I wrote a page a day, and the writing allowed me to articulate the things I had learned along the way about these leadership principles. I published it first as *The Keys to Leading* and then a year later, with revisions and all the corrections I somehow missed, as *The Leader's Journal*. I recommend it to anyone who thinks, even a little bit, about expressing his or her point of view. My conclusion was that, even if it's just for your kids, you should write down those thoughts.

The Leader's Journal

In 2006, the institute launched Foundations of Leadership, again for the emerging leader but this time extended over a three-year period. We had observed in Exploring Leadership the classic problem with one-off seminars and workshops – basically that some good learning can occur, but what people typically do is put the binder on the shelf and go back to their customary ways – their old habits. There might be a few takeaways but no substantial change would occur. We had become convinced that real transformation, real growth in one's leadership approach, would most likely occur over time. Thus, the three-year program commitment.

One other important lesson was woven into Foundations of Leadership: We reduced the group size from the typical class of eighteen to twenty-four down to just seven to eight. There is something about a large group that stymies real engagement. If you are in the back of the class, you can hide out, keep your head down, and sneak by without saying much. Frederic Hudson, through his executive coaching programs, showed us how groups of between six and eight people could be different. You could really connect with one another because you could look each other in the eye. It's weird and hard to explain why it works, but it does.

Over the next few years, eighteen groups formed, each facilitated by an experienced coach or mentor. Groups were put together around various organizing themes such as government, business, gender, faith, young entrepreneurs, nonprofits, etc. More than a hundred people participated in this program – some groups have continued to stay together well after their three-year commitment. Most of the annual retreats were hosted at Pat McConathy's Yarmony Creek Ranch outside of McCoy. Laura Emrich participated in a group in January 2010 and said, "The program allowed me to step away from the daily grind and to dig down deeper into myself than ever before. I found more strength, power, and wisdom than I thought I had. It was a breath of fresh air." [9]

During this period of the institute's growth, we came to see more clearly an important connection. While most people view leadership as relating to work – to their organizational role – we could see that it was really about looking at one's whole life. Gregg Vanourek, one of our trustees, wrote that "operating on a continuum between personal growth and leadership development allowed us to demonstrate the important, and often overlooked, link between how we lead our lives and how we lead our families, teams, organizations, and communities." [10]

WORKING ALONGSIDE FAMILY

All leaders knows they need to have good people around them. And I've been fortunate to always have strong, committed, engaged people on my team. Over the years, the best was my daughter Brooke. Maybe I'm a little biased, but here's why.

She came to the job with some experience as a leader. At Vail Christian, she had been captain of her volleyball team, taking them to regionals and then being selected as All State. While attending the University of Colorado, she coached the Boulder High School women's team. Handling the girls was one thing, but the parents were even more challenging.

As VLI's marketing and admin manager, not only was Brooke eager to learn, but I was keen to share my experience. It was different than traditional parenting in that now she was an adult. When she would ask about how to handle a certain project, I would say, "Here's what I did in a similar situation." Or the one she disliked the most was, "Don't worry, you'll figure it out."

She learned a lot in those few years, but so did I. Treating everyone like family, being patient, asking good questions, and providing encouragement was showing me how to mentor.

We learned from each rev (business speak for a revolution or turn) and made adjustments in the program. The curriculum was getting tighter and more robust. In 2010, we launched RoundTable of Leaders, a year-long peer learning program combining personal leadership development with real-world problem solving. Over the next few years, five groups were formed averaging seven senior executives from non-competing organizations. The same Inside First character-focused curriculum is used. The one addition to the program we labeled the "hot seat." At each monthly session, one member of the group presents an issue or opportunity he or she is dealing with. Over the next hour or two, that person receives candid feedback from trusted advisors. It's powerful and valuable – and probably worth thousands of dollars in free consulting. Mark Miller, Vail's fire chief and a participant in the Government RoundTable for several years, characterizes his experience this way.

Mark Miller holding court on his retreat

"The retreat was profound – I came away with an understanding of my core values, calling and purpose in a way that had never been revealed previously, despite my quest for transformational leadership for dozens of years prior. To say it was, and continues to be, life changing is an understatement. The focus was on integrating head and heart. Without question, every RoundTable meeting I attended with my trusted advisors was invaluable in my personal and professional leadership journey. Our 'hot seat' sessions proved to be as good as it gets, with honest, candid, feedback and thoughtful consideration as we each encountered challenging issues, individually and organizationally." [11]

Miller felt so strongly about his experience that he decided to take his entire command staff through a similar experience. It made a huge difference. He saw that the leadership essentials of character, competence, and vision start with having a clear understanding of one's personal values and purpose. He saw that this understanding was reflected in a quote from Nathaniel Hawthorne's writing that said, "No man, for any considerable period of time, can wear one face to himself and another to the multitude without finally getting bewildered as to which may be the truth." [12]

COMMENTARY: EARLY PROGRAMS

As I reflect back on the many lessons we learned in the unfolding of the Vail Leadership Institute (VLI), it was the indomitable spirit of the many young people that would stand out to set the stage for a learning community. As a new generation of leaders emerged to embrace the mountain lifestyle, they brought with them the same entrepreneurial spirit that defined the Vail Valley in its earliest days.

Their quest has been to create a sustainable and meaningful life that would contribute to their community while finding a work/life balance that would help move them through the many changes and challenges that define each of our lives. They are inquisitive and driven to seek out ways to connect with each other in order to share best practices in leadership and growth opportunities. VLI's Inside First model provided a format that allowed them to explore and clarify their individual commitments to a future that would help them achieve both their personal and professional goals.

Now as VLI and the idea of a learning community continues to evolve, there is a new sense of purpose, building on those who have gone before and driven by the needs of today with the simple idea that character-based practices can provide a good foundation for all of us.

William (Buck) Elliott
Principal – Paragon Guides
Founder – Vail Leadership Institute

Passing the Torch

The Vail Centre for Higher Learning – Realizing Our Vision

In 2014, a terrible accident became for me what psychologists call a "triggering event." My son, Conor, fell two stories from a fire escape outside his apartment in San Francisco. He was severely injured and blessed to be alive. I spent two months on his couch helping him move from a wheel chair to a walker and finally to a cane. Every morning and night as I prayed for his recovery, I had a realization; it seemed that now was the right time for me to implement a transition plan that was still two years out. As president of the Institute, I concluded I had done my part – it was time for someone else to lead. The board honored my request, and we hired Ross Iverson, a young entrepreneur who was a recent transplant from Minneapolis.

What Ross accomplished in a few years was pretty amazing. He opened a "co-working" space in Avon called BaseCamp that provided a place for entrepreneurs to develop their businesses. It now houses about sixty people who help one another. Very cool…and very much the Vail way.

The biggest advancement is just beginning to emerge and is called the Vail Centre for Higher Learning. Ross and his team took the University of Vail concept and shaped it into a viable, multi-disciplined entity modeled after the Banff Centre in Alberta, Canada. The Vail Centre includes four "sub-centers" in leadership (essentially a renamed Vail Leadership Institute): sustainability, longevity, and entrepreneurship. It's a big concept that will fulfill that lifelong dream of fostering a "learning economy" in the Vail Valley. And it will generate, hopefully, more utilization of our many assets.

Over these forty years, I have learned many leadership lessons beyond those I received as a young naval officer. I have come to believe that all meaningful human achievement begins from within. I've found that leadership is more about character than skills. Skills are important, no doubt, such as communicating, decision making, and strategizing. But without a solid foundation – basically, values and beliefs – a leader can be like a ship without a rudder. Leadership is not an individual undertaking but rather a team sport, and thus I've seen that relationships are key. Given that many hundreds of people have been touched by the Institute's Inside First philosophy, perhaps this thinking has become part of the Vail way.

For me, the experience of helping to build organizations, facilities, teams, and a family here in the Vail Valley has been a blessing. Participating with many others in building the Vail Leadership Institute has been wonderful, sometimes stressful, but always rewarding, especially when you see people have an "ah ha" moment or when they commit to a plan or find their purpose. It's like a breath of fresh air – you can see the change in their face, especially their eyes. I have only recently (in the last ten years, that is) realized that God had this plan for my life all along and being of service to others was at the core of it. I feel that this spirit of service to the community, this entrepreneurial spirit, is central to the Vail way.

Hopefully this story has surfaced a few thoughts about the Vail way. To further the thinking, here are several action steps from this chapter worth considering.

Also, the Questions for Dialogue, and the space to write, are intended to stimulate your thinking and generate conversations with friends and colleagues. Talking about your perspectives with others is a good way to learn.

ACTION STEPS:

- Take time to reflect on what you're doing and where you're headed.
- Keep your agreements and fulfill your commitments.
- Go through the open doors.

QUESTIONS FOR DIALOGUE:

- Can you articulate a purpose for your life and work?

  _____

- Are you doing what you really care about?

  _____

- What are you doing in your community to make a difference?

  _____

- What's the most transformative experience you've ever had?

  _____

  _____

213

CHAPTER 11

THE ATHLETES AND ADVENTURERS

PATROLMAN, INSTRUCTORS, RACERS, BOARDERS, AND CLIMBERS

"It is not the critic who counts; not the man who points out how the strong man stumbles, or where the doer of deeds could have done better. The credit belongs to the man who is actually in the arena, whose face is marred by dust and sweat and blood; who strives valiantly; who errs, and comes up short again and again, because there is no effort without error and shortcoming; who knows the great enthusiasms, the great devotions; who spends himself in a worthy cause; who at the best knows in the end the triumph of high achievement, and who at the worst, if he fails, at least fails while daring greatly, so that his place shall never be with those cold and timid souls who know neither victory nor defeat." [1]

Theodore Roosevelt

The thrill of the adventure

214

It might seem odd to think about this group of people as entrepreneurs, but given their attitude toward risk-taking, they qualify. The Vail way is not just about how businesses, nonprofits, or governments make things happens; it describes how people – in this case how athletes – envision a better future. This chapter will touch on the significant impact each of these groups of athletes have had on the community. The energy, passion, and fun that these individuals have brought over the years is part of our DNA.

INSTRUCTORS AND PATROLMEN

It's hard to say which bunch came first: the ski instructors, the patrolmen, or just the passionate ski bum. In the early years, everyone had one thing in common: being from somewhere else. And everyone loved skiing. Many people said the thrill of floating through champagne powder in the back bowls was the next best thing to you know what. One of the many instructors who felt this passion was Horst Essl.

Horst is a wiry, red-haired Austrian who is dearly loved by everyone who's ever skied with him. He has a gentle manner with a sweet smile that causes one to want to make the turn smooth just as he demonstrated. His quiet flair for teaching skiing makes it look so easy. Horst is at home in the mountains, but to make it home, like every ski instructor, he had to find summer work. Many became builders, some fishing guides, some realtors, but for Horst, painting was his second passion. Almost every mural around the Vail Valley is Horst's handiwork.

One of Horst Essl's murals at the Colorado Ski Museum

There are so many others who fit this same bill – a love of skiing and the mountains. Some are mentioned in the Glossary. But almost all the ski instructors, whether they came here in the 1960s and stayed or just arrived, they all seem to crave this lifestyle.

Ski Patrol – Jack's Kind of People

After service in Vietnam as a flight surgeon, Dr. Eck returned to Colorado to launch a less intense medical career. His trauma experience in Southeast Asia would be valuable when he found himself working with Vail's Ski Patrol in the early 1970s. After working during the week at his medical residency at either the University of Colorado Medical Center, Denver General, or Presbyterian Hospital, Jack would teach emergency and trauma medicine to ski patrollers, covering fractures, diabetes, seizures, and cardiac arrest. These ski patrollers were rugged individuals and great skiers, but they weren't doctors or EMTs.

It was a hardy, engaging life with these mountain men during the day. When "sweep" was complete and everyone was safely off the mountain, they would fully review the day's "trauma" at Donovan's Copper Bar on Bridge Street, their home away from home. In the summer, the camaraderie grew as they shared many hunting and fishing expeditions – and more than a few beers. The patrol embraced Jack, and many close friendships were built with Paul Testwuide, Chupa Nelson, Danny Welcher, Sandy Hinmon, and so many others that remain today. About Eck, Testwuide said, "He taught us techniques that would greatly influence the recovery or survival of accident victims. His experience and knowledge took the ski patrol's performance to a whole new level." [1]

Jack described the sense of ownership he and others felt for Vail Mountain, despite being public land. He said, "Most of us saw Vail Mountain as *our* mountain. We helped build it, and we felt like we shared in the ownership of it. There was a subtle pride in having participated in building things. We seemed to connect with the identity of the Vail Valley." [2]

The ski patrolmen have always been a wild bunch from the beginning. The stories are legend, like "Tuck 'em Inn," the ski patrol's secret hideaway near Riva Glade on Vail Mountain. It was a small yurt with throw rugs, a queen-sized bed, and a keg of beer where the patrol members would invite their girlfriends-to-be to check out for a little après ski "fun." It went on for years until "corporate" discovered it. A few of the early "users" included

Dickie "Pete" Peterson, Sandy Hinmon, and Dick Dennison. Its champion was Paul Testwuide.

Testwuide, better known as "Weed" to almost everyone, is as the creator made us all, unique. He stood out because of his raucous lifestyle and his good humor. At six-foot-four, he could out drink almost anyone – and he usually did. He loved life – and he loved skiing. Over a forty year period, Testwuide moved up the ladder at Vail Associates (VA) from the trail crew to head of the ski patrol to director of slopes and trails, and ultimately, to vice president of mountain operations. He used that modern-day management philosophy "managing by walking around," only in Vail it was "skiing around," to get out on the mountain and talk to people. He did it the old fashioned way with hard work and the ability to earn respect.

Andy Daly, a VA executive during much of Testwuide's tenure, said of Paul, "He is a big man who has had an equally big impact on our community. On the mountain, he led innovations in snowmaking, grooming and, most importantly, the overall guest experience helping transform Vail from a start-up experience to a world recognized resort today. He has been the friend of many over the years including Presidents and World Leaders, who have come to respect him for his thoughtfulness, immense knowledge of the wildlife and mountains, and his straight forward style that has become legend. He recognized at an early date the critical role water would play in the future of the Vail Valley and has done more to develop new sources and to work cooperatively with front range and west slope water users to insure the water is available for the valley to grow. He has been a wonderful friend over the years." [3]

Among the many other ski patrolman worthy of mention, Chupa Nelson stands out. The details of his heroism during the LionsHead Gondola accident in 1976, described in Chapter 5, has been become legend. But there were others that day, including Dave Stanish, Dennis "Buffalo" Mikottis, and John Murphy. Many other fascinating stories of the ski patrol are told in Pete Seibert's book and Shirley Welch's book *Vail: The First 50 Years*. Chupa went on to establish one of the most successful construction companies in Vail calling upon the same "we can do this" gusto mentioned by so many Vail pioneers.

THE RACERS

And then there were the ski racers. In many ways, Vail was built by and for ski racers. Almost every one of the founders spent time in the gates. From Bob Parker besting Bill Brown in Saalfelden, Austria, in a 1951 race (before either of them had heard of Vail) to Pete Seibert winning the coveted Roch Cup in Aspen in 1947 to Pepi Gramshammer being hired in 1962 to represent Vail on the pro circuit to the young ski racers coming out of today's Ski and Snowboard School, ski racing has been in the blood. Both Lindsey Vonn and Mikeala Schifferin, current Olympic and World Champions, call Vail home. And one who has built a life here is Cindy Nelson.

Cindy Nelson started skiing when most of us were learning to walk. Her father was a 10th Mountain veteran who brought the family to Vail in its very first season. In northern Minnesota at the Nelson family resort in Lutsen, winters could be long and bitter cold. Being active was one way of staying warm and developing a sense of determination and commitment. In time, she would use those traits in ski racing.

Cindy's accomplishments in skiing included lots of Olympic and World Championship medals. Beyond her winning way, she was a leader who used her natural confidence, technical prowess, and her quiet "can-do" attitude to encourage her teammates. One of the coaches travelling with the U.S. Ski Team said, "Cindy was older than her teammates and was constantly offering inspiration." [4]

But Cindy paid a huge price for her commitment to ski racing in multiple injuries. But as in most downsides, there are hidden blessings. For Cindy, her damaged body introduced her to Dr. Dick Steadman, and it would change the trajectory of her life. It happened this way.

Among many injuries, one of the first brought Cindy to Dr. Steadman's clinic in South Lake Tahoe, California, in July of 1974. Steadman had become an early advocate of minimally invasive surgery rather than the major reconstructive approach that was more typical at the time. Steadman's medical approach had two major parts: First was the "micro-fracture" surgery; that was followed almost immediately by an active physical therapy regime. Steadman took Cindy under his wing, and she became an early test case for this new approach. He encouraged her in overcoming the fear of more injuries. Cindy almost lived at the Steadman home in Lake Tahoe while she recovered; in fact, some of the physical therapy took place on his dining room table. That experience started a lifelong friendship.

On another occasion when Cindy had broken her ankle, Steadman worked his magic. Right after surgery, he said, "You're good to go." Cindy said, "What do you mean; I've got a broken ankle." The good doctor replied, "Not anymore – I fixed it." [5]

Richard Steadman was an "uber doctor" for Cindy. Beyond his groundbreaking procedures, he was a mentor and counselor constantly promoting the positive. In 1983 just eight weeks before the Sarajevo Olympics, Cindy tore another knee ligament. She flew to Lake Tahoe, and Dr. Steadman performed yet another miracle. Cindy was bummed because she thought it was over. But Steadman said, "You're going to Sarajevo." [6] And she did.

When Cindy retired from skiing in 1985, she decided to make Vail her permanent home, using the condo she bought back in 1979 as her home base. George Gillett, then the owner of Vail Associates (VA), made her director of skiing, which placed her in an envious PR role of squiring dignitaries around Vail. Skiing one day with Gillett, though, set events in motion. Getting off of Chair 4, Gillett got tangled up with another skier and tore his ACL. Having heard Cindy sing Steadman's praises, Gillett said, "What's the name of that doctor?" Cindy said, "I'll make the call." [7]

Cindy with Gay and Dr. Steadman

This began Gillett's relationship with Steadman. Over the succeeding months, Cindy urged Gillett to bring Steadman to Vail, beginning a multi-year courting or negotiation that would support the Steadman Clinic. The clincher was Gillett's commitment of several million dollars to help launch what Steadman really wanted – a research institute. Many people had a hand in bringing Dr. Steadman to Vail, but Cindy was the broker.

But it wasn't just convincing Steadman – and his wife Gay – to move; he had a whole team of people to bring with him. Cindy relays a conversation that Steadman had with Gay: "If anyone on the team declines moving to Vail, we're not going." [8] Topper Hagerman, John Atkins, John McMurthy, Cristal Adams, and a few others all agreed. And most of them are still here.

This whole episode is a blend of entrepreneurial vision and risk-taking, and Cindy was right in the middle of it. Her can-do attitude was at play here long before "the Vail way" became an expression.

Cindy has done what many former Olympic champions have done – they make a life around their sport. Vail is lucky that she made our little valley her home. Starting with her role with VA (now Vail Resorts), she began conducting corporate outings and giving motivational speeches. She continues to serve as a trustee of the U.S. Ski and Snowboard Foundation and on the board of the Steadman Philippon Research Institute.

In 1992, Cindy started her own business focusing her energies in television broadcasting, personal appearances, and consulting. She also partnered with Julie Young to form Here2Help, an organization that helps Dr. Steadman's patients navigate the Vail community when undergoing surgery. When not helping others, Cindy said, "I'll be in the mountains sharing the day with my family and yellow lab, Blaze. Or, I might be on the links...or the slopes still searching for that perfect turn." [9] Her determination, commitment, and willingness to take risks makes her an entrepreneur in the Vail mold.

Cindy in a World Cup GS without helmet

Ski racing may still be the first love in Vail, but there are other types of athletes and adventurers who have made this place home. Take the mountain bike variety. Mike Kloser is perhaps best known as a World Mountain Bike Champion and a four-time world champion of Adventure Racing. He could live anywhere, but the whole family has a passion for the outdoors and an inherent quest for adventure and travel that the Vail Valley satisfies.

Not all athletes are about speed. Climbers tend to call upon planning and caution as opposed to being the first to the top. And climbers come in several varieties: ice climbers, technical climbers, and your everyday champion of one or more of Colorado's "fourteeners" – those fifty-five mountains that exceed 14,000 feet in elevation. These adventurers are every bit entrepreneurs in their own right. Risk-takers for sure – but also people with a vision of accomplishment.

SKI NUTS

And then there are the regular, everyday athletes who just love their sport. One example among many is Gary Gilman. Gary is the owner of SteamMaster, a Minturn-based residential cleaning and restoration company that many locals know about because of his huge generosity to local nonprofits. Gary and his wife Julie, together with their CEO, Raj Manickam, run an intense business that responds to emergencies like flooded basements. But Gary still makes time to ski an average of fifty days every winter – and certainly most powder days. He craves the sensation of floating through dry, untracked snow. He loves the trees, the junk (tracked-up, unpredictable conditions), and certainly the back bowls. He's even an advocate of ski biking.

But Gary's ability to enjoy the mountain lifestyle didn't happen by coincidence. He did it the old fashioned, entrepreneurial way. Like so many, he stayed after that first winter season. He knew he needed time and financial flexibility to enjoy life. So, he created SteamMaster after realizing there was an unmet need for basic carpet cleaning in Vail. He didn't follow the traditional path (college, corporate job, home in the suburbs) advocated by his parents. Rather, he followed his passion. Gary's love for his sport (sports really) is shared by hundreds of others who have found this a place supportive of "sports nuts."

Vail's athletes and adventurers have found the lifestyle accommodating. Being healthy, active, and engaged are hallmarks of the "good life." This appetite is part of what makes the Vail Valley a vibrant community – their zest is yet another aspect of the Vail way.

Conclusion and Postscript

---

*"Never doubt that a small group of thoughtful, committed citizens
can change the world.
Indeed, it is the only thing that ever has."*

Margaret Mead

We are blessed with some much serenity

When the idea for this book was first hatched, I decided to test my hypotheses about the principles and practices that individuals and organizations called upon in making the incredible accomplishment of the Vail Valley come to life. I also wanted to know if there were certain qualities that continue to influence the current generation of younger leaders who are committed to taking this place to the next level.

Now I am convinced that there is a Vail way, but this approach is not thought of or phrased quite this way – not yet anyway. As one understands the full breadth of the history here, one realizes that the founders showed us the way. They set a tone and loosely followed an approach that continues to this day. Pete Seibert had a vision, he brought people together and got them to collaborate and innovate, and the company he started continues with that tradition. In the five decades that followed Vail's opening, entrepreneurs came from all over the country to build on that vision. They stay committed to that idea and continue to move it forward.

Entrepreneurship is deeply embedded in the Vail way. It's a way of going about building something extraordinary. It involves resilience, trust, and teamwork. Over time, an entrepreneurial mindset pervaded those who followed the founders, and that mindset exhibited an attitude that is resolute and determined, a recognition that we can do more collectively than individually.

An ancillary conclusion that came out of this effort is that the mountain lifestyle is a viable alternative to the urban. People who have chosen to live here call upon nature to rejuvenate the body, mind, and spirit. The pace is different here. I believe the European influence has helped make us diverse and worldly but also down-to-earth.

As I interviewed people, I usually ended with the question, "Do you feel there is a Vail way?" Almost everyone said something like, "Oh, absolutely," and then proceeded to give an example. As the process unfolded, I sensed some shared core values, like the love of being outdoors in God's creation, an interest in working hard and playing just as hard, in collaborating with others, and giving back to the many caring organizations that have popped up over the years.

Also, I heard an interest in continuing to learn and grow. Maybe I was simply selectively hearing what I wanted to hear, but life-long learning seemed to be a theme. As I thought about this, I was reminded of an observation that Agnes Sanford made in her book, *The Healing Light*, that urges us to sit by a pond for a while and observe what is happening with the water. She said, "Those who observe the flow of water see that in order to keep clean and fresh the water must have a continuing channel. A lake has not only a source but also an outlet. Without an outlet, it tends to become stagnant and unhealthy." [1] Linking this thought to the Vail way should urge us to share our insights with others. Rather than stifling the flow of knowledge, like a pond that stagnates, I feel called to spread this way of thinking. There is a secret sauce here, and my hope is that it gets shared.

As the book has unfolded, several people urged me to write about the problems as well as the successes we've seen. I acknowledge that I've highlighted mostly the positives in describing the Vail way, but we definitely have our share of problems and issues. Thus, I've decided to write a follow-up piece that will research and report on things like the economic disparity that exists in the Vail Valley, particularly in income and housing. In fact, affordable housing remains arguably our biggest challenge.

Another economic concern that I'll explore is diversity. The ability for people to secure good work, provide for their loved ones, and build a home is still at the center of the American dream. And it should be at the core of the Vail way. A strong economy that makes jobs available is foundational to a vibrant community. Simply stated, our local economy is flat and has been in need of diversification for years.

Yet another challenge that could be thought of as an opportunity is what I call the hispanic-anglo divide. We don't talk about it that much, but I believe it's there. It's like there are two communities: white, the Anglo's who recreate, and Hispanic workers who provide every kind of service imaginable. And there's not that much interaction. Some of it's caused by language, some by fear. Most people agree that the Hispanic community is incredibly hard-working and much appreciated. In fact, the resort economy would come to a screeching halt without hispanic employees. We need more integration – more communication.

John Gardner, the founder of Common Cause and the former Secretary of Education, once said, "The play of conflicting interests in a framework of shared purposes is the drama of a free society. It is a robust exercise and a noisy one, not for the faint-hearted or the tidy-minded. A community of diverse elements has greater capacity to adapt and renew itself in a swiftly changing world." [2]

This follow-up piece will not only address these challenges, but also take a stab at providing some prescriptions.

What will be required of the Vail Valley, or any community for that matter, to become truly vibrant? I believe that there are several integral conditions and components that must be in place to achieve this end. By most measures, we are not there yet, but we are definitely on a good path to becoming a vibrant community. In our second fifty years, we need to work on at least these things:

- Building a diverse and sustainable economy
- Creating life-long learning opportunities
- Maintaining a robust infrastructure
- Engaging a cadre of committed entrepreneurial leaders and mentors

Perhaps the Vail way is an idea whose time has come. But for it to take hold, we must continue to work at getting better. I like the way T.H. Watkins frames this challenge: "The most important truth to be found in this landscape is that earth's power and human understanding once built a long history together. Maybe if we bring a willingness to embrace what the land has to teach us of limits and possibilities, it can be rediscovered in our own lives, here in a place where earth meets sky in the long dream of life." [3]

How cool is that thought!!

P.S. I know there other stories out there that I have overlooked; I've just included the ones I know about. I want to issue a blanket invitation for anyone with a story about the Vail Valley's evolution to send me that information. I think we should develop the full history!

GLOSSARY OF PIONEERS, ENTREPRENEURS & UNSUNG LEADERS

Many people have been involved over this fifty year period in making the Vail Valley a special place. Some have been covered in one or more of the chapters and are not mentioned again here. Others were unsung and are listed here. These people are just a few who I actually met along the way and who stand-out to me in some way. There are so many more that could be mentioned here. Forgive me for running out of time!

- *Peter Abuisi*: The long-standing headmaster of the Vail Mountain School. He touched many of our children.
- *Buck Allen*: Vail's municipal judge for almost forty years who has served with distinction and humor.
- *Adam Aron*: The only CEO of Vail Resorts who didn't love skiing. Led the company through the complex planning for Vail's "New Dawn" developments.
- *Bob Barrett*: Served as President Ford's Military Aide in the White House and later as his Chief of Staff. Ruled access to the president with an iron fist.
- *Jim Bartlett*: A Stanford MBA who brought disciple and creativity to Dick Peterson's team at VA in the 70's.
- *Dick Bass*: Founder of Snowbird in Utah and prodigious Vail promoter. Gave President Ford his Mill Creek Circle home as the Western White House.

- *Harry Bass*: Chairman of Vail Associates from 1977 to 1986. His personal guarantee of the Beaver Creek Metro District bonds allowed the resort to open.
- *Don Berger*: A writer-editor for various publications over the years who always had a good thing to say.
- *Stan Bernstein*: Finance director for the Town of Vail from the mid-60's to the mid-'70s. Founder of the King of the Mountain Volleyball Tournament.
- *Lynn Blake*: Saved by a Vail fireman after suffering a sudden cardiac arrest in Vail Village. She started the non-profit, Starting Hearts that has placed hundreds of AED's around Eagle County.
- *John Boll*: An early Beaver Creek resident from Grosse Pointe, Michigan who led the fund raising campaign for the Vilar Center for the Arts.
- *The Borgen's*: Kathy and Erik have been steady hands for years; Kathy with the science school and Erik in the Vail Valley Foundation. They typify the best of those who give back.
- *Ross Bowker*: One of Harry Frampton's trusted lieutenants who continues to serve on the board of the Beaver Creek Resort Company.
- *Pam Brandmeyer*: Long-standing assistant town manager in Vail who kept the "trains running on time." She served the administrations of Rich Kaplin, Ron Phillips, Bob McLarin and Stan Zemler – with distinction.
- *Gordon Brittan*: A feisty retiree who took on numerous funding challenges at the Vail Valley Medical Center.
- *Byron Brown*: Long-time supporter of Ski Club Vail, and with his wife Vi, promoter of the Rummage Sale in Minturn for over 40 years.
- *Roger Brown*: Award winning filmmaker who often promoted a contrarian, but informed, view of the environment.
- *Bob Buckman*: The Beaver Creek property owner from Memphis who helped launch the Vail Leadership Institute.
- *Marge Burdick*: With husband Larry, built the Red Lion Inn, a favorite watering hole. Was instrumental in advancing cultural programming, including the original Vail Institute, and later, Bravo Colorado.
- *Pete Burnett*: The Town of Vail's "go to" maintenance man who kept the water running and the streets open in the early years.
- *George Caulkins*: Pete Seibert's "money man" who raised millions to get Vail off the ground.

- **Bev Christiansen**: Known to many as "Mother Bev" for her compassionate heart for battered women and seniors. Founder of the Women's Resource Center, now the Bright Futures Foundation.
- **Jim Clark**: Known to everyone as "JC," worked almost every job on Vail Mountain. Serves today as Ranch manager at MountainStar.
- **Pam Pettee Conklin**: Publicity director under Bob Parker who managed the White House Press Corps like the big-time professional she was.
- **Kevin Conwick**: Attorney from Holme, Roberts & Owen who managed the LionsHead Gondola litigation.
- **Jack Crosby**: A Texan who was the second donor in the Friends of Vail program. And another guy always smiling.
- **Art Currier**: A founder of the Vail Leadership Institute and former VP of Marketing for Salomon Skis and USIA, the ski industry marketing arm.
- **Andy Daly**: Former CEO of Vail Resorts and Mayor of Vail.
- **Susie Davis**: A long-time promoter of education who founded the Business-Education Partnership and later started the Youth Foundation.
- **Bob Dorf**: First ski school director in Beaver Creek who used his radio character "Beaver Bob" to promote the new resort.
- **The Donovan's**: John was the proprietor of the infamous Donovan's Copper Bar, ski instructor, and town councilman, his wife Diane was the one who kept John going, and who also served on the Vail Town Council. And Kerry followed in her parent's footsteps on the town council and now is a Colorado State Senator.
- **Earl Eaton**: The person known as the "finder" of Vail, but also a can-do handyman who built and maintained almost everything on Vail Mountain.
- **Jack Eck, MD**: Vail's second doctor who taught the ski patrol emergency medicine and helped build the Vail Valley Medical Center into a world-class community hospital.
- **Buck Elliott**: A founder of the Vail Leadership Institute and owner of Paragon Guides. He also led much of the fundraising for the Walking Mountain Science Center.
- **Carolyn Fisher, Ph.D.**: Assisted Bob Knous in executing the 1989 World Championships, as the unofficial "tooth fairy."
- **Ceil Folz**: The fourth President of the Vail Valley Foundation and key executive in two of our three World Alpine Ski Championships.
- **Harry Frampton**: The fourth President of Vail Associates, Inc. and chairman of the Vail Valley Foundation for the last thirty years.

In his spare time, he built East West Partners into a reputable developer. He also has his name on the door of Slifer Smith & Frampton.

- *John Garnsey*: The third employee of the Vail Valley Foundation who became President and led the 1999 World Championships. He later became President of Vail Resorts Global Mountain Development.

- *Charlie Gersbach*: The first manager of the VVI (the Vail Village Inn) and one of Vail's most enthusiastic salesmen.

- *George Gillett*: The second owner of Vail Associates who accelerated Harry Frampton's decision to bring detachable quad chairlifts to Vail. He also championed China Bowl and a variety of Disney-inspired innovations. He lost control of VA when he became over-extended in debt in his other ventures.

- *John Giovando*: Founder and Executive Director of Bravo Vail, the renowned music festival, and a guy who always has a smile and a good word to share.

- *Rene & Dave Gorsuch*: Former US Ski Team members who established Vail's iconic retail enterprise.

- *Sheika Gramshammer*: The vivacious wife of Pepi who together built the wildly popular Gasthof Gramshammer. Sheika's boutique in their sports shop is her special domain. Sheika's night club was the scene of many a chase. Pepi was the long-running ski instructor, guide and friend to President Ford.

- *Fred Green*: Lawyer, developer, golf nut who helped develop the neighborhoods west of Dowd Junction. Close friends of the Ford's and supporter of the hospital in the difficult years.

- *Dick Gyde*: A steady supporter of Vail Christian High School who led the board through the many challenges of growing an alternative educational institution/

- *The Hanlon's*: Bill and Sally came early and stayed. Sally ran Vail Village Travel and Bill still runs the Wild West hat store in the heart of town. And their kids, Joey and Meg are still here.

- *Topper Hagerman*: A sports physiologist who came to Vail with Dr. Steadman and built-up the Howard Head Sports Medicine Clinic touches thousands of people. He's another guys who's always smiling.

- *Dick Hauserman*: Not only brought Pepi Gramshammer here from Sun Valley, but also convinced Arnold Palmer to open a golf school on land that is now Eagle Vail.

- **Jimmy Heuga**: An Olympic champion who probably won his medal with MS in his system. He later established the Huega Center in Vail to give people his exercise and diet regimen for staying "healthy" even with MS.
- **Christy Hill**: Founded the Vail Blanche ski shop in 1962 with then husband, Dick Hauserman. Hill lived above that ski shop at the very base of Vail Mountain until her death in 2015.
- **Chris Jarnot**: A local boy, born and raised here, graduate of Eagle Valley High School, and the leading executive for Vail Resorts in Vail.
- **Frank Johnson**: Former vice president of the Vail Resort Association that morphed into the Vail Valley Convention & Tourism Bureau, and later the Vail Valley Partnership, where he served as president for fifteen years.
- **Paul Johnston**: Owner of the Christiania Lodge, operator of one of Vail's nightclubs, the Nu Gnu, and mayor of Vail in the mid-80's.
- **Chuck Johnsos**: The marketing guru who Bob Parker brought to Vail from TWA and later brought me to Vail. He subsequently changed his name to Charles St. John.
- **The Jouflas Family**: Chris and George, plus Jan and James were the most visible of this Greek clan who owner land up and down the Eagle River Valley, including Game Creek Bowl on Vail Mountain.
- **Rob Katz**: The Wall Street trained CEO of Vail Resorts who left the urban life behind after 9/11. Creator of the wildly successful Epic Pass program.
- **Brooks Keith**: The episcopal priest who championed the interfaith movement and helped build the Edwards InterFaith Chapel.
- **Art Kelton**: Real estate partner of Fred Green and Rod Slifer in building several neighborhoods west of Vail. Now serves as chairman of the Vail Valley Medical Center board.
- **Elaine Kelton**: Builder of the RamsHorn Lodge with husband Gary White. Became chairperson of the Vail Symposium. Co-author of *The Women of Vail*.
- **Walter Kirch**: With Jay Utter, built the Vail Racquet Club in East Vail. Sold me my first home in Vail.
- **Bob Knous**: The second president of the Vail Valley Foundation came to Vail after stints with Colorado Ski Country USA and the Governor's office.
- **The Knox's**: George, the father, also known as "the Skipper," founded the Vail Trail newspaper, son Alan run it for years before

selling-out to the Vail Daily crew, and son George who still operates the Vail Mug Shop on Bridge Street.

- **Ben Krueger**: Landscaper manager throughout Vail in the early years, including the Vail Golf Course. Brought color to town through the many flowers beds that his "crew" maintained.
- **Ludwig Kurz**: Vail Ski School director in the 80's who later served on the Vail Town Council, once as mayor.
- **Merv Lapin**: Vail's first, and perhaps only, stockbroker who invested his own money and built a substantial nest egg. All the while, he took hundreds of Vail hockey kids to China and Russia for an experience of a lifetime.
- **Bob Lazier**: Owner of the Tivioli Lodge and developer of numerous other early projects in Vail. Together with his son, Buddy, participated in numerous Indy 500 races.
- **Richard Leider**: An early influencer on the development of the Vail Leadership Institute who constantly pushed us to define our purpose.
- **Tom Leonard**: The human resources chief for VA in the 70's and 80's. Left Vail to become CEO at the Crystal Mountain ski resort outside of Seattle.
- **Chuck Lewis**: An early executive for Vail Associates who left to develop Copper Mountain. Served on the initial board of the Vail Valley Foundation.
- **Larry Lichliter**: Former CFO for VA and later partner of Mike Shannon and Henry Kravis in KSL Resorts.
- **Dale McCall**: An early Executive Director of the Vail Resort Association and impassioned promoter of Vail.
- **The Meyer's**: Luc and Liz brought fine French dining at the Left Bank, and for years, got away with a cash-only policy – but it was worth it. And Luc was always smiling!
- **Terry Minger**: Town Manager for Vail in the 1970's who left an indelible mark on the community. Helped start the Vail Symposium.
- **Mark Miller**: Former Fire Chief for the Town of Vail who advocated for more real leadership development in the fire service.
- **Tom Moorhead**: Former Chief Attorney for the Town of Vail and later Eagle County, and later as Chief Judge for the 5th Judicial District.
- **Jim Morter**: The architect who, with Rudi Fisher, designed the initial phase of Ford Amphitheater. His wife, Karen, was instrumental in building the Vail Symposium.

- *Chupa Nelson*: The ski patrolman who led the rescue of stranded passengers during the tragic LionsHead Gondola accident. He later built a successful construction company.
- *Sara Newsom*: Last standing executive assistant to VA's management team. Keeper of many secrets.
- *Andy Norris*: A member of Dick Peterson's team in the 70's and developer of the Cascade Village, also known as the original Westin. A great promoter, lover of life and superb volleyball player.
- *Kathy Macy*: Long-time Executive Assistant to Harry Frampton and whose other half is Joe Macy of ski patrol fame.
- *Jack Marshall*: The third president of Vail Associates (VA) who cemented the formal relationship with President Ford involving him in the development of the Vail Valley Foundation.
- *Pat McConathy*: A major contributor to Vail Mountain School and owner of Yarmony Creek Lodge that supported innumerable local organizations with a retreat setting.
- *Luc & Liz Meyer*: Owners of the Left Bank restaurant who set a tone for fine French dining. Later they opened the Mirabelle restaurant in the former Nottingham ranch house at the entrance to Beaver Creek.
- *Dave Mott*: An engineer who oversaw much of Beaver Creek's infrastructure development and later served as an Eagle County Commissioner.
- *John Murchison*: One of the original investors in Vail, but more importantly, the primary supporter of the Vail Valley Medical Center.
- *The Nottinghams*: Bill, Mauri and Allan of the family who owned huge tracks of land in the Vail Valley, including most notably, Beaver Creek.
- *ChuckOlgivy*: Builder and town council member. Supporter of many environmental programs.
- *Paula Palmateer*: Known to me as P², Paula was the former president of the Vail Resort Association, former Vail Town Council member, and founder of the Red Ribbon Project.
- *John Purcell*: Owner of Purcell's Restaurant (now Montauk) and friend and golfing buddy of President Ford. Ring leader of Vail's "restaurant mafia" including Ron Riley, Jim (JK) King, Michael Staughton and others.
- *Aldo Radimus*: The long-running Executive Director of Ski Club Vail who expanded the operation into one of the leading ski academies in the world.

- *Ron Riley*: Side kick of John Purcell and owner of Russell's and Los Amigos. Founding member of the Vail restaurant "mafia."
- *Leonard Ruder*: The operator of the "big iron" who cleared much of Vail Mountain and for whom Ruder's Run on Gold Peak is named.
- *Peter Runyon*: Staff photographer for VA in the 70's who later became an Eagle County Commissioner.
- *Willy Schaefler*: The German-born ski coach for the US Ski Team who opened numerous doors for Vail in the international ski community.
- *FitzHugh Scott*: Vail's original architect and land planner and consummate community advocate. Served on the early Vail Valley Foundation board.
- *Mike Shannon*: The fifth president of VA, and the youngest at 28, who led the company during an innovative phase under George Gillett. Left Vail in 1990 to start KSL with investor Henry Kravis and former VA executive Larry Litchliter.
- *Morrie Shepard*: First ski school director who was Pete Seibert's friend and dreamer from boyhood in Sharon, Massachusetts.
- *Suzanne Silverthorne*: Communications executive for the Town of Vail for several decades who has been a steady hand with a long view.
- *Don & June Simonton*: Don was the organizing force behind the Vail InterFaith movement from his position as the Lutheran pastor. Together with June, they became the unofficial historians of the Vail Valley writing several books and numerous articles. Don also helped start the Colorado Ski Museum.
- *Beth Slifer*: Married mayor Rod Slifer after a long distance courtship. Built Slifer Designs into a successful business then retired to serve on various community boards. Serves on the advisory board at the University of Colorado.
- *Jim Slevin*: An excellent restauranteur who started Up the Creek with Peter Stadler in 1988.
- *Mark Smith*: A marketing whiz and the middle name in Slifer Smith & Frampton. Founder of the Youth Foundation.
- *Roger Staub*: The Swiss Olympic champion who became Vail's second, and perhaps most loved, Ski school director who was taken from us in a hang gliding accident in 1970.
- *The Stauffer's*: Brothers Joe, Herman and Gottfried ran restaurants and hotels with a European flair. Joe later developed the Vail

Village Inn complex while serving multiple terms on the Vail Town Council.

- **Tom Steinberg, MD**: Vail's first doctor, coroner and ambulance driver. Served several terms on the Vail Town Council and later led the Eagle Valley Land Trust.
- **Howard Stone**: Lawyer turned impresario who started the Vail Jazz Foundation after his first concert when he realized "this is what I want to do with the rest of my life."
- **Oscar Tang**: A long-standing supporter of the arts and education, particularly Walking Mountains Science Center.
- **Paul Testwuide**: Ski patrolman turned VA executive who embodies the wild and yet responsible lifestyle that Vail has become known for.
- **Jim Thompson**: President of Arrowhead and prime-mover behind Bachelor Gulch.
- **Barbara Treat**: A prolific volunteer for the Vail Valley Foundation and others. Wife of Sandy Treat, a 10th Mountain veteran and a fixture in the community.
- **Packy Walker**: The long-standing GM of the Lifthouse Lodge and mastermind behind the Great Race, the annual spring "fling" in LionsHead. Partnered with Dave Garton on pranks over many years.
- **Karin Weber**: With Alison Knapp, raised many millions to build the Roundup River Ranch, a camp for children with chronic illnesses.
- **Lisa McGraw Webster**: The philanthropist who funded the first ice rink that was later built upon creating the Dobson Arena.
- **Bill Whiteford**: Builder and operator of the Casino nightclub, Vail's first discotheque that also served as an interim church on Sunday mornings.
- **Jeanne Reid White**: Started as "number two" at the Vail Associates Foundation. Became the chief fundraiser for Bravo over many years.
- **Vicki Notaro**: The long-standing receptionist and "voice" of Vail Associates and Vail Resorts. Has been answering 476-5601 for close to 40 years.

ACKNOWLEDGMENTS

Writing this book has been a real joy. Visiting with people I worked with over the years has been both fun and enlightening. I have tried to select what I thought were the most compelling stories to understand and convey the Vail way. I'm sure I've missed a few, and for that I offer a blanket apology to anyone offended. I've tried to mention a whole host of others in the Glossary of Pioneers, Entrepreneurs, and Unsung Leaders. Again, forgive me, if I overlooked you or someone you love.

The most important acknowledgement of this book goes to the "three amigos," Pete Seibert, Bob Parker, and Bill Brown. Each of these World War II veterans contributed mightily not only to Vail's founding but also to me personally. I worked with each of them, traveled with them, and, most importantly, admired them for their commitment to a vision.

At Pete Seibert's memorial in 2002, this poem from T.E. Lawrence was shared, and it spoke volumes about his dream:

"Those who dream by night in the dusty recesses of their minds
wake in the morning to find that all was vanity;
but the dreamers of the day are dangerous,
for they may act on their dream and make it possible."

A huge "thank you" to everyone who met with me to uncover the Vail way: Vail pioneers, community leaders, those who have written commentaries, including, Kathy Borgen, John Garnsey, Buck Elliott, Art Currier, Charlie L'Esperance, Art Kelton, Elaine Kelton, Gerry Flynn, Alan Danson, Bob Parker, Paula Palmateer, George Lamm, Carroll Tyler, and Jen Wright.

And to key stakeholders of the Vail Leadership Institute, especially to Dr. John Feagin who encouraged me along the way to uncover the uniqueness of the Vail way. Also, a big thank you to Ursula Gross, my editor, who tried her best to bring some discipline to my informal style. Lastly, I acknowledge the creator for all of the blessings of this life but, particularly, for calling me to "stay the course" here in the Vail Valley.

CHAPTER NOTES

Preface

[1] Wikipedia
[2] The Bible: New International Version; James 2:17
[3] Thomas Edison.com: Gerald Beals; February 11, 1997
[4] Shirley Welch: Vail – The First Fifty Years; Arcadia Publishing, Charleston, SC; 2012
[5] Interview with Rod Slifer, February 12, 2015
[6] Stephen R. Covey: The 7 Habits of Highly Effective People; Simon & Schuster, London, 1990
[7] Robert Jarvik, MD: Wikipedia
[8] Burt Nanus: Visionary Leadership; Jossey-Bass, San Francisco, 1992
[9] David Gergen: Quoting an African Proverb; Beaver Creek, 2008
[10] Jim Collins: Good to Great; HarperCollins, 2001
[11] Walter Issacson: The Innovators; Simon & Schuster, 2014
[12] Ibid
[13] Robert Greenleaf: The Servant Leader; Paulist Press, 2001
[14] The Bible: New International Version; Matthew 20:28
[15] William Hutchinson Murray: The Scottish Himalayan Expedition; 1951

Introduction

[1] Vince Lombardi: Coach, Green Bay Packers; 1962

Chapter 1:

[1] *The Triumph of a Dream*: Peter Seibert – Mountain Sports Press – Boulder, CO – 2001
[2] Ibid
[3] New York Times: November 1962
[4] *Another Kingdom* – Not Proudly: Robert W. Parker – Rio Grande Publishing; Santa Fe, NM
[5] Interview with Pam Conklin Pettee, October 26, 2012
[6] Interview with Bob Parker, August 15, 2015
[7] Ibid
[8] Ibid
[9] Pam Conklin: Ski Area Management: November 1984
[9] Ibid
[10] Ibid
[11] Stephen L. Waterhouse: Passion for Skiing; Dartmouth, 2010
[12] Tom Washing: Correspondence from March 2015
[13] Interview with Art Kelton, March 2, 2015
[14] Interview with Paul Testwuide, April 2015
[15] Larry Buendorf: Comments at Bill Brown's Memorial; September 2008
[16] Interview with John Garnsey, May 2015
[17] Interview with Harry Frampton, October 2014

Chapter 2:

[1] Conversation with Frank Lynch, December 1988
[2] Interview with Pepi Gramshammer, January 1990
[3] Conversation with Bobby Albrittan, Bormio, Italy, February 1985
[4] Comments by Paul Johnston, Vancouver, BC, June 1985

Chapter 3:

[1] Don Berger: Vail Symposium program; "Exploring Today's Realities," September 1990
[2] Interview with Terry Minger, October 2014
[3] Vail's First 50 Years: *A Retrospective*; Suzanne Silverthorne and Allen Best
[4] Rene Dubos: Vail Symposium, June 1971
[5] *Vail's First 50 Years: A Retrospective*; Suzanne Silverthorne and Allen Best

[6] Conversation with Don Simonton, December 2012
[7] Celebration of Life Program for Don Simonton: May 2015
[8] Interview with Jen Wright, May 2015
[9] Tom Moorhead, September 2015
[10] Ibid
[11] Cheryl Jensen, September 2015
[12] Kevin Dubois, June 2015
[13] Jen Wright, July 2015
[14] Ibid
[15] Jim Lamont, Vail Homeowners Newsletter,

Chapter 4:

[1] Interview with Rod Slifer, June 2014
[2] Interview with Morrie Sheppard, July 2014
[3] Interview with Rod Slifer, June 2014
[4] Vail's *First 50 Years: A Retrospective*; Suzanne Silverthorne and Allen Best
[5] Interview with Rod Slifer, June 2014
[6] Ibid
[7] Interview with Terry Minger, April 2014
[8] *Vail's First 50 Years: A Retrospective*; Suzanne Silverthorne and Allen Bes
[9] Ibid
[10] Interview with Rod Slifer, June 2014
[11] Interview with Paula Palmateer, July 2014
[12] Interview with Bill Wilto, July 2014
[13] Interview with Beth Slifer, September 2014
[14] Interview with Mark Smith, August 2014
[15] Interview with Harry Frampton, July 2014
[16] Interview with Rod Slifer, June 2014
[17] Interview with Mark Smith, August 2014
[18] Interview with Rod Slifer, June 2014

Chapter 5:

[1] *The Triumph of a Dream*: Peter Seibert – Mountain Sports Press – Boulder, CO – 2001
[2] Interview with Morrie Sheppard, July 2014
[3] Vail's *First 50 Years: A Retrospective*; Suzanne Silverthorne and Allen Best
[4] Interview with Terry Minger, April 2014

[5] Interview with Bob Parker, August, 2012
[6] Interview with Dick Peterson, June 2014
[7] Ibid
[8] Interview with Bob Parker, August, 2012
[9] Interview with Harry Frampton, July 2014
[10] Jim Robinson: American Ski Classic, March 1986
[11] Harry Frampton: American Ski Classic, March 1986
[12] Interview with Mike Shannon, November 2014
[13] Interview with George Gillett, September 2014
[14] Interview with Andy Daly, January 2015
[15] Interview with Charlie L'Esperance, March 2015
[16] Interview with Rob Katz, June 2015
[17] Interview with John Garnsey, October 2014
[18] Interview with Rob Katz, June 2015
[19] Interview with Mark Gasta, November 2014
[20] Vail Resorts' CEO: Transforming the Business of Skiing: Barron's; November 2014
[21] Interview with Rob Katz, June 2015
[22] Voices of Experience: University of Denver; April 2013
[23] Interview with Rob Katz, June 2015
[24] Ibid
[25] Voices of Experience: University of Denver; April 2013
[26] Comment from Pete Seibert, Jr., November 2014

Chapter 6:

[1] Interview with Joe Stauffer, September 2015
[2] Interview with Karl Feassler, July 2014
[3] Interview with Johannes Feassler, August 2015

Chapter 7:

[1] Conversation with Jack Marshall: August 1978
[2] Conversation with Harry Frampton: July 1982
[3] Conversation with Graham Anderson: June 1982
[4] Conversation with Graham Anderson: April 1983
[5] High and Mighty Meet: Meeting Planners International: January 1983

Chapter 8:

[1] Kim Langmaid: Exploring Entrepreneurship: October 2013
[2] Interview with Kim Langmaid, November 2013
[3] Interview with Terry Minger, September 2013
[4] Interview with Kim Langmaid, November 2013
[5] Jack Shea: Teton Science School; June 2001
[6] Oscar Tang as relayed by Kim Langmaid: August 2005
[7] Oscar Tang as relayed by Alan Danson: June, 2015
[8] Interview with Kim Langmaid, November 2013
[9] William Hutchinson Murray: The Scottish Himalayan Expedition; 1951
[10] Interview with Markian Feduschak, January 2014
[11] Correspondence from Kim Langmaid, June 2014
[12] Interview with Kim Langmaid, November 2013
[13] Ibid
[14] Interview with Terry Minger, June 2015

Chapter 9:

[1] Interview with Bob Parker, August 2015
[2] Interview with Tom Steinberg, March 2015
[3] Interview with Jack Eck, August 2015
[4] Interview with Topper Hagerman, May 2015
[5] Vail Health Magazine: 2014
[6] Conversation with Steadman Fellow: Head Residence; April 2013
[7] Interview with Jack Eck, August 2015
[8] Ford Frick: Vail Daily; February 2012
[9] Interview with Jack Eck, August 2015
[10] Interview with Mike Shannon, August 2015
[11] Interview with John Feagin, August 2015
[12] Interview with Doris Kirchner, August 2015
[13] Mike Shannon: Vail Health Magazine, 2014
[14] Merv Lapin: Vail Daily, April 2005
[15] Mike McClinton: September 2015
[16] Kathy Langenwalter: Vail Valley Medical Center magazine, Summer 2011

Chapter 10:

[1] Richard Leider: Minneapolis, October 1997
[2] The Bible: New International Version; Matthew 23:26
[3] Parker Palmer: The Courage to Teach; Jossey-Bass, 1987
[4] Carl Sandburg: Bob Vanourek in Words of Wisdon; September 2015
[5] Conversation with Tom Moorhead, August 2014
[6] Conversation with Frank Johnson, September 2014
[7] Smartest Guys in the Room: Bethany McLean and Peter Elkind; Portfolio Trade, 2004
[8] Board of Trustees: Vail Leadership Institute; September 2006
[9] Laura Emrich: Foundations of Leadership retreat; September 2010
[10] Gregg Vanourek: Positioning Matrix; November 2011
[11] Mark Miller; RoundTable retreat; July, 2013
[12] Nathaniel Hawthorne: The Scarlet Letter

Chapter 11:

[1] Interview with Paul Testwuide, November 2014
[2] Interview with Jack Eck, August 2015
[3] Comment by Andy Daly; September 2015
[4] Interview with Topper Hagerman: May 2015
[5] Interview with Cindy Nelson, August 2015
[6] Ibid
[7] Ibid
[8] Ibid
[9] Cindy Nelson, LLC: Web-site, August 2015

Conclusions & Postscript:

[1] Agnes Sanford: The Healing Light
[2] John Gardner: Building Community – American Leadership Forum reading
[3] T.H. Watkins

Photo Credits

Cover.........Vail Resorts, Dann Coffey and the author

Dedication

p. vii.........By the author

Preface

p. xiii...........Colorado Ski & Snowboard Museum

Introduction

p. xxi...........By the author
p. xxiii.........Wikipedia
p. xxv..........Vail Trail
p. xxvi.........Vail Resorts

Chapter 1

p. 1...........Colorado Ski & Snowboard Museum
p. 2.........Vail Resorts
p. 3.........Colorado Ski & Snowboard Museum
p. 5..........Colorado Ski & Snowboard Museum

Chapter 2

Chapter 3

Chapter 4

Chapter 5

Chapter 6

Chapter 7

Chapter 8

Chapter 9

Chapter 10

Chapter 11

Conclusion and Postscript

INDEX

C

L

M

Printed in the United States
By Bookmasters